Dieter Rams:
As Little Design
as Possible

Dieter Rams:
As Little Design
as Possible

Sophie Lovell

'Indifference towards people
and the reality in which they
live is actually the one and only
cardinal sin in design.'

Dieter Rams

Preface

During the early stages of working on the first edition of this book, I travelled to Osaka, Japan, for an exhibition about the work of Dieter Rams in the context of twentieth-century design. On the evening after the opening we were sitting in a bar at the top of a high-rise hotel, looking out through huge plate-glass windows at the nocturnal panorama of the dense industrial Osaka cityscape. It had been a long day of press conferences, opening speeches and seminars followed by a Japanese banquet in Dieter Rams's honour, and now I was in the company of a small group of people including Klaus Klemp, the exhibition's co-curator, Mark Adams and Daniel Nelson from Vitsœ, Dieter Rams and his wife, Ingeborg, and Rams's good friend and advisor Britte Siepenkothen, enjoying a nightcap of Japanese whisky.

We were quietly discussing the day's events when Dieter Rams, who had worked hard all day and appeared tired, suddenly said, 'Why on earth do we need another book about me?' Then aged seventy-six, Rams had been famous as a designer since he was twenty-five and, despite acknowledging that having people interested in your work and ideas is no bad thing, he hated all the limelight and media attention. 'I want nothing to do with this star designer machine,' he added, suddenly getting rather worked up. We all looked at him. Apart from the fact that, as one of the most respected industrial designers in the world, he was a 'star' whether he liked it or not, the reason why the world needed another book had been made absolutely clear earlier in the day in the huge auditorium packed with young designers and design students hanging on to Rams's every word. A particularly beautiful and precise speech at the symposium by the Japanese designer Naoto Fukasawa, who praised Rams's oeuvre of what he aptly called 'correct design', highlighted the level of respect there is for his work among today's top professionals in the field. Klaus Klemp was the first to speak up: 'Dieter,' he said, 'you still have work to do – to communicate and bring your message across to the young people.' There was a chorus of assent from all those present. Mollified, Rams agreed that this was a good reason to do another book. 'But,' he added, looking at me very intently, 'it should be an empty book that says something important.'

In this respect, I perhaps failed in my task. How do you write an empty book about someone whose working life has covered more than half a century and who has designed well over 500 products, and at the same time transmit all the complex interrelationships and contexts in which these products came into being? It would all be much simpler if one could state that Dieter Rams's work and principles arose from him alone. But Rams would be the first to say that what constitutes his 'work' as an industrial designer is inseparable from the systems and networks through which it was produced. As such, assigning individual authorship to his work is, to some extent, meaningless. He could never have resolved his concepts without the ideas of his predecessors and his contemporaries, in what was an extraordinary era of worldwide growth and change. He could not have produced the things he did without the other designers at Braun, nor without the technicians, the managers, the materials manufacturers, the vision of the company's original owners and even the marketing department. The same goes for his furniture design with Vitsœ, albeit on a smaller scale. Even beyond this vast network of people required to create his products, the designs themselves were modular and thus system-related. In nearly every instance, there are complex interrelationships within and between his designs: the improvements of individual components, how the products work with one another, how they are related aesthetically and in terms of intent, and how they function in the home. Last but not least, Rams's products – in fact, his whole attitude and his principles – are geared towards the end user: they have to fit into the social systems, the lives and homes of a multitude of different kinds of people, and serve all of them discreetly, reliably and comfortably. It would be wrong to remove the work of Dieter Rams from these contexts and yet trying to explain them has involved many words and many pictures. I set out to write an empty book, but there was much that needed to be said about Rams's extraordinary life and work in order to transmit the essence of his message: 'less but better'.

The world has changed since then, but the message within it has not. It seems a more fragile place than ever, yet much more in need of context. It would be even harder to write an empty book that says something important in 2024 than it was in 2011. Dieter is now in his nineties. He moves a little more slowly but his passion for mending the world through design is undimmed. Ingeborg sadly passed away in 2022; Britte, his manager, who kept the show on the road and secured the sound basis for Dieter's historical legacy through the Rams Foundation, is enjoying her well-earned retirement. Klaus is now running the Foundation. Mark, along with his family and the Vitsœ team, continues to put Rams's principles into practice, including placing people and planet first.

Although design has also moved on a great deal in terms of technology, materials and requirements since Dieter's heyday, the internet has helped to make him into something of an 'icon', a synonym for values, principles and the capacity for reflective intelligence in industrial design. Long after most of the products Dieter and his team designed have gone out of production (but not use – there is a thriving vintage market for certain objects), his name remains a benchmark for younger designers in a field flooded with change and responsibility.

Why is that? Of course, it's true to say that, as a designer of consumer goods, Dieter Rams helped to fill the world with more 'things' at a time when commercial production exploded towards the environmental tipping points we are faced with today. But it is also true to say that he did this with a passion for quality and usability that was often at odds with the interests of company profits. Dieter has been expounding for years to anyone who would listen about the need to make 'less but better' in the face of catastrophic over-consumption. Now, at long last, the world might just be starting to listen.

Sophie Lovell

Foreword
Jonathan Ive

p.305

When I was a young boy growing up in London, my parents bought a wonderful juicer. It was a Braun MPZ 2 Citromatic [+]. I knew nothing about Dieter Rams or his ten principles of good design. But to a little boy uninterested in juicing, I remember the Citromatic he and his team designed for Braun with shocking clarity. It was white. It felt cold and heavy. The surfaces were without apology, bold, pure, perfectly-proportioned, coherent and effortless. There was an honest connection between its blemish-free surfaces and the materials from which they were made. It was clearly made from the best materials, not the cheapest. No part appeared to be either hidden or celebrated, just perfectly considered and completely appropriate in the hierarchy of the product's details and features. At a glance, you knew exactly what it was and exactly how to use it. It was the essence of juicing made material: a static object that perfectly described the process by which it worked. It felt complete and it felt right. While my memories are, of course, in the past tense, the product remains all these things. I was completely enchanted with it then, and I now find, with surprise, that this object resonated so deeply with me that nearly forty years on I remember my sense of it with startling clarity.

While studying design in the 1980s I read about Dieter Rams and his work with his team at Braun. But the reading was never as powerful as seeing and using his products. Prolific and consistent, Rams is defined by what he does rather than what he says. And what Dieter Rams and his team at Braun did was to produce hundreds of wonderfully conceived and designed objects: products that were beautifully made in high volumes and that were broadly accessible. He defined how it was supposed to be: how industry could responsibly bring useful, well-considered products to many.

In so many ways Dieter Rams's work is beyond improvement. Although new technologies have since offered new opportunities, his designs are not undermined by the limits of the technologies of their time. The concave button top, necessary to stop your finger from slipping as it made the long travel necessary for earlier mechanical switches, does not point to obsolete mechanisms. Instead, it reminds us how immediately and intuitively form alone can describe what an object does and suggest how we should use it. So profoundly good is his design of music players, cameras and kitchen tools that it somehow transcends their technical capability. Some of these products are now over fifty years old.

Rams's ability to bring form to a product so that it clearly, concisely and immediately communicates its meaning is remarkable. The completeness of the relationship between shape and construction, material and process, defines his work and remains a conspicuously rare quality. And although there is no inherent virtue in consistency, Rams's application and resolve to pursue his vision over time also led to a remarkable cohesiveness of design throughout his career.

His products seem inevitable, challenging you to question whether there could possibly be a rational alternative. It is this clarity and purity that leads to the sense of inevitability and effortlessness that characterizes his work. The CSV 12 amplifier rotary switch, for example, is perfect. It could not be better, simpler, clearer, or more beautiful. It brings order and explanation to what is a far more complex problem than the user could possibly conceive. Simplicity, of course, is not the absence of complexity. Just removing clutter would result in uncomplicated but meaningless products. Rams's genius lies in understanding and giving form to the very essence of an object's being – almost describing its reason for existence, as so perfectly illustrated by the Citromatic juicer of my childhood.

Ironically, while he relegated these products to the status of tools, he elevated them by imbuing them with clarity, simplicity and consequent beauty. In doing so he defined the new relationship between the object and the user. He and his team created objects that were neither vehicles of self-expression nor purely a means to make money. He addressed the issue of our relationship with our manufactured environment, articulating important rules of engagement between user and product.

For a designer to produce a couple of objects this significant and influential in their lifetime could define a movement. To produce more than 500 borders on the absurd. This speaks to perhaps a less obvious but critically important attribute of Rams – his ability to collaborate. The fact we know Rams primarily by his beautifully engineered and mass-manufactured products rather than his credo of good design, speaks volumes about his extraordinary collaborations within Braun. In defining individual products he also defined Braun. His was not an academic experiment in modernism. He lived every day with the commercial realities and consequences of what he and his team designed. Equally, he lived with the organizational and structural consequences of the way he and his team worked. When you think of Braun, you immediately think of the products, not some abstract mission statement or charter. Our perception of these products is our perception of the brand. In a profession with more than its fair share of rhetoric, Dieter Rams succeeded in making his philosophy tangible by giving form and, ultimately, the relevance of mass production to his ideas. He remains utterly alone in producing a body of work so consistently beautiful, so right and so accessible.

Who is Dieter Rams?

Dieter Rams was a child of World War II. Like so many of his generation, he experienced a childhood affected by totalitarianism, bombs, separation, confusion and hardship. But during his teenage years and early adulthood he was caught up in an era of new hope and optimism, in which many people passionately believed that they had been given a new chance to build a better, more egalitarian and modern world. This new world, full of light and new buildings, with hot and cold running water and labour-saving devices for all, was to be as far removed as possible from the dark days of the recent past.

Rams was born on 20 May 1932 in Wiesbaden, Germany. His parents, Martha and Erich Rams, separated when he was very young. His father was an Elektroingeneur (electrical engineer) who travelled around the country for much of the time, installing hilltop radio stations. An only child, he spent much of his childhood being shunted between parents, grandparents and, at one point, a foster family. Even at an early age Rams showed himself to be somewhat wilful and stubborn. 'I was an absolute outsider,' he recalls, and often got into trouble with authoritarian figures. His early school career was somewhat mixed due to the War and his frequent moves. At one point he says he was sent to a military-style Jungvolk[1] boarding school, but he was demoted and ran away because he refused to fit in, hating all the military manoeuvres and field training in particular – an act of rebellion that could not have been easy under a totalitarian regime in wartime.

Rams's memories of his childhood are not particularly rosy but could easily have been worse. Aged thirteen, he was just young enough to miss being called up by the Volkssturm[2] to fight at the end of the War. His paternal grandfather, Heinrich Rams in Wiesbaden, had a significant influence on his early years. Heinrich was a master joiner and the young Dieter Rams spent many long hours with him in his workshop, learning about making traditional furniture and polishing it by hand. Through his grandfather, Rams developed a lifelong love of honest, simple handmade wooden furniture. 'My grandfather had no machines. He rejected them. He preferred working alone. Workers did not do the job well enough for him … Now and again he would make small pieces of furniture, individual items. He took great care in selecting the wood he used at specialist dealers and shaped and planed it by hand. So in a totally natural way something straightforward arose, which did justice to his work … Needless to say, back then I did not register this consciously, but I adopted it and even today have not given it up. I was always concerned that things should be plain, straightforward. For as long as I can remember that was what I wanted.'[3]

[1]   The Deutsches Jungvolk (German Youth) was the junior branch of the HJ or Hitler Jugend
        (Hitler Youth), for children between ten and fourteen years of age.

[2]   The Volkssturm ('People's Storm Troop') was a militia established by Hitler's decree in late
        1944, which mobilized all civilian men born between 1884 and 1928.

[3]   Dieter Rams, 'Erinnerungen an die ersten Jahre bei Braun' ('Memories of the first years at Braun'),
        an open letter to Erwin Braun (July 1979), reprinted in *Weniger aber Besser / Less But Better*
        (Hamburg, 1995), 13. Translation modified by the author

In 1946, Rams's father came back from a brief spell of captivity as a prisoner of war and was soon working for the Americans, helping to set up radio antennae for the media. He must have recognized his young son's creative talent, for he helped to secure a place for him at the re-opened Handwerker-und-Kunstgewerbeschule (Arts and Crafts College) in Wiesbaden. Thus at the tender age of fifteen, Rams went to college to study architecture and interior design together with a mixed bag of war veterans and survivors of one of the most shocking phases in his country's history.

The head of the Wiesbaden college was Professor Hans Soeder. In a complete break from the Nazi-era attitude towards design, in which it was more or less reduced to handicraft, Soeder developed a new school concept for Wiesbaden based on the Bauhaus model, emphasizing the relationship between architecture and design. Students there were required to complete a full training in craftsmanship before going on to do two years of master classes. In 1948, Soeder had the school reclassified as a Werkkunstschule (Applied Arts College). Several other colleges in Germany followed his example and, as the instigator of this pedagogical shift, he can be considered as an important figure in the development of post-war German design education.[4]

Rams completed two semesters at Wiesbaden before doing a three-year practical apprenticeship as a carpenter, which he completed as 'best of year' in the whole state of Hessen in 1951. He then returned to Wiesbaden (by then an applied arts college) for four semesters. There he began to learn about German modernism in art, architecture and design from teachers, such as Gerhard Schrammer, Hugo Kückelhaus and former Bauhaus student Hans Haffenrichter. By the time Rams graduated with a diploma in interior design with honours in July 1953, he was firmly intent on a career in architecture. 'I wanted to stay in architecture,' he remembers. 'I wanted to be a town planner. In fact if I could do it all again, I would have liked to do landscape planning – dealing with the whole system (Gesamtkonzept), not individual elements, such as reclaiming industrial landscapes and uncontrolled urban development. It is all still far too uncoordinated.'[5] Even as a student he was gripped by the idea of tidying up the world and making it a better place.

Initially Dieter Rams's career remained in the field of architecture. After a brief sojourn at a small local practice, he took a job with Otto Apel (1906–66) in 1953. Apel was the leading representative of the 'International Style' of architecture in Frankfurt at the time. Rams was particularly influenced by the industry-orientated post-war modernism that came back to Germany from the United States through Apel's collaboration with the Chicago-based firm Skidmore, Owings and Merrill on the construction of US consulates in Germany at the time. These years were 'decisively important for me,' he recalled in 1979. 'Here I could work just as I had

---

[4]   Klaus Klemp et al., eds, *Less and More: The Design Ethos of Dieter Rams* (Osaka, 2008), 317

[5]   In conversation with the author (June 2009)

imagined. And here I could expand my knowledge of high-rise building. I must emphasize the influence that the co-operation between Apel and the office of Skidmore, Owings and Merrill, which was just beginning at the time, had on me. I believe that this is what allowed me to cope with what I came up against later with Braun and industrial design.'[6]

The rest of this book examines Dieter Rams's life and work, his ideas and products, his ethos and influence. He began his career wanting to be an architect but ended up, almost by accident, in the post-war manufacturing industry, and quickly went on to become one of the most important industrial designers of the twentieth century. Indeed, the name Dieter Rams is almost synonymous with that of the German domestic appliance manufacturer Braun. He worked for the company from 1955 until he retired in 1997 and during that time designed or co-designed more than 500 products, from hairdryers and coffee makers to hi-fi systems and televisions, many of which have been hailed as masterpieces of contemporary product design. At the same time, Rams created furniture for a small company called Vitsœ, including a shelving system that is still in production and selling well today, half a century after first hitting the market. British designer Jasper Morrison calls Vitsœ's 606 Universal Shelving System [+] the 'endgame in shelving' – as close to perfect design as it is possible to get.

p.202

The pure, rather masculine utility of Dieter Rams's products is unmistakable and has led to many imitations of his work. His exquisite attention to detail, genius for interface reduction and almost poetic sense of harmony and balance means that few come close, even today, to the level of refinement that he achieved. This applies to many hundreds of products that have served thousands of individual consumers faithfully all over the world for many years. His legacy is a design that is entirely directed towards the comfort of the user, to improving their lives in small but important ways, Dieter Rams is what good design is all about.

[6]   Rams, 'Erinnerungen' in *Weniger aber Besser*, 15. Translation modified by the author

Dieter Rams, 1957

Braun

The Beginning of Braun

The life story of Max Braun reads like a cliché of industry and entrepreneurship. The son of a farmer and sailor, he started out with little more than initiative and a good idea and went on to build a company that became one of the most famous and successful household appliance brands of the twentieth century. But this seeming cliché contains a story worth telling. It offers an insight into the success of certain types of German industry, despite all the horrors of war, totalitarianism and economic setbacks. It also represents a particular kind of industrial family business format that encouraged a philanthropic atmosphere of experimentation and entrepreneurship, untrammelled by corporate hierarchies, and which could lead, under certain circumstances, to true innovation and genuine progress.

In 1921 a young East Prussian named Max Braun set up a small workshop in Frankfurt called Max Braun Maschinen-und Apparatebau to produce a gadget of his own invention that could repair the large drive belts used for numerous manufacturing machines at the time. His invention sold well and other ideas soon followed. By 1929 Braun had set up a modern factory with 400 workers, focusing on the production of household radios for a growing market, and by 1933 he had brought out the rather innovative 'Phonosuper Cosmophon 777', one of the first radio-phonograph combination units. Success was swift: more factories in Belgium and England followed the one in Germany, along with outlets in the Netherlands, France, Spain, Switzerland, Tunisia and Morocco. With this expansion abroad, Braun became one of the first European manufacturers, and a version of the famous Braun logo with the outsized 'A', designed by Will Münch, made its inaugural appearance. 1935 saw the launch of Braun's first battery-driven portable radio receiver, the BK S 36, which helped to win the company two gold medals and a Grand Prix at the Paris World's Fair in 1937, along with international critical recognition.[1]

By 1938, Braun had 1,000 employees and was busy developing his first concept for a pioneering electric razor with an oscillating cutter and a foil shearing head. It was a significant improvement on most of the sheep shearing machine-like appliances available at the time. But World War II arrived and the company was forced to concentrate on manufacturing products for the war effort, such as mine detectors, portable two-way radio sets and transmitters. Braun was no friend of the Nazi regime[2] and he often had difficulties with the administration: his home was seized, his factories were searched and he was placed under house arrest on several occasions, but his factory was considered important for the economy and so it continued to function.

[1]   Hans Wichmann, *Mut zum Aufbruch: Erwin Braun, 1921–1992* (Munich, 1998), 34

[2]   Klaus Klemp et al., eds, *Less and More: The Design Ethos of Dieter Rams* (Osaka, 2008), 323

Nevertheless, by 1945 the War was lost and the Frankfurt factory had suffered considerable damage from Allied bombing. Yet the indefatigable Max Braun had continued to think about his electric shaver idea and, together with 150 employees, set about rebuilding the company. His two sons, Erwin [←] and Artur, helped to develop new domestic products and again business began to flourish. By 1948 the factory had been rebuilt and the company had 600 workers. They began to produce their first kitchen appliances in the form of juicers and mixers (known as the MultiMix) and, in 1950, the first Braun electric razor, the S 50, designed by Max and Artur, was launched at the Frankfurt Fair and proved yet another market coup for the company. However, Max's presence in the story ends here: he died suddenly at his desk of a heart attack in 1951, aged only 61, leaving a thriving company at the cutting edge of the shaver industry to his two sons: Erwin, then aged thirty, who had planned to become a doctor, took over the commercial side of the business, and Artur, then aged twenty-six, became responsible for the technical and engineering department.

p. 31

Braun in the 1950s

Erwin and Artur Braun clearly had their father's touch when it came to business and invention. New electronic flashguns for cameras were added to the company's repertoire and an improved version of the Braun De Luxe shaver led to a ten million dollar licence with the US company Ronson in 1954 (a huge sum at the time). These and other new products contributed to massive increases in turnover for the company in the early 1950s.[3] But Erwin, in particular, was not only interested in running a profitable company. He had progressive ideas, particularly when it came to product design and marketing. Soon after his father's death, he began restructuring the company, initiating a new design-driven approach, [←] expanding the product range (especially in the audio segment) and, equally importantly, establishing a network of contacts and collaborations with like-minded individuals who understood and believed in a modern approach to business. The fresh start was reflected in the company's logo, which was redesigned in 1952 by the graphic designer and photographer Wolfgang Schmittel, who gave it the familiar shape that it still takes today [←] – one of the most famous logos of the twentieth century.

Erwin also believed in a corporation's responsibility to its workers. The factory site in Frankfurt boasted a staff canteen serving organic, healthy food, a staff health service and a company clinic, tennis courts and a sauna, as well as various other social facilities. All of this was part of Erwin's holistic approach to Braun. He applied the maxim of 'A sound mind in a healthy body' to staff, products and

p. 36

p. 34

[3]   Marlene Schnelle, 'Braun Design – ein Beispiel des Industrial Design in der BRD nach 1945', thesis manuscript (University of Bochum, 1978), Dieter Rams archive, 3.3.1

the firm as a whole, believing only that which is fit and healthy inside – whether it be man, appliance or corporation – can function optimally on the outside.

Prior to the establishment of the Bauhaus in the first half of the twentieth century, the design of industrial products was not considered to be much of a priority. Many appliances tended to be devised by the company engineers and even by the 1950s, the concept of the industrial designer had not caught on either as a profession or as an essential element of the industrial process. The War interrupted much activity in Germany. The Bauhaus closed and many of its members fled abroad, particularly to the United States, to continue their work. But afterwards, certain designers, architects and teachers in Germany began to pick up the threads of functionalist thinking that had been left behind, this time in a rather more sober, rational, practical, and even a political manner. For them, design was no longer about making things pretty, nor was it a quasi-esoteric pastime; their intent was to create a large number of products that served a function and improved the quality of life for everyone – the aesthetics would come later.

p. 32

In Darmstadt in 1954, Erwin attended a speech by the designer and former Bauhaus teacher Wilhelm Wagenfeld [+] that was to have a significant impact on the design direction of his company. It was a speech that challenged the accepted role of the manufacturer and outlined a holistic approach of a different kind: one in which the quality of products was bound to the attitudes and actions of their creators, as well as being the natural outcome of a function-orientated process involving many individuals working in different disciplines within the framework of one company. '[Better products] need intelligent producers who should thoroughly think through every product in terms of its purpose, its utility and longevity, and then consider how to fabricate what is required and right, with the minimum production and cost outlays, and bring it to the market,' Wagenfeld said. 'Industry and the market often understand creative input to be a decorative attachment, a kind of fashion design according to the latest patterns ... The result is that the displays in the shop windows of our cities are overflowing with unchanged, meaningless junk ... The wares have got louder, brasher, more intricate, but not better. In order to sell, people want to be "up to date". The desire is understandable ... when we consider that our industrial production is largely dependant on specialists, from manufacturers and managers who may know how to produce and sell, but can only judge the quality of their products in terms of how much profit they make.'

He argued that factories manufacturing consumer goods make a vital contribution to determining the quality and usefulness of products. This quality is located inside the objects, and results from both visible and invisible work. Wagenfeld ended his speech by saying that the simpler an industrial product, the harder it is to make, because simplicity comes from a degree of self-assuredness on the part of the designer. A 'simple' industrial product has a clarity that is free from the desires and constraints of each of its creators. He said: 'An industrial product that arises out of my activity thus only meets my own standards if a great distance causes it to seem almost unknown to me. It has to exist for itself, have its own being, completely purged from the individual influences that let it come into being. It should embody the company's achievement as a whole, the joint searching and discovering.'[4]

Wagenfeld was in effect advocating an objective design-driven approach to manufacturing, whereby the purpose of design should not be to increase profit, but to serve the consumer. The kind of practice he was talking about should not be autocratic: too much ego on the part of the creator can only have a negative effect on the end result, since the product will reflect the whims of the maker more than the purpose. His rejection of fashion and decoration and the suggestion that integrity of form, utility and thus quality could only be achieved if the will and participation of an entire company was bent towards it must have chimed with Erwin's sympathies. Immediately after the lecture he asked Wagenfeld to join him in helping Braun to search for a new formal product language, starting with radios and phonographs.

p.61

That same year, Erwin commissioned his former wartime comrade and creative mentor, the art historian, theatre and film director Fritz Eichler, [•] to take the company's cinema commercials in hand. This was to be the beginning of a long and fruitful collaboration. Eichler guided the firm's creative and cultural outlook and he maintained an association with Braun well into the 1970s. Like Wagenfeld, he took a systematic approach and was gripped by the idea of creating a fresh generation of products for a new, contemporary way of living. He began by observing and giving advice, but then, together with Artur, set about modernizing the entire p.37 design section of the firm. The first Kleinsuper SK 1 and SK 2 [•] radios with bakelite casings and perforated fronts, designed by Artur and Eichler together, plus some appliance redesigns by Hans Gugelot, such as the G 11 superHet radio with a maple p.37 wood housing, marked the beginning of the new Braun product world. [•] Eichler was a key figure at Braun: he helped to commit the company to a path of 'honest, understated, functional design' and guided the creation of a corporate identity that reflected those values.

Still in 1954, Erwin brought the recently founded Hochschule für Gestaltung (HfG) Ulm on board at Braun. The 'Ulmers' were also strong proponents of a rational, p.33 objective approach to design. Otl Aicher, [•] co-founder of the college, also became involved in developing the Braun corporate identity through the creation of printed material and trade fair exhibition stands. The highly talented architect and p.33 designer Hans Gugelot, [•] who taught at HfG Ulm, introduced his concepts of system-orientated design to Braun along with a number of other significant ideas, including new forms and materials for the casings of radios and phonographs.

[4]   Wilhelm Wagenfeld, 'Kunsterlische Zusammenarbeit mit der Industrie' lecture at the 'Bund Deutscher Kunsterzieher' convention at the Technical University of Darmstadt (18 September 1954), reprinted in Wichmann, *Mut zum Aufbruch*, 178–80

Another early Braun associate who deserves recognition at this point is Professor Herbert Hirche, who was head of the interior and furniture design department at the Academy of Art in Stuttgart. Hirche, who had studied with Mies van der Rohe and worked with Egon Eiermann and Hans Scharoun, devised cabinets for Braun audio appliances that were elegant items of furniture, with clean lines and stripped-down forms intended to harmonize with a modern interior. Through these pieces Hirche created a no-nonsense functionality for household appliances that was nevertheless aesthetically highly attractive. His design for the Braun HF 1 [+] television from 1958 is a particularly stunning example of his work.

p.286

All these designers had been recruited to the company in just six months. Erwin, Aicher and Gugelot were all in their early thirties at the time, whereas Hirche was forty-four, Eichler forty-three and Wagenfeld was fifty-four. They were all key contributors to Braun design but, with the exception of Eichler, none them worked in-house, which meant that the design presence within the company was still limited and non-continuous.

As the engineer in the family, Artur, like his father, was fascinated by technical innovation, as well as being more than capable of generating it himself, and so he was the ideal partner to support Erwin's creative vision. He and his technicians worked closely with the growing number of individuals giving design input to the company, collaborating on products involving new technologies and on the use of innovative materials to help solve particular design problems. Thus Wagenfeld's vision of a factory at which products and the quest for ideal functional form took precedence over departments, management and egos was beginning to take shape. Thanks to the commitment and forward-thinking attitude of its owners, Braun had become a giant experiment, testing a highly inclusive design theory. Now all that remained was to find out whether the buying public were interested in being part of it as well.

In a spectacularly short period of time, Braun developed a new range of products that was first presented to the public at the 'Rundfunk-, Fernseh- und Phono-austellung' (German Radio, TV and Phonographic Exhibition) in Düsseldorf from 16 August to 3 September 1955. Earlier, in June, Otl Aicher and the HfG Ulm had been commissioned to design a new trade fair stand, poster and catalogue for the show. The resulting stand, D 55, [+] developed together with the HfG student Hans G. Conrad, consisted of a system of steel profiles and plywood panels that could be slotted together in various formats.[5] It was a minimal and powerfully geometric set-up that was to be used many times in later exhibitions [+] until 1970 and is now on display at the Braun headquarters in Kronberg. The construction was almost a skeleton of a space, like an architectural sketch. Thin steel supports and intermediate spaces defined living areas furnished with pieces from Knoll

p.38

p.38

[5]   Jo Klatt and CC Cobarg, 'Der "ungewöhnliche" Braun-Messestand auf der Düsseldorfer Funkausstellung 1955', *design + design* magazine (undated), Dieter Rams archive 3.3.3

p.40

International, such as Harry Bertoia's Bench 400, and Wohnbedarf Zürich, such as the 1963 armchair by Gugelot, alongside potted plants in Rosenthal vases. A functional, recessed ceiling completed the backdrop for the Braun products redesigned by Wagenfeld, Hirche and Gugelot [+], including the TS–G and G–11 radios, G–12 phonograph, FS–G television and PK–G music cabinet. Also featured were the MS 1 music cabinet and a FS 1/2 TV set with control panels designed at Ulm, and the SK 1 and SK 2 radio devised by Artur and Eichler.[6]

Gugelot later described the effect that the new stand had on fair visitors: 'the brightly lit object right in the middle of the stands of the competition that were decorated with fountains and garlands caused a real shock.'[7] But it was still hard to gauge whether the 'shock' was ready to become a sensation. Although the media reaction to the new Braun products and image was positive and there was strong international critical interest, this was not immediately reflected in sales. Braun had to put considerable effort into educating sales departments, outlets and customers about the virtues of an approach based on design quality and technical concept, especially since the resulting products were certainly not cheap to buy. But ultimately it was up to the marketing department to convince the public. From 1956 onwards, special display systems for outlet shops and showrooms, [+] similar in style to the D 55 stand, were designed by Aicher and Conrad, alongside printed material [+] to reinforce the brand image. Erwin Braun cultivated alliances with like-minded companies such as Knoll International and Rosenthal, which helped further the cause, but at the beginning Braun was out on its own in completely unexplored marketing territory. Emphasizing functional quality and product placement in such a straightforward, Spartan manner was not the practice of its competitors. This was the beginning of 'Braun design' – the idea of basing the company's corporate identity on 'good design' – and it would never have been possible without the total commitment of hands-on owners who were prepared to risk putting quality before profit for a while.

p.42
p.43

In 1957, two years after the 'Rundfunk' exhibition, Braun participated in the West German international building exhibition in Berlin called 'Interbau', and it was here that the modernist and domestic context intended for the Braun design appliances became apparent. The Interbau was one of most interesting of the various worldwide post-war utopian modernist living experiments. It incorporated a completely new urban district called the Hansaviertel, which was an experiment in future living, called the 'City of Tomorrow', full of light and space and showcasing every modern convenience. Fifty-three high-profile architects from all over the world, including Alvar Aalto, Le Corbusier, Egon Eiermann, Walter Gropius, Arne Jacobsen and Oscar Niemeyer, were invited to contribute to the project, and Hirche and Gugelot were involved as interior designers.

[6]   Klemp et al., *Less and More*, 341

[7]   Hans Gugelot, lecture in Stockholm (May 1962), reprinted in Wichmann, *Mut zum Aufbruch*, 63

About a third of Berlin had been destroyed during the War. By the mid-1950s, much of the centre was still a treeless bomb-site divided between two political ideologies, each with a huge housing crisis. West Berlin needed new homes for families, but it also had to set an ideological standard: a break with the past, a fresh way of living based on the principles of freedom, democracy and internationality, not to mention a symbolic counterpoint to the socialist blocks of flats and monumental architecture being built around the Stalinallee in the east of the city.

As the thirty-six commissioned buildings went up, from low-rise single residences to high-rise apartment blocks, more than a million visitors came to gaze in wonder at the model apartments with under-floor heating, hot running water, functional fitted kitchens, rubbish chutes and unbelievably large windows: 'You would perhaps find it hard to understand today,' says resident Hanna Knebusch, who bought one of the first atrium houses in 1959, 'but it was absolutely amazing for us then – we had never seen such huge panes of glass before!'[8]

Visitors could go to the Interbau information centre and attend various exhibitions, including one held by the German Design Council that featured Braun products, to examine new styles of furniture and learn how to live in this modern set-up. Most importantly for Braun, around 60 per cent of the show apartments were fitted with Braun household appliances.[9] It made sense to put the objects in modern interiors: they constituted a 'natural habitat'. The product placement allowed people to see the full potential of this new kind of uncluttered interior and to understand that it was intended to be a space for self-expression where the user occupied the foreground. The effect of this Interbau exhibition on the German people and the international public cannot be underestimated. Here was a blueprint for a new way of living that picked up on the Bauhaus ideas of the past but included all the latest technologies and materials that were to be part of the future –, and Braun was being placed firmly at the heart of the new home. From here on, the term 'Braun design' started to be conflated with 'German design'. Dieter Rams, who had joined Braun two years earlier, remembers clearly the impact that visiting the Interbau had on him as a young man: 'It was my first-ever flight in an aeroplane and there was this city of rubble, tidied-up rubble but rubble nevertheless, and in the middle were these Interbau houses with their restrained interiors that were all about living in contrast to the encrusted, overloaded interiors from before that were all about possessions'.[10]

Shortly after the opening of the Interbau, Braun showed its new products at the eleventh Milan Triennale in 1957. This time the critical resonance was huge: Wagenfeld received the 'Gran Premio' gold award for his complete works and Braun won another for its entire new range of products. Over the subsequent

[8]   'Modern Love', *Wallpaper** magazine, no.104 (November 2007), 144–49

[9]   Klemp et al., *Less and More*, 351

[10]   In conversation with the author (August 2007)

Braun trade fair stand in Berlin, 1954

Max Braun

Artur and Erwin Braun

Wilhelm Wagenfeld

Otl Aicher   Hans Gugelot

BRAUN

0.1. Firmensignet
Das Firmenzeichen soll auf allen werb-
lichen Kommunikationsmitteln erscheinen.
Es darf in seiner Zeichengestalt nicht
verändert werden.
Es darf weder im laufenden Text noch in
Verbindung mit anderen Zeichen
erscheinen.

0.1.1. Konstruktion

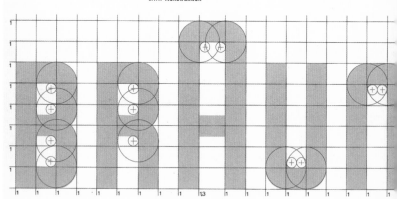

Balkenstärke und lichte Weite der Buchstaben sowie die Buchstabenabstände
haben ein Verhältnis von 1:1. Die Konstruktion kann somit auf einem Quadrat-
netz angelegt werden. Eine Ausnahme
ist die lichte Weite des Buchstabens A;
sie steht in einem Verhältnis von 1 : 1,3.
Die Höhe der normalen Buchstaben ist
6mal die Balkenstärke. Die Höhe des
Buchstabens A 8mal die Balkenstärke.
Die inneren Rundungen haben ihren
Einstich auf den Schnittpunkten einer
gedachten Vierteilung des Quadratnetzes.
Die Zirkeleinstiche der äußeren Rundungen liegen auf den Schnittpunkten
des Netzes.

Braun logo, 1935   Guidelines for the new Braun logo, designed by Wolfgang Schmittel in 1958

5

0.1.2. Größen und Proportionen

Zur besseren Lesbarkeit auch in den klei-
neren Größen wurde das Braun Zeichen
in 3 Schnitten angelegt, wobei die Schnitte
2 und 3 in ihrem Duktus lichter sind.
Der erste Schnitt, wie er in der Konstruk-
tionszeichnung angelegt ist, darf nur
dann verwendet werden, wenn die Länge
des Zeichens größer ist als 22,5 mm.
Der Zweite Schnitt ist für die Größen
17,5·20 und 22,5 mm, der dritte Schnitt
für die Größen 5·7,5·10·12,5 und 15 mm
angelegt.

BRAUN

BRAUN   BRAUN   BRAUN
35   30   25

BRAUN

BRAUN   BRAUN   BRAUN
22,5   20   17,5

BRAUN

BRAUN   BRAUN   BRAUN   BRAUN   BRAUN
15   12,5   10   7,5   5

Diese Schnitte dürfen fotografisch nicht
verkleinert oder vergrößert werden. Sie
sollen bei ähnlichen Drucksachen-
Formaten in gleicher Größe verwendet
werden.

Top left: FS 1 television, 1955
Above left: SK 2 radio, Artur Braun and Fritz Eichler, 1955

Top right: G 11 radio, Hans Gugelot, 1955
Above right: PK-G radio / phonograph, Hans Gugelot, 1956

A mockup of the D 55 Braun pavilion at Ulm, 1955

The Braun D 55 pavilion in use c.1964,
displaying audio products including the TP 1, SK 4, RT 20, T 22, T 52, and 'studio 2'.

Top: The D 55 pavilion at the Düsseldorf 'Rundfunk' exhibition, 1955
Above left: The D 55 pavilion in Zurich, 1962

Above right: The D 55 pavilion, Frankfurt Fair

Top: Display system for Braun showrooms, c. 1965
Above: Guidelines for using the display system

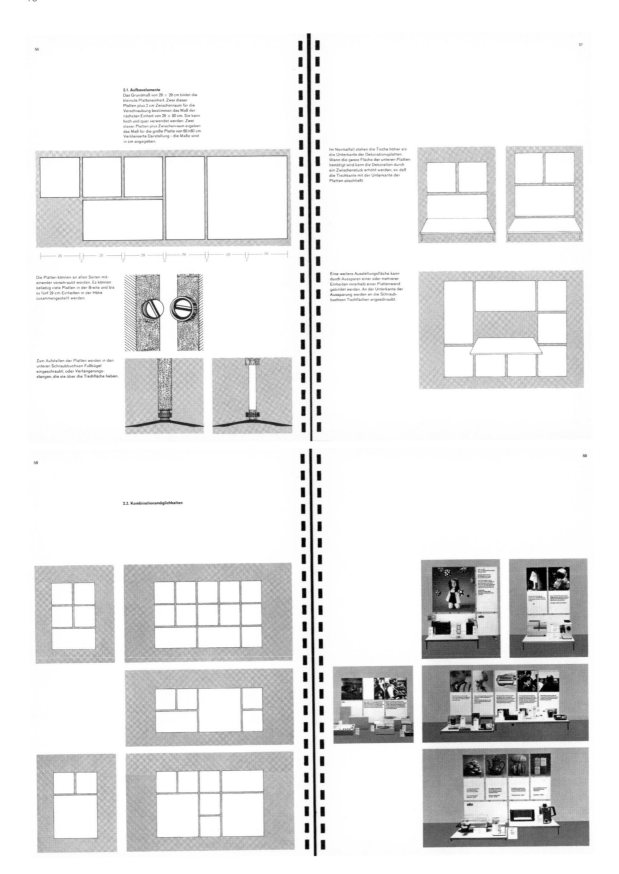

years, the company's international reputation and presence continued to flourish. In 1958, sixteen Braun appliances were shown in the German pavilion of Brussels World's Fair, including a new radio and phonograph combination called Studio 1. In the same year The Museum of Modern Art in New York (MoMA) included five Braun products in its permanent design collection: the SK 5 Phonosuper, the KM 3 food processor, the Transistor 2 portable radio, the T 3 pocket-sized receiver and the PA 2 projector, and they were shown in an exhibition of outstanding twentieth-century design. The Braun experiment, it seems, was beginning to deliver exceptional results.

Dieter Rams Joins Braun

Dieter Rams never intended to be a designer. Architecture was the profession he had chosen and his interests beyond this field tended towards environmental design and town planning: he was drawn to the big picture rather than individual elements. But in 1953, unable to afford the luxury of extended academic study, Rams left college at the age of twenty-one with a diploma in interior architecture. Soon afterwards, he secured a position with the architecture office of Otto Apel in Frankfurt, which he held for the next two years. It was pure chance that led him to Braun. A colleague in the office had found an advertisement in the local newspaper from the company, which was looking for an in-house architect. 'I didn't know anything about Braun,' recalls Rams in an open letter to Erwin Braun in 1979, 'but I applied anyway. My colleague did too: it was a bet to see which of us would get an answer – and I won.'[11]

At his interview, Rams met Erwin, who gave him an idea of his plans for the company. Erwin also showed Rams prototypes of products and this piqued his interest: 'It must have been the models of the appliances that were later presented at the Internationale Funkausstellung (International Radio Exhibition) in 1955. I was enraptured by Gugelot's work – like many architects after me.' Following an interview, a number of short-listed candidates were asked to come up with a design for a company guest room. So Rams made his sketch and sent it in. [*] Fritz Eichler picks up the story in another letter, this time addressed from him to Rams in 1980.[12] He relates how he, together with Erwin Braun, Hans Gugelot and Otl Aicher, examined the short-listed drawings, some of which were inviting, and some of which were clearly intended to look as prestigious as possible: 'Your design comprised just two A4 sheets with a simple floor plan and elevation that were realistic

p. 54

[11]   Dieter Rams, 'Erinnerungen an die ersten Jahre bei Braun' ('Memories of the first years at Braun'), an open letter to Erwin Braun (July 1979), printed in *Weniger aber Besser / Less But Better* (Hamburg, 1995), 15. Translation modified by the author

[12]   'Dear Dieter', letter from Fritz Eicher, *Design: Dieter Rams* & (Berlin, 1980 and 1981), 11–16. Translation modified by the author

– without any razzmatazz – drawn with the same simple and sparse lines that I encounter today when I come into your office and see a first sketch for a new appliance on your desk. Our conclusion back then was unequivocal: he fits in with us."[13]

Rams was given the job and a space with a drawing board in the graphic design department alongside Wolfgang Schmittel, who had redesigned the Braun logo. Schmittel helped define the company's corporate image until he left the firm in 1980. He developed the sparse, functional graphic style that defined its identity: often monochrome, typography-led print media with images that explained the products to the user. As with the products, this approach was radically different from that of the competition. The starkness of the Braun corporate imagery made it stand out a mile.

The only element of frivolity in Schmittel's work for Braun were his use of jazz images. Jazz held a significant meaning for Braun: throughout the War, a somewhat subversive jazz scene survived in Frankfurt, and it blossomed after the Allies took over. Erwin and his crowd, which of course included many individuals from Braun, were very much part of this scene that, in the 1950s, had its social centre at a place called the 'Jazz Keller'. Schmittel was also a photographer and he took many images of the illustrious jazz musicians who played in Frankfurt during this time, quite a few of which were used to advertise the company's audio products. Jazz suited the Braun image well: adventurous, daring and unconventional, yet highly disciplined and rigorous; constrained by set patterns and guidelines yet totally free to find new paths between them; intellectual yet undeniably wild, cool and modern. Associating Braun with jazz not only came naturally to the individuals defining the company, but it also provided a superb visual counterpoint to the rather dry, technical minimalism of the products.

Rams was initially occupied with working on designs for various interiors in the Braun factory complex and a private residence for Erwin (which was later taken over by Gugelot). It was not long, however, before he got swept up in the general creative excitement surrounding the new products. Because the profession of 'industrial designer' did not really exist yet, many of those involved with designing Braun appliances had an architecture background and the novelty of Braun's approach tended to blur even the professional categories that did exist. For the individuals who had been invited into this environment by Erwin, for those who 'fit in' at Braun, there seems to have been a feeling of 'all hands on deck', and Rams was soon involved in the redesigns of the TS 2 radio and colour concepts for the SK 1 and SK 2 series.

p. 57 The PA 1 first automatic slide projector [←] was the first appliance that Rams designed solely. His signature muted chromatic greys, soft edges, superb detailing, colour highlights for button controls and haptic sense for the surface qualities of component materials were all present in this first piece, which came on the market

---

[13]   Ibid., 12. Translation modified by the author

by 1956. It attracted a great deal of interest at the 'Photokina' trade fair in Cologne that year and must have made it clear to the Braun brothers – if they didn't know already – that their new architect had quite a talent for objects at the smaller end of the construction scale.

p.53
p.60

Still in 1955, Artur Braun was looking for a model-maker who could work in plaster to assist with the development of kitchen appliances. Rams recommended his friend and former fellow student from the Werkkunstschule Wiesbaden, Gerd A Müller, [+] who joined the team later that year. In 1956, another Wiesbaden graduate, Roland Weigend [+], came aboard to help out with the model-making and Rams's ever-increasing workload. So even though Rams barely knew the designers from Ulm when he started at Braun, he soon had some familiar faces to keep him company. The three of them were given a studio together and were later to form the nucleus of the permanent Braun in-house design department.

—

The SK 4 – 'Snow White's Coffin'

p.58

1956 was also the year in which Dieter Rams began working on a product that became legendary for Braun, and raised his profile considerably. The super phonograph SK 4, [+] nicknamed 'Snow White's Coffin', was a combined radio and record player that is widely considered to mark the beginning of the modern domestic music system. Like all Braun products, the SK 4 was born out of a team effort. The design of the record player was based on an earlier model by William Wagenfeld, but the rest of the product was entirely new. Instead of being hidden away in a piece of furniture, the controls and the functional aspects of the device were not only on display, but they were the predominant feature of the design. Rams, under Fritz Eichler's guidance, was the main designer assigned to the development of the SK 4. He developed a wooden housing with a metal facing, as well as the arrange-ment of the turntable and controls on the top. The story goes that Erwin Braun sent Eichler to HfG Ulm with the prototype so that he could show it to Hans Gugelot, who proposed the wooden end panels and an entire casing made in bent sheet metal, including a lid that was later dropped because it disturbed the acoustics.[14] The Braun brothers were still not 100 per cent convinced of the design until, back in Frankfurt, Rams suggested making a transparent lid from a new plastic that had just come on the market and was being used for advertising displays. It was an inspired thought and lent the phonograph just the lightness needed to balance the metal and wood of the base, as well as helping to define the acoustics. It also set the standard for all record players that followed – a turntable without a Perspex dust cover is now almost unthinkable.

[14]   See CC Cobarg and Dietrich Lubs, 'Wie entstand der SK 4, wer gab ihm den Namen Schnee-wittchensarg?' (2005), Dieter Rams archive; quoted in Klemp et al., *Less and More*, 345

—

The Braun Design Department

Towards the end of the 1950s, Braun concentrated increasingly on the development of its in-house design team. This was probably for practical reasons as much as anything else. The HfG Ulm designers had made an invaluable contribution to the company's product line but business was growing at an extraordinary pace and Ulm was more than 300 kilometres away. 'I am often asked how we designers at Braun succeeded in creating our own expertise, in gradually relieving the Ulm designers until finally all the design assignments were solved by Braun's product design department,' wrote Dieter Rams in his 1979 letter to Erwin Braun. 'It was a completely organic process. When I started at Braun, the Ulmers dominated of course. The co-operation with them had been going on for some time. I wasn't involved that much... But gradually I got into the work. I had the advantage of being in-house.'[15]

Rams went on to add that he understood the importance of, and thus cultivated the relationship with, the technical department, taking great care to convince the technicians that the designers were not there to take their work away from them but to support them. 'Naturally it was also an advantage that when an acute problem came up, the technicians could reach me more easily. I could go with them to the drawing board and find solutions with them more quickly and easily – as I would still argue today – than an external designer could ever do,' he wrote. 'The decisive factor in this kind of co-operation is always human consensus... But this can only be arrived at if you understand the other's work completely, respect achievement and repeatedly familiarize yourself with their ideas... I would maintain that even today Braun depends on these kinds of personal relationships. Without them you cannot make reasonable design. Nothing can replace them – not even the most cunning marketing ploys.'[16]

Braun took on two graduates of Ulm as permanent members of the design team: Reinhold Weiss in 1959 and Richard Fischer in 1960, when they were also joined by Robert Oberheim, [+] another Wiesbaden graduate. Rams, who had a number of significant design achievements for the company already under his belt (not to mention a successful independent 'sideline' in designing furniture systems for the company Vitsœ + Zapf), and an ability to bring together individuals from different disciplines into a cohesive unit, was a natural candidate to lead the Braun design team. In 1961, when the company became a joint-stock corporation, his position became official: chief designer and head of the Braun product design department.

p. 60

[15]   Rams, 'Erinnerungen' in *Weniger aber Besser*, 19. Translation modified by the author

[16]   Rams, 'Erinnerungen' in *Weniger aber Besser*, 20. Translation modified by the author

—   The Braun Design Team

Teamwork is vital in any company and the way members of the Braun design
team collaborated among themselves as well as with other teams, such as the
technicians and the marketing department, made a significant contribution
to the ongoing success of the company in the following years, even after the
departure of the Braun brothers. The firm remained committed to a design-
driven approach and this was reinforced by the role of the design team within
it; the department led by Dieter Rams held a high position in the company hierarchy. It was independent of other sections and answerable only to the management, of which, as of 1968, Rams himself was a member.

The design team at Braun also remained remarkably stable. After the initial
comings and goings, many employees stayed on for long periods of time. Rams
himself worked in the Braun Design Department from 1955 until 1995 – almost his
entire working life. The team was also relatively small: at its peak it comprised
only 17 staff. The individual designers tended to specialize in certain product areas

p.60
and often co-designed pieces with other team members, [*] including Rams.
Although he could easily have withdrawn to a managerial role, he continued to design
many Braun products himself throughout his career and was always actively
involved in the decision-making process and supervision of the rest. Although
the media often tends to conflate 'Braun design' with 'Dieter Rams design', Rams
himself always points out that the appliances created during his time there were
the result of teamwork. When authorship is assigned to a particular product
it is important to bear this collaborative design approach in mind. Nevertheless
there is rarely the time and the space, nor the documentation available, to name
all those who should be mentioned. Between 1955 and 1995, Rams and his team

p.62
designed more than 1,000 products for Braun. [*] Just as there is limited space
here to credit all those involved, so too is there not enough space in this book
to examine every product. Included here is a selection of the team's main pro-
tagonists; the 'Detail' chapter contains a closer examination of some of the significant Braun products that Rams was directly involved with.

One of the first key figures in Braun's design team was Gerd Alfred Müller
p.53
(1932–91) [*] who had studied interior design with Rams at Wiesbaden. Rams first
recommended him to Artur Braun for a post in the model-making department,
but he too was to become an important designer for the company. Müller's
approach was a sculptural one; he made the forms of the appliances he worked
on rather than drawing them. One of his first products for Braun was perhaps his
p.66
most famous, the KM 3 food processor [*] from 1957. This was followed by other
kitchen appliances, which became his speciality, including the first versions of the
p.67
MP 3 juice extractor (1957), the MX 3 mixer (1958) and the M 1 hand mixer [*] (1960).
Müller also worked with Rams on the development of the combi DL 5 shaver (1957)
and with Hans Gugelot on the famous matt black and chrome SM 31 Sixtant

shaver, launched in 1962. Müller was one of the few team members who chose to pursue a career beyond Braun. He went freelance in 1960 and set up his own design studio in Eschborn, near Frankfurt, where he designed a series of pens for Lamy in 1966, the 2000 series, which are still in production today and have rightfully earned their place as a German 'design classic'.

Like Dieter Rams, Reinhold Weiss (b. 1934) studied carpentry and then architecture. He later attended the HfG Ulm, where his dissertation project was the design of an iron with an innovative handle for easier use, which was later purchased by Braun. He joined the company in 1959 and his first design for them, a radically new type of desk fan called the HL 1, [+] went on sale in 1961. He also devised an absolute Braun classic, the black plastic and chrome HT 1 toaster, [+] which was the first of its kind for the company. His HLD 2 hairdryer from 1964 had a compact and revolutionary form but tended to overheat when the user inadvertently covered the air intake slits with their hands and so was redesigned by Rams in 1970. Several of Weiss's designs were highly innovative, both in form and in engineering, and were much imitated by the competition. The toaster was one example, and the HE 1 express kettle [+] (1962) was another. So too were the elegant KSM 1 and KSM 11 coffee grinders. Weiss left Braun in 1967, and moved to the United States to take up a post as vice-president of product design at Unimark International before going freelance in 1970.

Richard Fischer (b. 1935) was another former Ulm student. He joined the team in 1960 and worked on a variety of products, ranging from kitchen appliances and photographic equipment (including a film camera line with Rams, the EA 1) to razors. He left in 1968 to pursue a freelance design and academic career and teach as a professor at the nearby College of Design in Offenbach.

Robert Oberheim (b. 1938) joined Braun in 1960 and remained with the firm until 1994. He took over the development of the film camera line from Rams and Fischer. His first Nizo camera, the S 8 [+] (1965) was a highly attractive and easy-to-operate device with a matt aluminium housing, a black lacquered grip and clear operating elements. The design was so successful that it changed little through various updates right up until 1981, when the film camera and flashgun production was sold to Robert Bosch and video camcorder technology began to make them obsolete. Oberheim also designed a timelessly attractive film projector, the FP 30, [+] in 1971, which used the same matt anodized aluminium and black painted finish as the cameras, and clear plastic film reel spools. Like numerous other Braun products from this era, the FP 30 would look at home alongside contemporary designs such as Apple Macintosh laptop computers.

Dietrich Lubs (b. 1938) [+] was one of the last of the first generation of designers to arrive at Braun. He grew up in East Germany and, after fleeing to the West in 1953, trained to be a shipbuilding engineer in Cologne. On reading an article about Braun in the German magazine *Form* and seeing Braun products on display with Knoll International furniture in their Düsseldorf showroom, he decided to apply for

p.76
p.65

p.65

p.73

p.72

p.60

a job at Braun, where he was interviewed and hired by Rams in 1962. Lubs was initially assigned to work on *produktgrafik* (appliance typography) in collaboration with Roland Weigend. He spent his early years at the company soaking up the atmosphere, learning by doing and labelling appliances and control panels with the distinctive in-house, lower-case sans-serif typeface 'Akzidenz Grotesk'. By 1971 Lubs was head of product typography but, like most other employees, this was not to be his only area of responsibility. In 1972 he designed a mains-powered alarm clock, the 'Phase 3' and in 1975 he designed the distinctive mains-powered 'functional' digital

p. 79

alarm clock. [+] They marked the beginning of a range of clocks, watches, clock radios and travel alarms that at times commanded the highest product recognition for the firm – beyond even the shavers – and Lubs, occasionally working in collabo-ration with Rams, designed most of them. The AB 1, the ABR 313 sl travel radio

p. 80

alarm, and the AW 10 wristwatch [+] were among the best-known. Lubs' clocks even gave Braun a corporate sound: how many hundreds and thousands of people all over the world have woken up to the distinctive peep peep peep of the Braun travel alarm?

Clocks were the perfect product area for Lubs. There were few appliances at the time where typography had such a vital role to play in a product's function. Lubs' first clock designs were digital but, ironically enough for such a technically forward-looking company, it was the analogue versions that were to prove most popular. 'The human is an analogue creature,' explains Lubs. Braun's design approach to clocks was just like its method of creating other products. They were not intended to be decorative; they were chronometers whose primary purpose was to show the time.

Rams and Lubs also designed the first pocket calculator for Braun in 1975 and they quickly improved on it in 1976 with the ET 22. Various redesigns followed

p. 80

as technology improved, but it is perhaps the ET 66 [+] from 1987 that is the most refined version. Like the clocks, it is the immaculate sense of proportion in the typography and the form, as well as the clear yet restrained colour-coding, that make the ET 22 not only enjoyable to use but also a pleasure to look at.

Lubs was greatly inspired by the Braun design environment. He describes the work atmosphere in the early 1960s as being 'very serious but with lots of energy'. The department, he adds, was like an apartment: 'you had to ring a doorbell to come in'. The team worked very hard at their individual projects, but communication between them was constant, so there was little need for group discussions. Although Rams was the boss, remembers Lubs, everyone else had a voice. The studio appears to have been rather like a college workshop. 'If Dieter did not like something, he would say, "Is that good?" or "Do you think it is finished?",' he recalls. 'After work the team socialized together as well,' he adds, 'bringing along their girlfriends, going out for drinks, to listen to jazz, celebrating birthdays together … The com-pany had a hierarchy but it was also open house. There was constant discussion, taking and giving, we were all filled with the same goal.'[17]

[17]   Interview with the author (May 2009)

Braun becomes Gillette

Being a Braun designer was clearly as much a way of life as an occupation in the first decade of its existence. Throughout the 1960s business boomed for Braun AG. By 1964 it had a turnover of 173 million deutschmarks and nearly 5,000 employees.[18] Despite its size, the company continued its benevolent approach and offered good wages, a pension scheme, profit-sharing and a comprehensive health service to employees, who worked hard to contribute towards a system that they clearly felt was worth believing in. Therefore it must have come as quite a shock in 1967 when the Braun brothers sold the company to the US concern Gillette. The Braun brothers had previously gone to the US several times looking for a partner. These trips became a search for a buyer, however, with news of an impending act from President Lyndon B Johnson that would, starting on 1 January 1968, forbid US companies from direct investment in certain countries, including Germany. As a result, Gillette made a quick decision to buy Braun in 1967.

Now Dieter Rams could no longer rely on a good relationship with like-minded owners. He had to consolidate and maintain his role and that of the design department in the company. The design historian Klaus Klemp states: 'Apart from his own design work, this is the second greatest achievement of Dieter Rams: establishing a design department within a company, which succeeded for decades in preserving its own individual approach and rigorously advancing it, without really being influenced by changing market interests.'[19] He is right; it was a remarkable feat. It takes a considerable degree of doggedness and conviction to follow the ungratifying and difficult path of insisting on a consistently long-term view in a corporate world that is constantly shifting and full of short-term decisions.

Although it happened remarkably quickly, the change of ownership at Braun seems to have been a friendly affair, particularly from the viewpoint of the design team, since it was precisely the quality of design that was so interesting for the new owners. According to Dietrich Lubs, the main obstacles for the design team were having to battle more intensely with the differing priorities of the marketing department and the fact that the company managers tended to change every couple of years, 'which meant we had to re-convince them all the time'. A significant aid in this Sisyphean task was the designer's excellent understanding with the technicians – a situation that is often difficult to create in creative teams, and one that existed at Braun thanks to Rams's cultivation of interdisciplinary co-operation right from the beginning.

During the 1970s, Rams strengthened the position of the design team in various ways. He was now travelling more and giving talks as an ambassador for Braun but, more importantly, as a representative of 'good design'. When asked to discuss

[18]   Wichmann, *Mut zum Aufbruch*, 113

[19]   Klemp et al., *Less and More*, 437

the Braun 'philosophy', he talked increasingly about his philosophy and that of his team: 'We are economical with form and colour, prioritize simple forms, avoid unnecessary complexity, do without ornament. Instead [there is] order and clarification. We measure every detail against the question of whether it serves function and facilitates handling.'[20] As the public face of Braun, on view every time the company picked up yet another design award or critical acclaim, Rams fused the idea of the company with the goals of the design team. His team *was* Braun.

p.84 Behind the door with its own doorbell, the team continued its work [+] as it always had: in somewhat Spartan surroundings, its members created technical drawings to communicate ideas with the technicians, and built models in wood, plaster and plastic to communicate with each other and sell each new idea to the management, sales and marketing departments. But as the product range increased during the late 1960s, the product design department expanded further and individual designers began to need to specialize more. By 1977 the product design department, still headed by Rams, was split into three sections to accommodate this: Product Design (PG–P) was led by Robert Oberheim, Product Graphics (PG–G) by Dietrich Lubs and the Model Workshop (PG–M) by Roland Weigend.

Florian Seiffert (b. 1943), who studied design at the Folkwangschule in Essen, joined the team in 1968 after becoming joint winner of the inaugural 'BraunPrize', which was the first international industrial design award in Germany. He went on p.69 to design the colourful Aromaster KF 20 coffee maker [+] and was in charge of the shaver section until he left in 1972. His Aromaster design was later updated as p.69 the even more successful KF 40 version [+] by a fellow former Folkwangschule student at Braun, Hartwig Kahlcke (b. 1942). Both Seiffert and Kahlcke later left Braun and opened their own design office together in Wiesbaden. A third Folkwangschule graduate in the team was Ludwig Littmann, who won the BraunPrize in 1972, and went on to head up the hand-mixer category and later the steam iron section.

The designer Jürgen Greubel (b. 1938) was another former Wiesbaden student, just as Rams was before him. He worked at the company full-time from 1967 until 1973 and later on a freelance basis after he went on to design for other clients such as London Transport. He collaborated with Rams on the Citromatic citrus p.71 press and devised the almost-sculptural HLD 6 hairdryer [+] before specialising in the production of steam irons together with Littman.

Roland Ullmann (b. 1948), who joined Braun in 1972, specialized almost exclusively in electric shavers – which were among Braun's strongest products right from the beginning. Perhaps his most famous design is the 1976 micron electric shaver with a knobbly grip made of a specially developed combination of hard and soft plastics, which remained in production for more than 15 years.

[20] In response to the question: 'What is the Braun philosophy?' in an interview with Hans-Hermann Kotte, *taz* magazine (29 August 1989). Reprinted in Uta Brandes, ed., *Dieter Rams, Designer. Die leise Ordnung der Dinge* (Göttingen, 1990), 190

Gerd Alfred Müller and Dieter Rams in Frankfurt, c.1950.
Wartime rubble is visible behind them.

Dieter Rams and Gerd Alfred Müller in West Berlin, c.1980

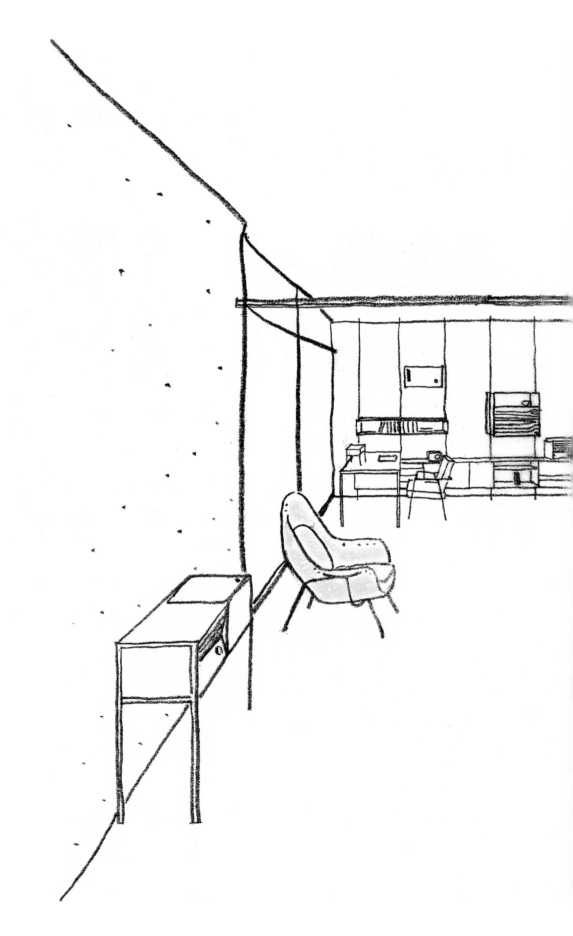

Dieter Rams's first sketch for a Braun showroom, 1955. Knoll furniture.
The idea for a shelving system is visible on the back wall.

1955 jul

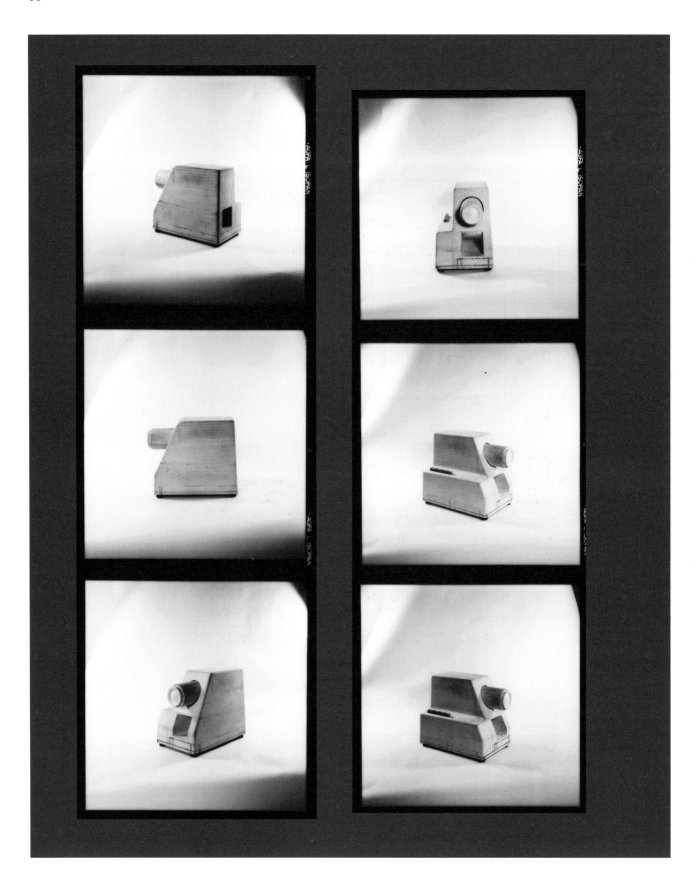

Model for the PA 1 slide projector,
Dieter Rams, 1956

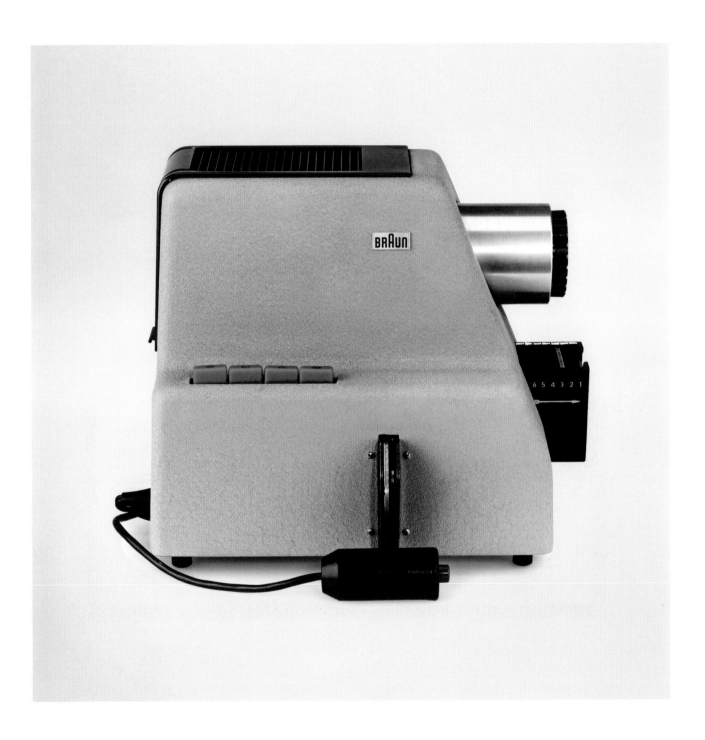

PA 1 slide projector

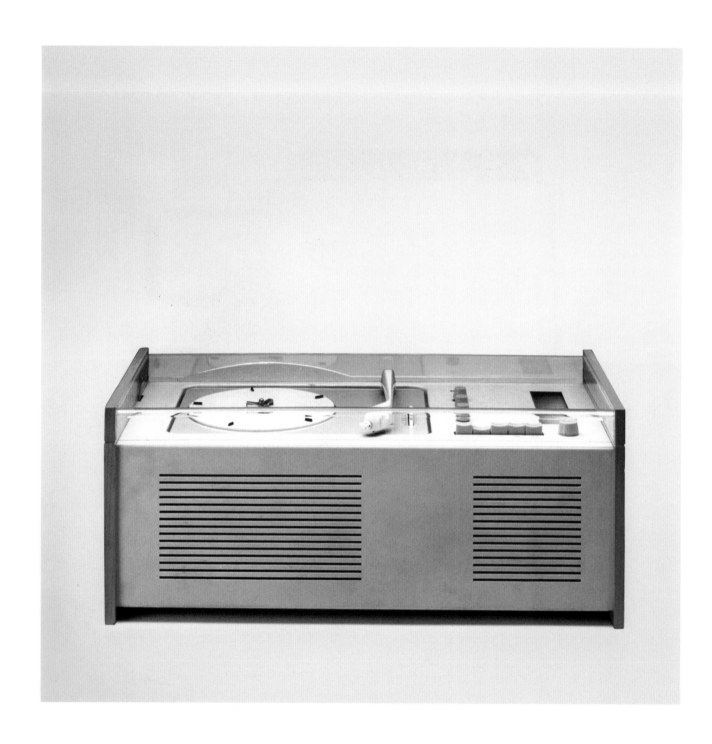

SK 4 record player,
Dieter Rams and Hans Gugelot, 1956

Wolfgang Schmittel, Dieter Rams and Fritz Eichler, c.1964

Top left: Gerd Alfred Müller, c.1957
Above left: Robert Oberheim, c.1970

Top right: Dietrich Lubs, c.1979
Above right: Roland Weigend, c.1970

Top: Fritz Eichler and Dieter Rams, c.1968
Bottom: Dieter Rams (centre) and Fritz Eichler (right), c.1964

Centre: Dietrich Lubs, c.1979

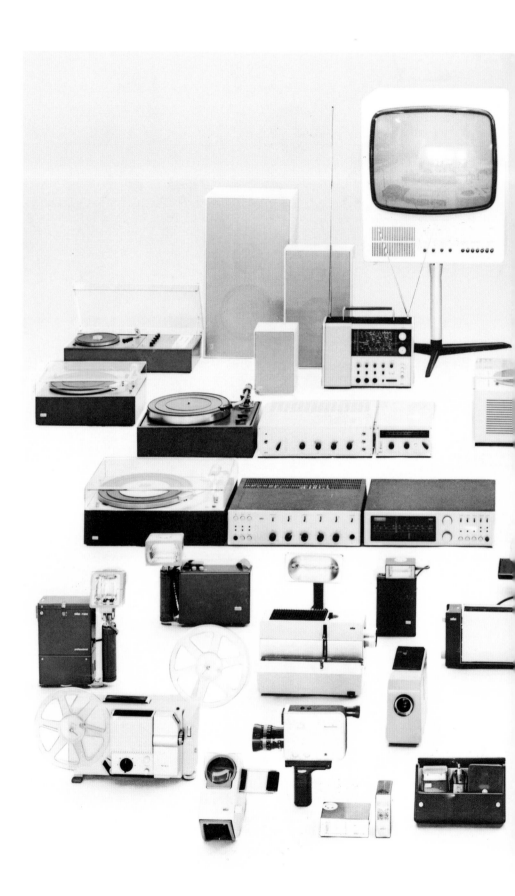

Braun product range, c.1970

Braun product range, c.1963

HE 1 kettle,
Reinhold Weiss, 1962

HT 1 toaster,
Reinhold Weiss, 1963

KM 3 kitchen machine,
Gerd Alfred Müller, 1957

M 1 mixer,
Gerd Alfred Müller, 1960

MPZ 2 'citromatic' citrus press,
Dieter Rams and Jürgen Greubel, 1972

KMM 2 coffee grinder,
Dieter Rams, 1969

KF 20 coffee maker,
Florian Sieffert, 1972

KF 40 coffee maker,
Hartwig Kahlke, 1984

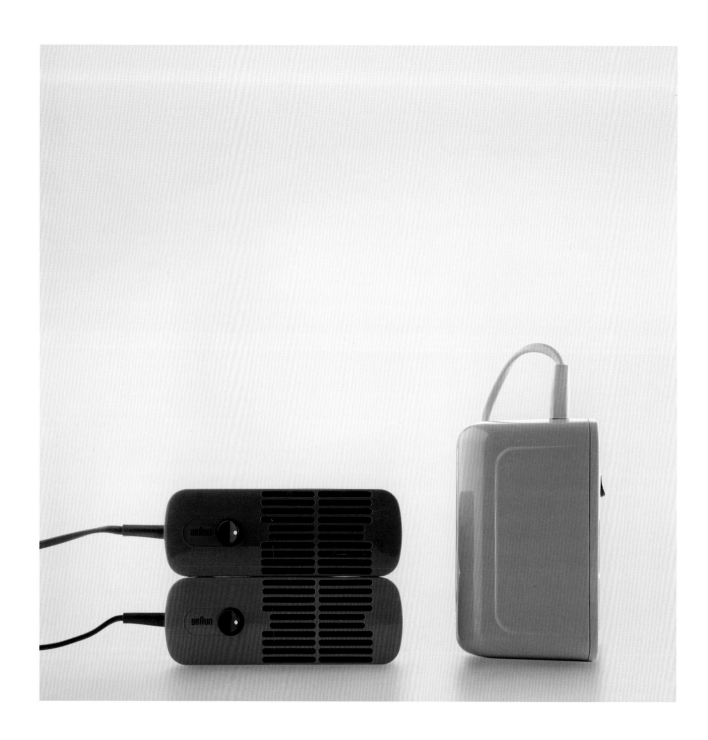

HLD 4 hairdryer,
Dieter Rams, 1970

HLD 6 hairdryer,
Jürgen Greubel, 1971

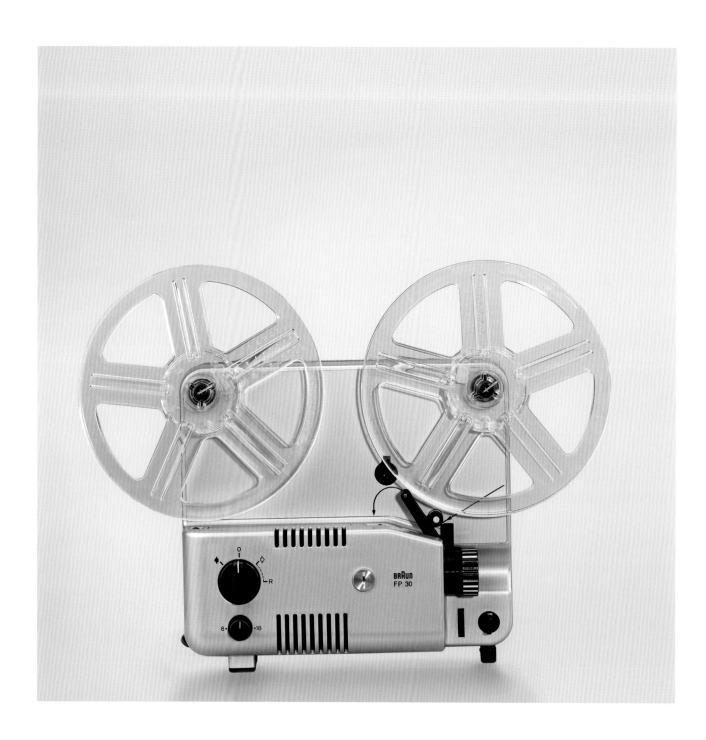

FP 30 film projector,
Robert Oberheim, 1971

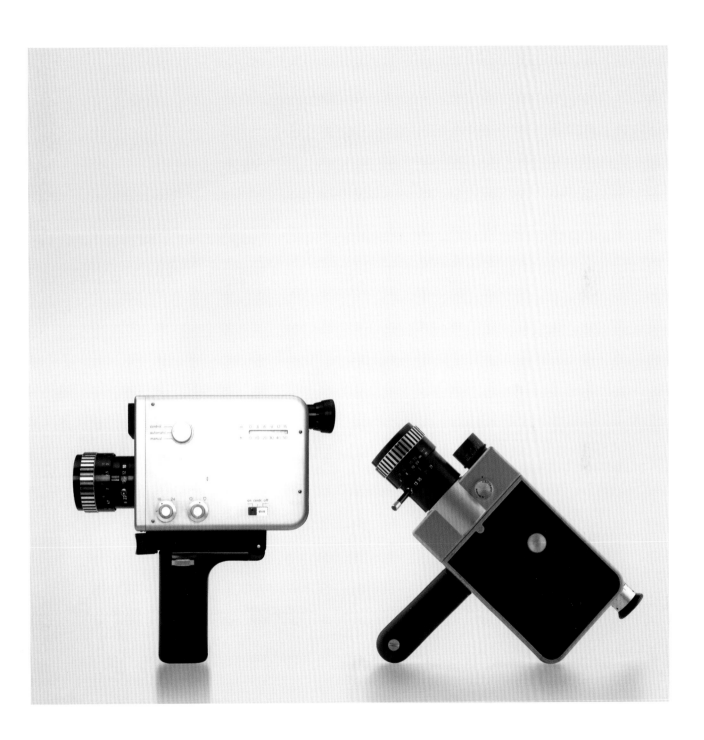

Nizo S 8 camera,
Robert Oberheim, 1965

EA 1 camera,
Dieter Rams, Richard Fischer and Robert Oberheim, 1965

8008 'sixtant' shaver,
Dieter Rams, Florian Seiffert,
Robert Oberheim, 1973

DL 5 'combi' shaver,
Dieter Rams and Gerd Alfred
Müller, 1957

'micron' shaver,
Roland Ullmann , 1976

'domino' lighter,
Dieter Rams, 1976

T 2 / TFG 2 lighter,
Dieter Rams, 1968

F 1 mactron lighter,
Dieter Rams, 1971

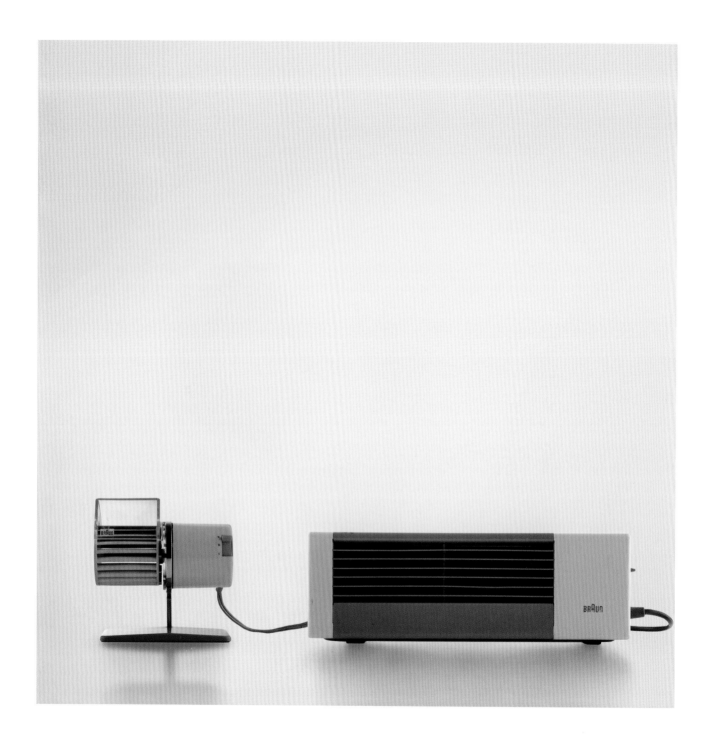

HL 1 fan,
Reinhold Weiss, 1961

H 1 heater,
Dieter Rams, 1959

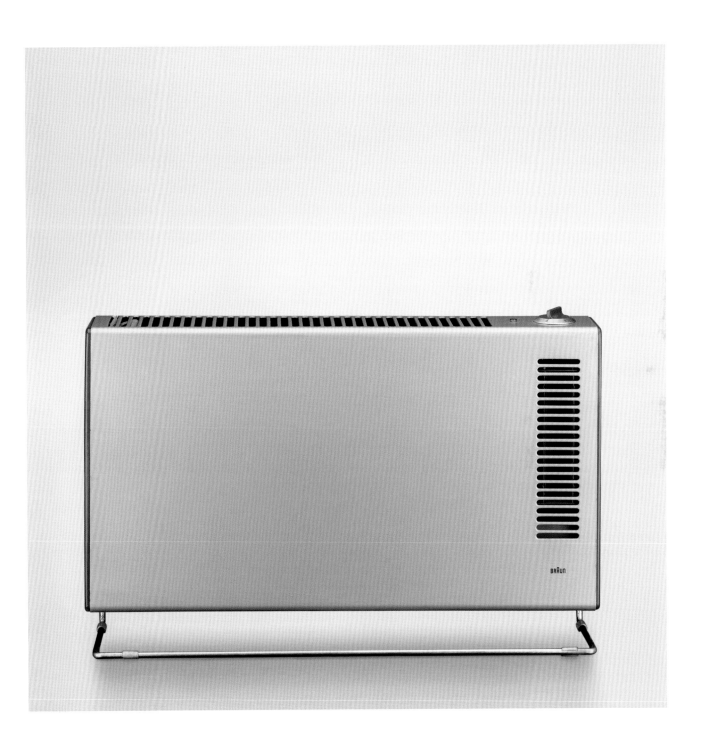

H 6 heater,
Richard Fischer and Dieter Rams, 1965

EF 1 flash,
Dieter Rams, 1958

F 111 flash,
Dieter Ram, 1970

EF 300 flash,
Dieter Rams, 1964

AB 31 alarm clock,   phase 3 alarm clock,   'functional' alarm clock,
Dietrich Lubs, 1979   Dieter Rams, 1972   Dietrich Lubs, 1975

Top left: ET 88 'world traveller'
calculator, Dietrich Lubs, 1991

Top centre: ET 66 calculator,
Dieter Rams and Dietrich Lubs, 1987

Top right: ET 55 calculator,
Dieter Rams and Dietrich Lubs, 1983

Above: AW 10 watch,
Dietrich Lubs, 1989

Peter Hartwein (b. 1942) joined Braun in 1970. He came from a carpentry and architecture background, which must have endeared him to Rams. He started off working on camera technology but soon moved on to hi-fi systems and loud-speakers – a domain that originally belonged exclusively to his boss. Hartwein and Rams developed a highly successful partnership while working on music systems. The late Braun hi-fis were expensive, top-of-the-range dream machines for techno fans: a far cry from the simple, affordable tools for living, they had become exercises in the interface between design and technology. Over the course of Rams's career, music systems evolved rapidly, from the early phonographs such as the SK 4, into the first off-white components in neat boxes, for example

p.278
p.268

the 'studio 2' [+] from 1959, and the almost scientific, steel-clad, wall-mounted systems (TS 45, TG 60 and L450) [+], and eventually the stackable black modules such as the 'atelier', 'studio', 'regie' and 'audio' series, covered in knobs yet inscrutably sleek and compact. So many design features that we take for granted in hi-fis come from Rams: the components, the silver or black casings and the stacking elements, for instance. Rams, like no one else, defined the look of music in the home for the twentieth century.

The last person to join Rams's team was Peter Schneider in 1973 (which, rather incredibly, meant there were no more significant staff changes at the company for the next twenty-two years). Born in 1945, Schneider was another BraunPrize winner. He took over the last generation of film cameras, repositioning the handles for easier use and updating the control features. He was in charge of external design commissions that came from the Gillette corporation, including the Oral-B toothbrushes and a cosmetic brand called Jafra, plus a competition design for in-flight tableware for the German airline Lufthansa. Schneider took over from Rams as head of product design at Braun in 1995 and retired from the post in 2009.

In between guiding a design team for an international company, defending its position vigorously, overseeing the production of many hundreds of products and devising furniture for another company on the side, Rams also managed to find time to come up with stunning designs of his own, particularly in the hi-fi area. He

p.258
p.262
p.78
p.75,75
p.70,68
p.261

devised several versions of portable radios, such as the T 52 [+] from 1961 and the T 1000 [+] world receiver from 1963; an electronic flashgun range for cameras, a nota-ble model being the EF 1 Hobby Standard [+] from 1958; cigarette lighters such as the F 1 Macron [+] and the T 2 Cylindric TFG 2 [+]; as well as the KMM 2 Aromatic coffee grinder and the HLD 4 [+] hairdryer. Back in 1959, Rams also developed a remarkable portable transistor radio and record player, the TP 1 [+], which he now affectionately terms 'the first Walkman', and this was twenty years before the advent of the first micro-stereo systems from Sony, themselves the ancestors of the tiny mp3 devices we now take for granted.

—   What was so special about Braun design?

Trying to pinpoint the reasons for success is always a slippery task. There were so
many factors that made 'Braun design' work well: the right moment in history,
inspired company CEOs, smart decisions, committed staff, enthusiastic customers,
brilliant designers and a stable design team, led for more than forty years by a
man who was not only enormously talented but an unbelievably stubborn perfec-
tionist, all combined with a generous portion of luck. Without just one of these
elements the whole Braun phenomenon could never have happened.

    When talking about Braun design, Dieter Rams often likes to quote a simile
that he says came from Erwin Braun: 'Our electrical appliances should be humble
servants, to be seen and heard as little as possible. They should ideally stay in
the background, like a valet in the old days, that one hardly noticed.' He describes
his own approach in equally understated terms: 'I try to develop appliances for
daily use, that do not hurt the eye (or other sensory organs); and I try to make sure
that they are then produced and sold for an acceptable price that the normal
consumer can afford. That's about it really.'[21] But this humble statement invites
practical questions: is it really that simple? Do you just have to be idealistic and
socially aware to make good design, and more than that, to be successful with it?
Braun design under Rams was all about reduction and simplicity, but it came at
a high price in terms of time and painstaking effort. Rams's even simpler motto
'Less but better' is all about striving for a result that appears as light and effortless as possible.

    Convincing customers to pay more for less because it had to be better was
also no mean achievement. Braun design was expensive and Rams is the first to admit
that it costs more to make 'good design' because of all the work involved. Some
of the Braun products, the hi-fis in particular, were right off the scale when it came
to the average consumer budget. Not many people can afford a luxury limousine,
let alone a stereo system in the same price bracket. On the whole, people who bought
Braun products wanted tools, not toys. But they were also people who tended to
be discerning and could afford something 'better'. You either needed to be well-off
to buy Braun or, like the founders of the company, and Rams in particular, committed to the long-term view because in the end quality lasts longer.

    Braun design had a beauty that was more than skin deep. It would be wrong to
say that because the Braun approach spurned fashion in an ongoing quest for
functional and useable perfection, it ended up with this beauty by accident. There
is a very strong aesthetic sense in both the proportion and materials of nearly
all the products of the Rams era. They have a 'restrained beauty', he admits. And
in their modesty, these appliances stood out from the competition. But aesthetics
tends to refer to just a visual effect. Braun products designed by Rams and his

[21]   Brandes, *Dieter Rams*, 115

team have a haptic aesthetic as well: when you pick them up, handle them, and use them as the tools they are supposed to be, you become aware of the effort that has gone into making them sit comfortably in the hand, of the texture, weight and balance they possess, and of the satisfying click of the control buttons.

But there is also something austere and uncompromising about these appliances. They clearly belong to a family and subscribe to a strict, rigorous and highly disciplined system of economy, harmony and order. They have one voice. The people in the team who designed them were all men from similar educational backgrounds and experiences. They all worked with the same methods and had similar views and tastes. Rams chose people to work for him, and with him, carefully: he chose people that were like himself.

Braun was never interested in making pretty boxes for its products, or in decoration for its own sake. Theirs was a much deeper approach, prioritizing the needs of the user (whether the user was aware of them or not). It required starting with individual components and the inner structure of the appliances, coming up with considered solutions that focused on functionality and technological quality, all of which resulted in a reduced aesthetic language. Braun's household appliances were designed from the inside out. As a result, they almost could not help but fit – and, more than that, help smooth the transition – into a modern domestic life that was increasingly intertwined with technological tools at nearly every level: listening to music, shaving, cooking, hair-drying or documenting life through photography and film. Braun's approach belonged to its time, and the new way of living to which Braun products clearly belonged was powerfully attractive for a generation that grew out of hardship and wanted something better but still valued quality and longevity.

There is an old joke about the definition of a camel being a horse designed by a committee. When you look at the consumer products generated by many other manufacturers, and even by Braun today, there seem to be an awful lot of camels around. Maybe these companies are too diffuse, have the decision-makers in the wrong places or are continually making the wrong decisions and have no one to stop them. They make products with short-term goals in mind, seducing the eye of the buyer with fashionable colours, sensational curves or exotic surfaces. They may have external designers and, perhaps most significantly, the brand identity is defined by marketing concerns, rather than design or user-related issues. The lesson to learn from Braun is that allowing a consistent philanthropic design approach to define a company can be extremely successful if it is executed with discipline, flexibility and good timing combined with hard work and, not least, great talent.

Dieter Rams, c.1979

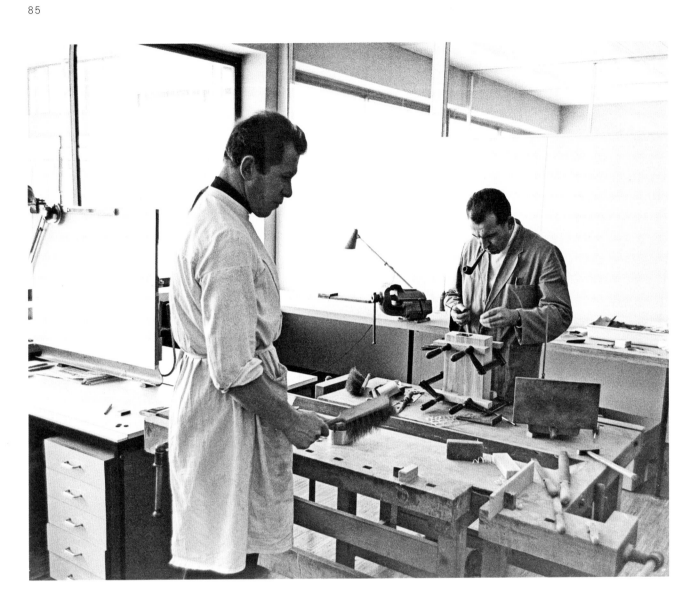

Robert Kemper and Roland Weigend, c.1970

Dieter Rams, c.1979

Dieter Rams, c.1979

The following photographs were taken in the Braun archive.
All products are from Braun unless otherwise noted.

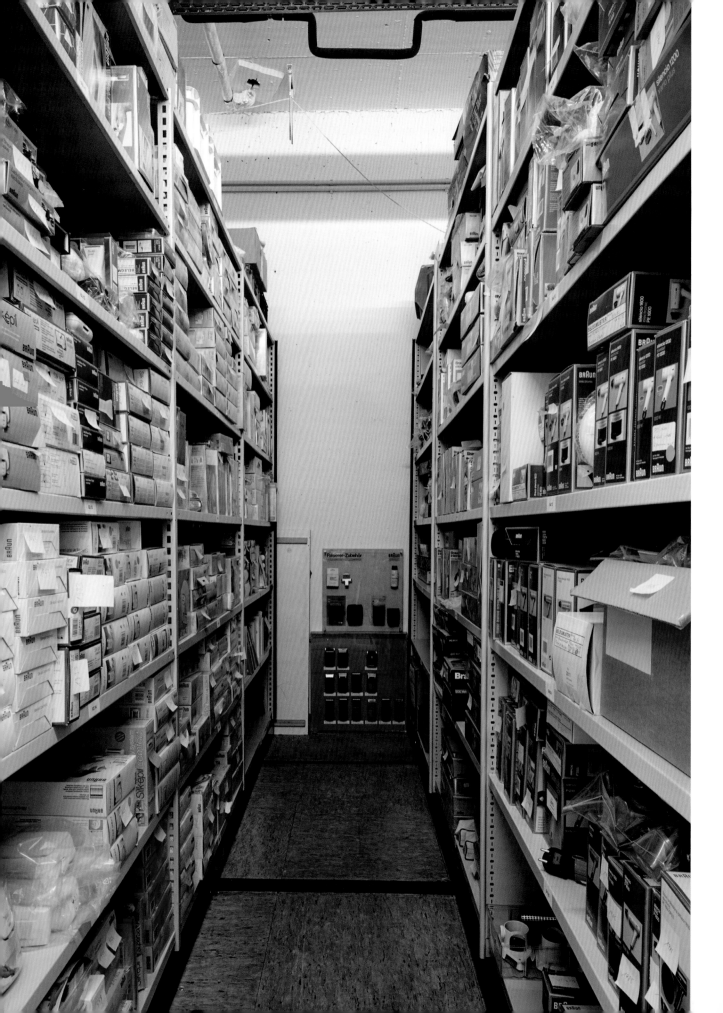

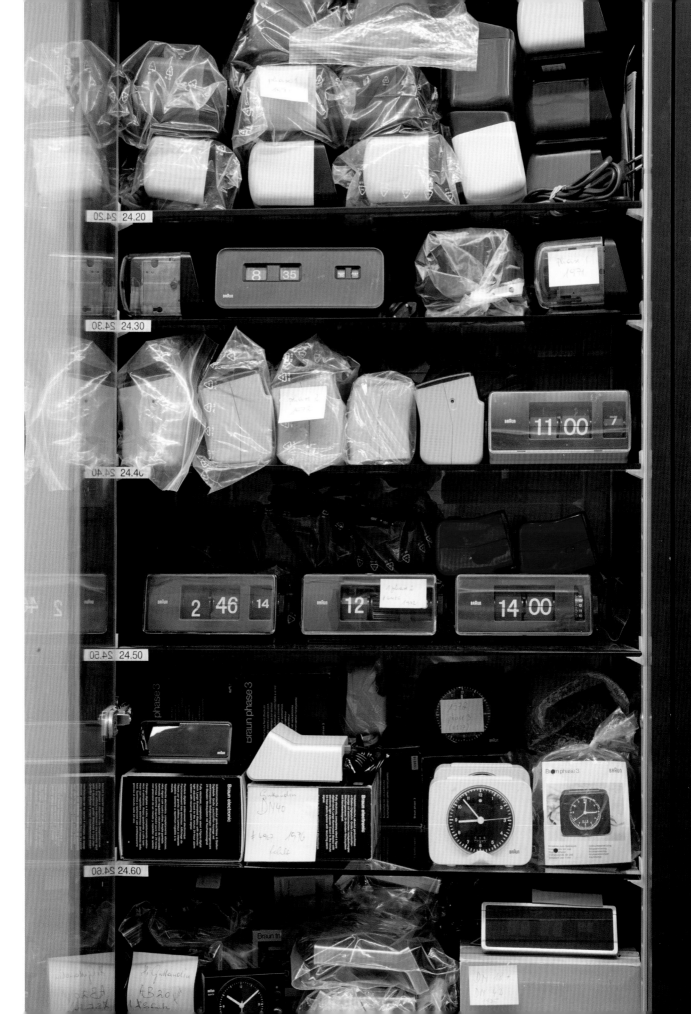

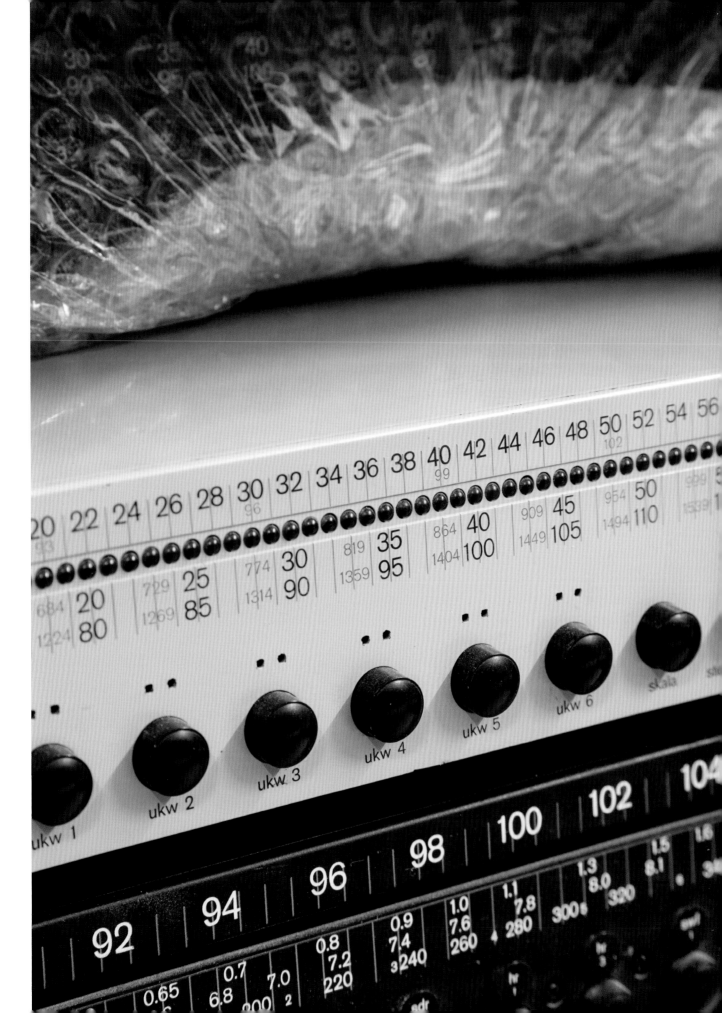

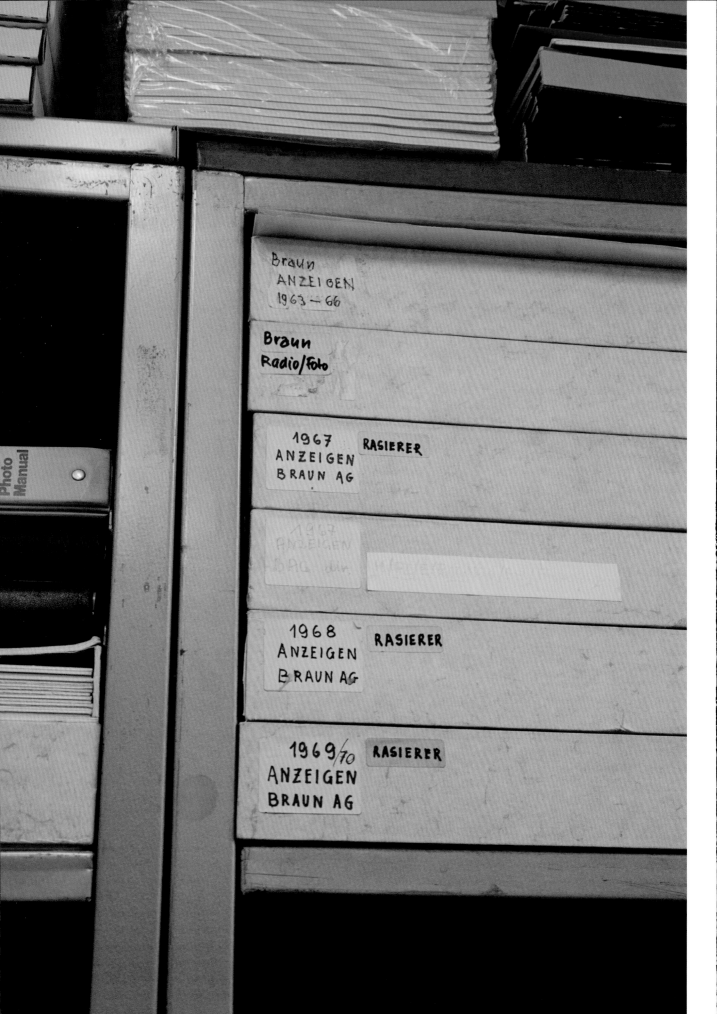

Braun sixtant S
BRAUN
Belegmuster
Type 5330
VDE
1957
1960
1955/66
S 61

Braun HLD 4

1970

BRAUN

BRAUN

BRAUN

...ur-Set

Haartrockner-Styler
Hairdryer/Styler
Sèche-Cheveux/...

BRAUN

11.13

11.14

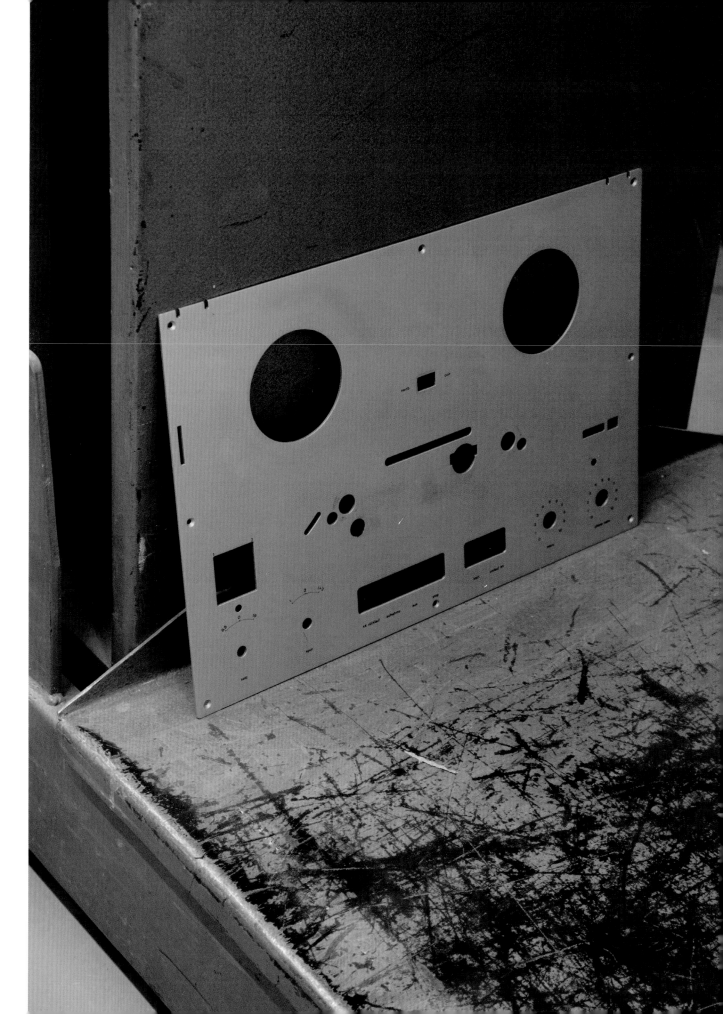

The Kronberg House

Erwin Braun's holistic approach to life, work and business found expression not only in pension schemes, profit-sharing, health centres, cultural experiences and canteens for his employees, but in architecture as well. In 1958, with approximately 3,000 employees and an annual turnover of 100 million deutschmarks[1], Braun bought up large areas of land in Kronberg, a town in the Taunus area just outside of Frankfurt. He initially commissioned the Hochschule für Gestaltung (HfG) Ulm to come up with a suitable site plan to include housing with 3,000 living units, although they did not end up designing the large complex that was eventually built there. The company buildings that comprised that scheme were later designed by the architecture firm Apel, Beckert and Becker, among others.

Erwin also commissioned two private residences in neighbouring Königstein for himself and his brother Artur from Hans Gugelot. These were modular, prefabricated and rather experimental. Erwin was not particularly pleased with the result. He gave his house to Fritz Eichler and asked Herbert Hirche to design a larger, four-unit bungalow complex and a physiotherapy practice instead. Dieter Rams and his wife Ingeborg lived here from 1962 until 1971 along with their neighbours: Werner Kuprian, the health director at Braun (who operated the physiotherapy practice) and his family, and Peter Siepenkothen (an employee of Braun from 1965–69 and President of Braun North America from 1965–66) and his wife Britte. Erwin Braun kept a flat there until 1967, when he moved to Switzerland to set up a clinic for preventative medicine after selling the company to Gillette.

On another piece of land bought by Erwin, called the 'Rothen Hang' which was near the company headquarters in Kronberg and bordered the Taunus forest, there were plans to build a housing estate for friends and colleagues at Braun. Rams had been impressed by the Halen Estate near Bern in Switzerland designed by Atelier 5 between 1955 and 1961, which had its own petrol station, communal swimming pool and a dense building format that still afforded privacy. He discussed the idea of designing something similar himself with Erwin, who was enthusiastic. The HfG Ulm and the Apel office (Rams's former employers) also submitted designs, but it was Rams who was offered the commission for what was to be his first serious building project: a planned system with many communal features including underground parking, a centralized heating system and recreational spaces.

But luck did not smile on Rams the architect as it had on Rams the industrial designer. Although he completed the initial plans, the project was abandoned after the Braun brothers relinquished control of the company. A private investor later took on the project, commissioning their own architects to do the detailed planning, and even though some of Rams's plans are still recognisable, much was changed. Determined not to lose the idea entirely, Dieter Rams bought a double plot on the site to build his own house to his own specifications. His earlier neighbours, the Siepenkothens, bought the plot next door[2].

[1]   Hans Wichmann, Mut zum Aufbruch: Erwin Braun, 1921–1992 (Munich, 1998), 99

[2]   Britte Siepenkothen was Dieter Rams's business advisor and manager.

p.144

p.145

Rams's house in Kronberg is his only significant, realized architectural project. [+] It is a two-storey, L-shaped bungalow that was completed in 1971 with an entrance at street level and a subsequent drop down the slope below. The two wings of the house partially enclose a walled, Japanese-style garden [+] that is accessible from both levels. On the top floor, almost fully glazed walls with large sliding doors facilitate maximum interaction between outside and inside. The garden is not overlooked by any other building, and this privacy allows it to be used as an outdoor living room in the summer months. The house is flat-roofed, white and densely embedded in the garden landscape. Rams's architecture is somehow nearly invisible, and it is not the building that is noticeable but the spaces it contains.

The visitor enters the apparently windowless residence from a tiny private road at the top of the hill. The front door, and indeed the house itself, is almost concealed by tall, well-kept bushes. A small mossy path leads from a tiny gate to the dark-painted front door. The contrast to this upon entering the house is considerable: a small hallway opens up directly into an open-plan kitchen and
p.147
main living room, [+] that is painted white and is flooded with light. The compact yet expansive interior seems far larger than the entrance as a result of the almost entirely glazed back walls. The ceilings are relatively low and the strong horizontal lines of the angular architecture are balanced by the flow of the building as it spills down the hill and into the split-level courtyard garden. The master bedroom and
p.149
bathrooms are hidden behind doors leading off the main space on the ground floor. [+]

As one would expect, the entire interior is furnished with great precision and attention to detail. Rams's own Vitsœ furniture dominates. Although there are a few other pieces of furniture such as Thonet dining chairs, the rest is clearly Rams – even the door fittings. There is absolutely nothing frivolous about any of the decoration. In fact the house is not 'decorated' as such at all. The organic softness, pattern, colour and texture that make this such an inviting space derive from the garden vegetation, which becomes part of the home thanks to the large picture windows. The feeling of interior blurring with exterior is enhanced by house plants and a number of artworks on the walls, which include black-and-white photographs taken by Ingeborg, his photographer wife, and pieces by the German artist A.R. Penck and the Dutch Gruppe nul co-founder Jan Schoonhoven among others. A small silver-framed snapshot showing Dieter and Ingeborg on one of their many skiing holidays perched on the bookcase is one of the few personal details that gives a hint of a private life beyond design. Even the vertical louvred fabric blinds at the dark framed south-facing windows are reminiscent of the air vents on Rams's earlier wood and metal audio appliances.
p.151
The lower two floors of the house contain Rams's office and workshop. [+] The rather cool, white interior is filled with Rams's products and prototypes, including a 606 shelving system made of successive generations of component designs. On Rams's 570 desk downstairs and scattered around the room are a number of objects. They are not so much decorative as inspirational, and include

an iPhone and a laptop (both unused), a set of beautifully crafted Japanese boxes, an old slide rule that used to belong to one of his grandfathers, as well as a few maquettes of ideas for chairs and numerous Braun cigarette lighters and ashtrays. Mounted on one wall is one of Rams's iconic early silver-coloured audio systems. Only the lack of CD player and the reel-to-reel tape player betray its age. This is a house of a man whose life is clearly his work. The topography, the proportions, the furniture, the fittings – everything belongs to Rams. But it is nevertheless a comfortable dwelling and workspace. When one sees many of Rams's products isolated in a display setting they often seem masculine and slightly lacking in emotion. Here, in their 'natural habitat', they make sense: the 'family' relationship between all his designs and their soothing qualities of colour and form. It becomes clear in Rams's own house that he completely understands interfaces: between outside and inside, between nature and technology, between public and private, between user and surroundings.

Dieter Rams, on his house

My house in Kronberg, bordering the Taunus woodlands, is part of a concentrated housing development that I had originally helped to plan. The house is built and furnished according to my own design and I have lived here with my wife since 1971. It goes without saying that we live with Vitsœ furniture systems. Firstly, because I have only ever designed furniture that I myself would like to have and secondly to get to know them during daily use to better recognize where they might be improved or developed further. In instances where the Vitsœ programme is not complete, I have selected furniture from other manufacturers that have been designed from a similar perspective, such as the bent wood 214 Thonet chairs around the Vitsœ 720 table that we use for dining, or the Fritz Hansen stools at the breakfast bar between the kitchen and living area.

In the centre of the living room area there is a loose group of 620 armchairs, my version of a seating landscape. It is a lively and much-used area with a view of the garden. Here we sit together, talk, entertain our friends and watch television. Plants, books and pictures lend atmosphere. The composition of these rooms represents the basic intention behind my design: simplicity, essentiality and openness. The objects do not boast about themselves, take centre stage or restrict but withdraw into the background. Their reduction and unobtrusiveness generate space. The orderliness is not restrictive but liberating. In a world which is filling up at a disconcerting pace, that is destructively loud and visually confusing, design has the task in my view to be quiet, to help generate a level of calm that allows people to come to themselves. The contra position to this is a design that strongly stimulates, that wants to draw attention to itself and arouse strong emotions. For me this is inhumane because it adds in its way to the chaos that confuses, numbs and lames us.

Inside my house, just like in my office at Braun, I can adjust my senses and my sensitivity. I often work at home – in a room that opens out on to the garden, just like the living room. Working for me does not mean so much designing in the usual sense of the term, but more contemplation, reading and talking. Design is in the first instance a thinking process.

In traditional Japanese architecture, living spaces are designed from a position that is similar to my own. The aesthetic of an empty room with its clear and precise organisation of floor, walls and ceiling and careful combination of materials and structure is much more sophisticated then the European aesthetic of opulence, pattern and loud forms.

In the design of my relatively small garden, I have allowed myself to be inspired by Japanese gardens. It is not a copy of any specific garden, rather a homage to the essence of the Japanese garden, a translation into our time, our landscape and our climate. I find working in the garden stimulating – it is a kind of design work that is comparable with that of a room, a furniture system or an appliance. The small swimming pool in the garden is delightful but no luxury, rather a therapeutic necessity for me.

It may seem surprising that I, as a designer of the late twentieth century, as a designer of technical products, also draw inspiration from design cultures such as traditional Japanese architecture and view their achievements with total respect and recognition. But it would be even more surprising if there was nothing in the long history of design that had inspired me or helped strengthen my beliefs. The lack of historic interest in many contemporary designers is, in my view, a weakness.

Just as with the old Japanese design culture, I feel equally drawn to the architecture of the romantic period. The medieval Eberbach Monastery in Rheingau, is one of the pearls of Romanesque architecture and lies not far from my native city of Wiesbaden. I visited it often when I was young. Another most exceptional architectural achievement is, to my mind, the octagonal thirteenth-century Castel del Monte in Apulia, Italy, built by the emperor Frederick II of Hohenstaufen. Years ago I became acquainted with Shaker design, which deeply impressed me with its straightforward approach, its patient perfection and respectful regard for good solutions[3].

[3]   This text was written in 1994, and first published in Weniger aber Besser / Less But Better (Hamburg, 1995). New translation by the author, completed in 2009.

Dieter Rams at his house, c. 1973

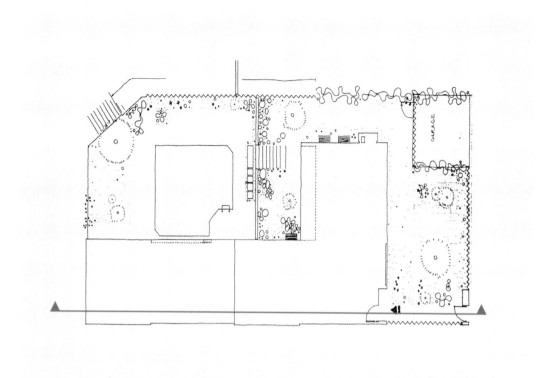

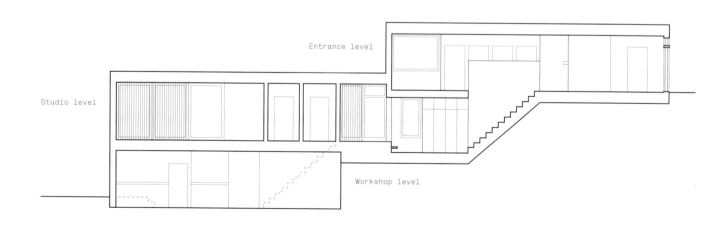

Top: Site plan
Above: Schematic section, showing the entrance level (top), the studio level (middle) and the workshop level (bottom)

Top: View from entrance level to backyard
Above: View from backyard to entrance level

Top: Top level of Rams house. View from entrance towards living room
Above: View from living room towards entrance and kitchen

Top: Living room looking towards 606 shelving programme
Above: Living room, looking towards backyard

Top: Middle level of Rams House. View from landing showing the stair leading up to the entrance level
Above: View from landing towards the workshop

Top: View towards studio, showing stairs leading down to the workshop level
Above: Studio

Top: Middle level of Rams House. View from studio towards the backyard
Above: View from studio towards 606 shelving programme

Top: Bottom level of Rams House. Workshop
Above: Workshop

The following images were taken in the Rams House:

1	Dieter Rams seated in chair from 620 chair programme
2	Braun promotional material and image of the 606 shelving programme
3	Dieter Rams with T 1000 radio
4	Dieter Rams with T 2 lighter
5	Dieter Rams with Braun packaging material
6	Dieter Rams with TG 550 reel-to-reel tape recorder
7	Detail of TG 550 reel-to-reel tape recorder and TS 45 receiver
8	T 52 radio aerial and control knobs
9	TP 1 record player and radio
10	T 3 'domino' lighter
11	Detail of 620 chair
12-13	Drawing board details
14	Dieter Rams archive room
15	T 22 radio
16	D 5 slide projector
17	Prototypes for digital alarm clock numerals
18	Workshop level
19	SK 4 record player
20-23	Prototypes and tools in the workshop level
24	Braun sign with a magnet forming the 'A', one of many birthday presents the team made for Dieter over the years.
25-29	Prototypes and tools in the workshop level
30	606 shelving programme
31	Speaker
32	Dieter Rams seated at 570 desk

BRAUN

Was wäre Deutschland ohne Dieter Rams (Jahrgang '32). Er legte den Grundstein dafür, dass Design aus der Bundesrepublik heute weltweit geschätzt wird. Jahrzehntelang prägte er die Produkthandschrift des Elektrogeräte-Herstellers Braun. Bis heute sind seine Entwürfe legendär und bei Sammlern heiß begehrt. Für SDR+ entwickelte er u. a. das zeitlose Regalsystem '606' (o.).

„Gutes Design macht ein Produkt verständlich."

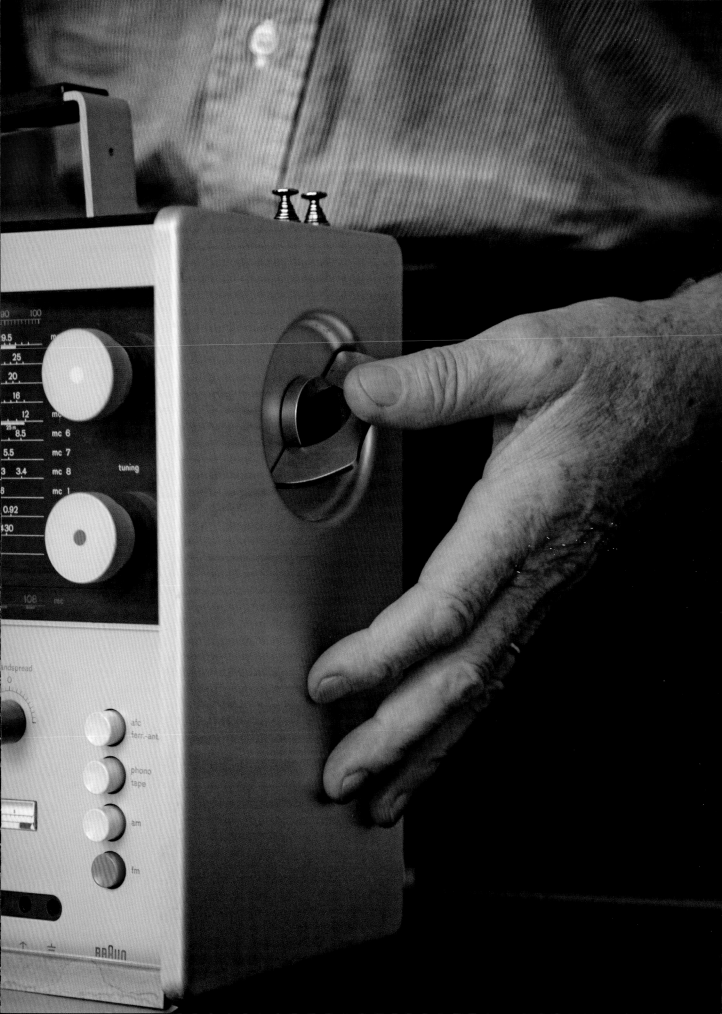

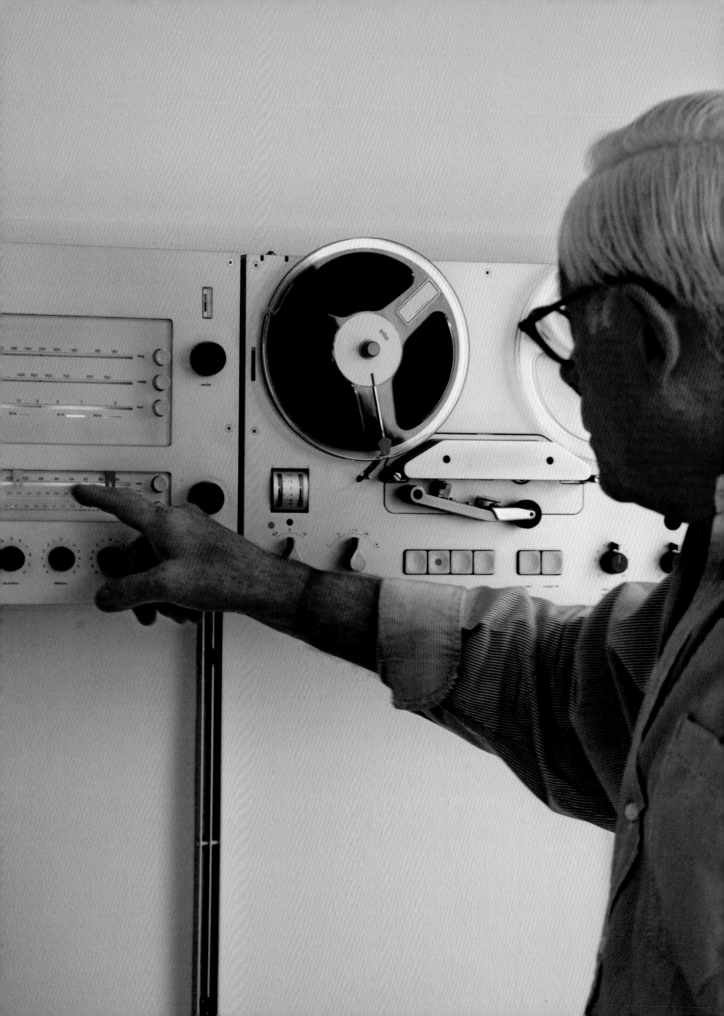

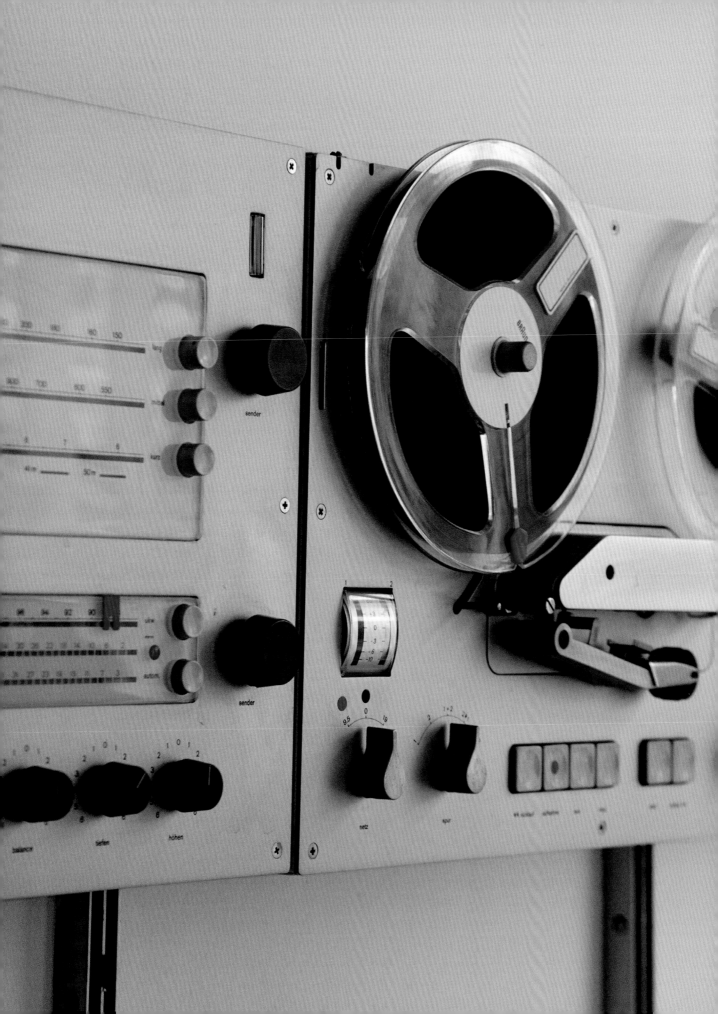

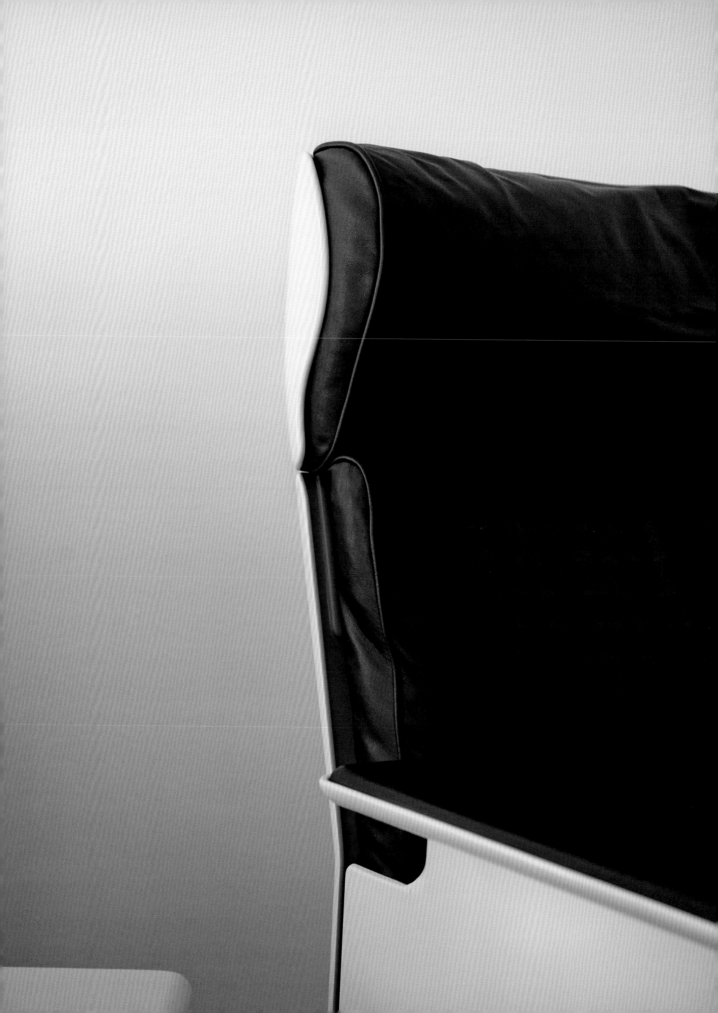

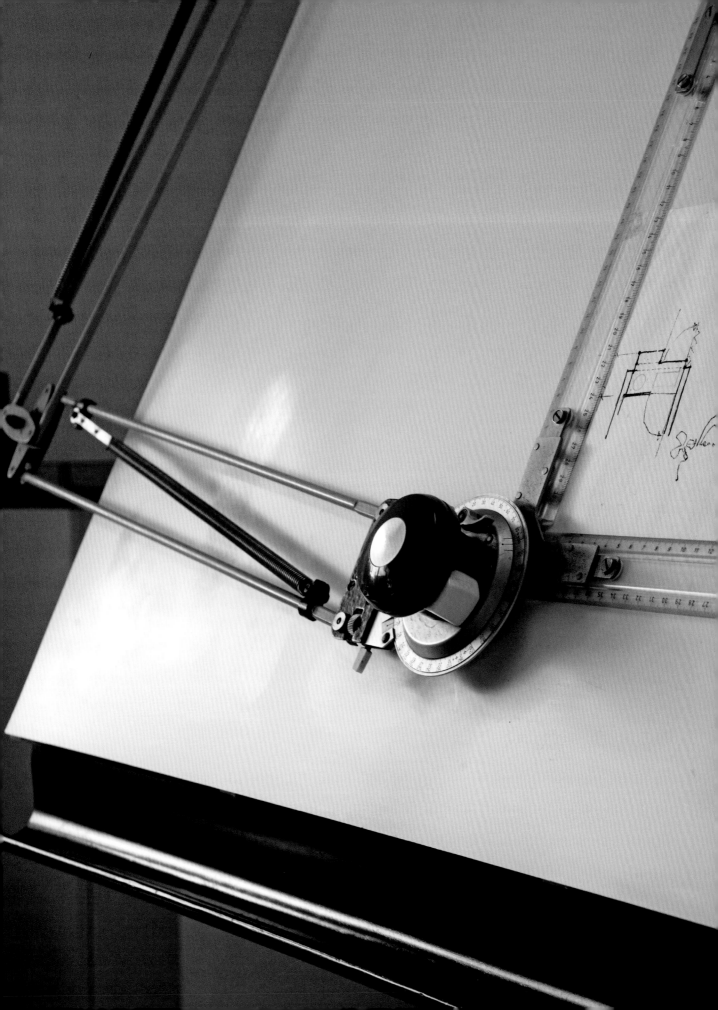

Universal Sägeblatt für Handkreissägen und Kappsägen. Nachschärfen möglich!

ANWENDUNG:
- Sägeblatt für Stahl, Eisen, Holz, Holz mit Nägeln, harte Kunststoffe usw. Die Anwendung ist Universell!
- Schneller und sauberer Schnitt.
- Gradfreie Kanten.
- Feinste Schnittbreite mit niedrigstem Widerstand, motorschonend.
- Kein Verhaken, keine Nacharbeit.

Universal Sawblade for hand- and tablesaw machines. Resharpening is possible!

APPLICATION:
- Metal, Wood, Wood with nails, Plastics, Aluminium.
- Quicker and finer cut.
- Cuts without hooks.
- Thinnest possible cut, with very few resistance, saves your motor.
- No hooks, no afterwork.

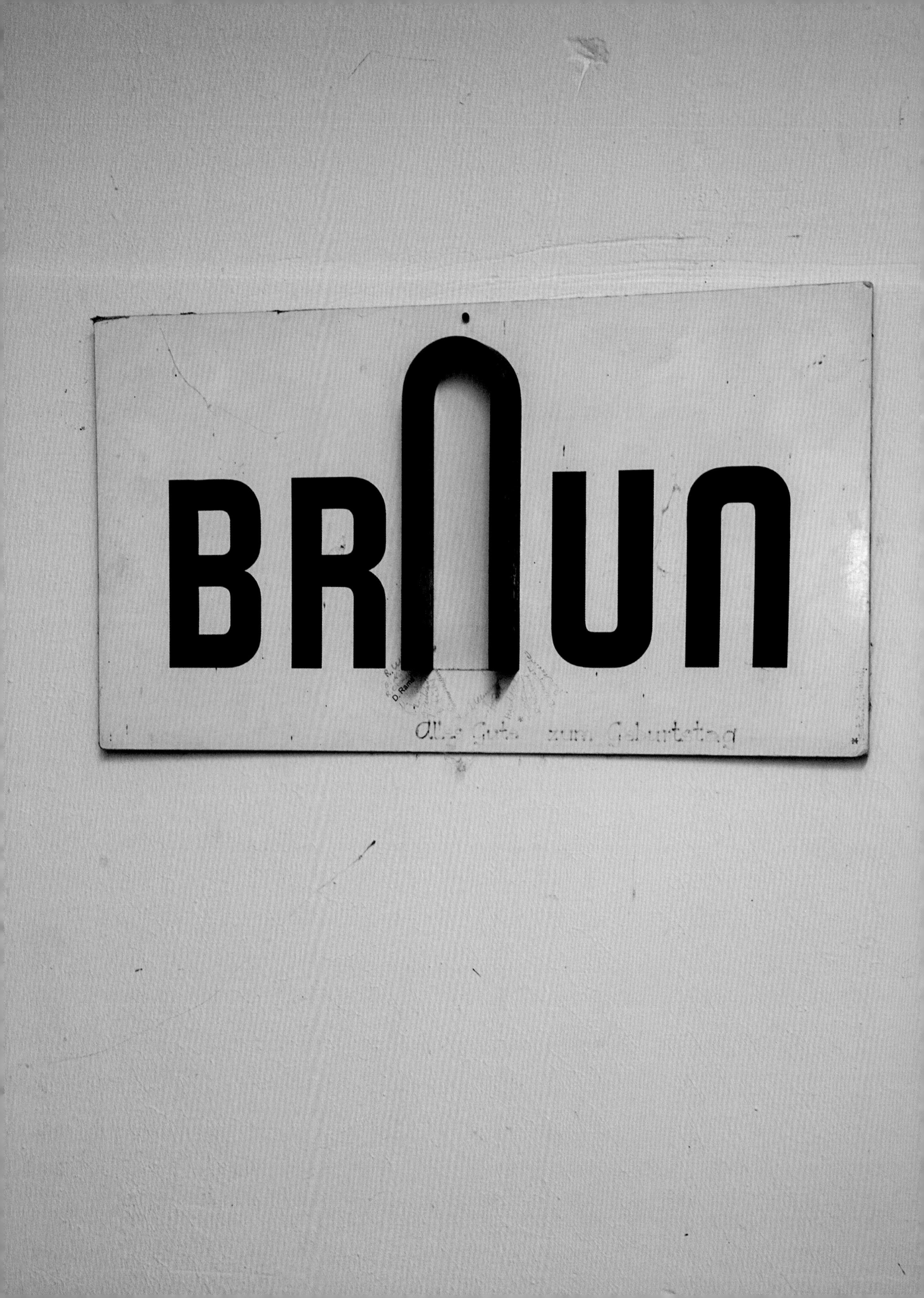
BRAUN
Alles Gute zum Geburtstag

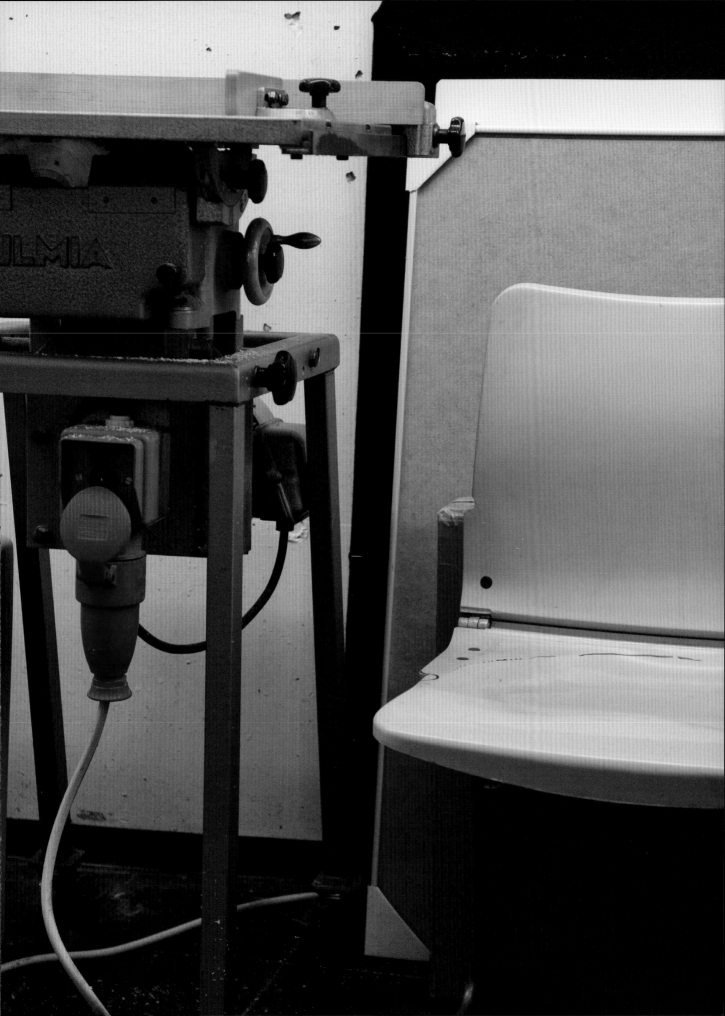

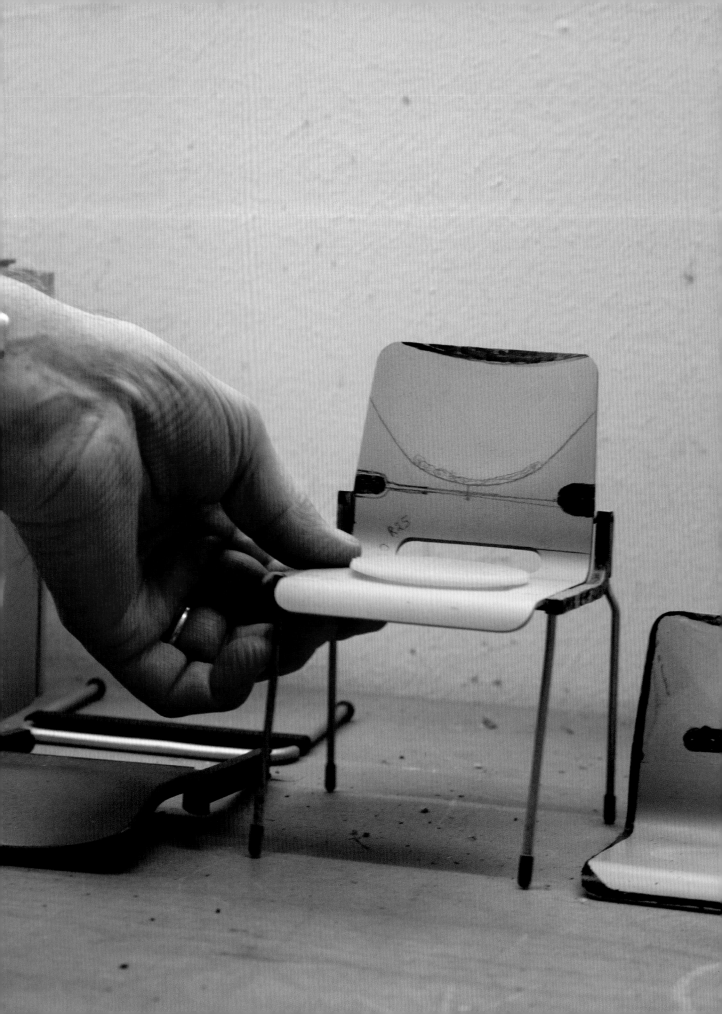

Vitsœ

Dieter Rams gained fame and worldwide recognition as a designer early on in his career at Braun. After achieving success with his first products for the company and attracting wider international acclaim at venues such as The Museum of Modern Art (MoMA) in New York, he could easily have chosen a path that many designers would have found desirable and made a highly successful international career by designing products across a broad field. Instead he chose to remain focused on household appliances at Braun in Frankfurt for more than forty years, developing and refining his work and riding out all the company's internal changes. This career decision was made possible by three significant factors: Rams's own methodical and determined nature, his relatively high status in the company, which allowed him enough control to follow his own approach and, perhaps most importantly of all, his parallel occupation as a furniture designer for a small company initially known as Vitsœ + Zapf.

In 1957 a young physics student called Otto Zapf (b. 1931) was looking for ways in which to improve his father's modestly sized furniture-making business in Eschborn (near Frankfurt). He had been impressed by the recently launched SK 4, nicknamed 'Snow White's Coffin', a super phonograph with a radio and record player that Braun had publicly credited to Dieter Rams (together with Hans Gugelot) and decided to visit Rams at Braun. Rams recalls that Zapf turned up with a portfolio of furniture designs by the architect Rolf Schmidt under his arm, opened it up and asked Rams what he thought. Rams said that, first of all, the prototype photographs were of poor quality and offered to come around and re-shoot them with Marlene Schnelle, a good friend of his and Braun's in-house photographer at the time.[1] At this second meeting, Zapf asked Rams if he would consider designing some furniture for him and Rams agreed. It was not a surprising progression. Rams had, after all, trained as an interior architect and his initial role at Braun was to design interior spaces for the company. In fact, in some of his early sketches for Braun [←], Rams combined Knoll International furniture with his own designs for shelving and storage to house the new Braun products. Braun had already developed a strong collaboration with Knoll by this time (thanks to a contact that Rams made between a friend of his who worked there and Erwin Braun), as well as showrooms that mixed contemporary furniture with their new product range to demonstrate the 'modern' way of living to customers. So furniture was already very much part of Rams's design thinking at the time.

The placement of Braun products in sympathetic interiors was viewed as an essential aspect of the company's marketing strategy by Erwin Braun and his creative team. Indeed, some of the impact of the first presentation of new Braun appliances in Düsseldorf in 1955 can be credited to its appearance within the highly innovative, modular D 55 trade fair stand designed by Otl Aicher and Hans G Conrad. Its versatile, flexible and lightweight definition of space was neutral

p. 54

---

[1]   Dieter Rams, in conversation with the author (July 2009)

enough to show off the appliances to their advantage, and the design echoed the angular, minimal pavilions of the former Bauhaus architect Mies van der Rohe, taking inspiration from his use of proportions. The stand was furnished with Gugelot-designed pieces from Wohnbedarf AG in Zürich, as well as objects from Knoll International, which at that time also held the rights to the production of furniture designed by Mies – then at the height of his career in the United States. This strategy of Braun – linking its products to other innovative modern designs in a variety of scales, ranging from furniture to architecture – was part of a contemporary trend towards an expanded field of design that picked up from pre-war modernist examples. In this new professional world, the designer's and architect's mandates were expanding, and there was growing interest in creating living elements and utensils that were not confined to strictly defined fields but instead were part of complete environments for a new, more flexible, way of living.

Much to his surprise, when Dieter Rams went to his boss Erwin Braun in 1957 and asked for permission to design furniture for Zapf in addition to his work at Braun, the response was immediate and positive. 'It was not usual in those days when you were employed by a company to work externally for someone else as well,' recalls Rams,[2] 'but Erwin Braun thought it was a good idea. I can still hear his words: "Let Rams make furniture, it will be good for our radios".' But there was considerable resistance to the idea within the company from colleagues and technicians. 'He [Erwin] was the only one to think outside the box and see that it could only be an advantage. Without his support I would never have been able to do it,' says Rams. Erwin was already a firm believer in an integrated approach to modern life and design. Perhaps he also understood that allowing his valuable young designer this 'hobby' outside of the company would help to keep him at Braun in the long term.

Systems Furniture

p.206 Dieter Rams's first design for Zapf was not a piece of furniture at all but a system: the so-called 'Montage system' (assembly system) RZ 57. [•] This was a small collection of mass-produced components that could fit together in a large variety of ways to create customized furniture landscapes for all sorts of situations – a clear ancestor of the flat-pack, self-assembly fitted kitchens and modular furniture that is so familiar today. It was a rather plain-looking but highly flexible system of shelves and cupboards, composed of perforated anodized aluminium profiles and white beechwood panel elements based on a grid width of 57 cm or 114 cm (a little less than 2 ft and 4 ft, respectively). It had both hinged and sliding door modules. The RZ 57 was intended for use in the living room, bedroom, dining room or office. As there was no left or right, back or front, top or bottom to any of the individual sections, the storage system could be assembled

---

[2]   Dieter Rams, interview with the author (October 2008)

in a variety of ways, either against a wall or as free-standing units. This degree of flexibility required a high degree of precision and quality in the execution and finishing of all of the components.

Rams wanted to design 'utility' furniture with a 'variety of functions and auxiliary functions'.[3] The versatility of his system allowed the user to arrange and re-arrange the units to their heart's content, creating a living environment that can be adapted to a changing lifestyle. His aim was that manual input during manufacture should be kept to a minimum so that the system could be affordable. He also intended for the component aspect of the system to greatly reduce storage and transport costs between manufacturer and customer. Finally, the reduced nature and visual neutrality of this furniture, believed Rams, should also liberate the owner from an environment that is dominated by furniture and allow for freedom of individual expression. 'My intention is to omit every unneeded element in order to place the essentials in the foreground. Forms will then become placid, soothingly comprehensible and long-lasting,'[4] he said. Thus, by creating a highly standardized system, he hoped to deliver a versatile, low-cost, bespoke furniture solution that would be available to a large number of people.

Rams's strategy for his furniture naturally mirrored his approach and the design environment at Braun. It is also worth noting that Rams specifically considered his Braun products in his RZ 57 design. With the addition of metal side panels, the furniture system could house the compact 'atelier' radio system that he had designed around the same time. There were also aesthetic parallels between the RZ 57 and the 'atelier' system (as well as the earlier SK 4). These similarities were not an attempt to humour his main employers, but were the natural outcome of Rams being gripped by the idea of a comprehensive interior system: modular furniture and appliances for everyone, a standardized system that afforded equality in respect to quality and standards of living, yet allowed for individuality: the same but different.

This idea of furniture systems has its origins in pre-war German modernism. In particular, the 'New Frankfurt' housing programme between 1925 and 1930 had a significant impact on Dieter Rams's hometown. Under the direction of architect Ernst May some 12,000 apartments were built by the city council to relieve the city's acute housing shortage in the 1920s. These dwellings, made from pre-fabricated components to reduce costs, were furnished with the first-ever fitted kitchens – the *Frankfurter Küche* designed by the Austrian architect Margarete Schütte-Lihotzky – and other standardized furnishing elements by Ferdinand Kramer that were manufactured in municipal workshops. The aim was to make complete living spaces that were attractive yet functional with an optimum use of space for people on low incomes.

[3]   Dieter Rams, 'Zurück zum Einfachen, zum Puren' ('Back to the Simple, the Pure'), interview with Gina Angress and Inez Franksen, *Work + Zeit*, no. 4/79, reprinted in François Burkhardt and Inez Franksen, eds., *Design: Dieter Rams* & (English edition, Berlin, 1981), 205 (207 in the German edition)

[4]   Ibid., 206 (208 in the German edition)

However, it was not until after World War II that the modern idea of furniture systems for the home and office took off on an international scale. In 1950, while working in Max Bill's office, Hans Gugelot designed a furniture system called the M 125 for Wohnbedarf AG in Zürich. It was based on 125 mm (5 in) modules and multiples thereof, used to make shelves, cabinets and room dividers. In 1956 an improved version of the M 125 went into industrial production with Wilhelm Bofinger in Germany, where it continued to be manufactured until 1988.[5] Gugelot was later to expand and expound on his ideas of systems furniture as head of product design teaching at the Hochschule für Gestaltung (HfG) Ulm from 1953, and, of course, in his contact with Braun.

Meanwhile, in the United States, Hermann Miller introduced the Eames Storage Units (ESU) by Charles and Ray Eames in 1951. According to the accompanying brochure at the time, their storage units offered 'a frank and forthright answer to a basic furniture need'. The units came in two widths and three heights and offered a desk system as well. But they were far more decorative and colourful in appearance than their European counterparts and were delivered fully assembled to the consumer.

Vitsœ + Zapf

While designing the RZ 57, Dieter Rams quickly realized that Otto Zapf's father's workshop was not equipped for manufacturing such a system. They made a number of prototypes there but possibilities were limited. Meanwhile, Zapf was still studying physics but made time to extend his contacts in the world of graphics, architecture and furniture. At the Cologne Furniture Fair in 1958 he met the Danish furniture salesman and entrepreneur Niels Wiese Vitsœ (1913–95) [•] who was selling popular, high-quality contemporary Danish furniture in Germany at the time and who had influence and good connections in the business. Zapf then introduced Vitsœ to Rams and his ideas for system-based furniture. This meeting brought a 'whole new dimension' to the budding business, recalls Rams. Vitsœ's contacts with a number of German manufacturers and retailers suddenly made the furniture idea an economically interesting proposition. Now there was not only the possibility to manufacture components in a range of materials to the required degree of precision, but also access to outlets to sell the resulting furniture to the public.

p.214

Vitsœ had been looking for a chance to establish his own business in the German market, separate from the Danish furniture companies for whom he had worked for the past 20 years, and in 1959 he formed a partnership with Dieter Rams and Otto Zapf called Vitsœ + Zapf, with the sole purpose of realising and manufacturing Dieter Rams's furniture designs. Zapf gave up his studies to concentrate on the technical side of the business and Vitsœ dealt with sales. The first furniture

[5]   Guus Gugelot, ed., *gugelot.de* ‹www.gugelot.de›

p.206 that the company produced was the RZ 57 system (later known as the 571 / 72),[6] [+] which was to be expanded and improved over the following years until it became almost a complete domestic interior. The final system had thirteen different heights, two widths and three different depths as well as two different versions: Model 571 had pale grey lacquered panel elements and a slight structuring to the side panels and shelves; Model 572 had beech veneer side panels and shelves with doors and back panels in light grey or matt black. The set-up included a *Tischpro-gramm* (table programme) of tables and floor units and even a sofa / daybed. The table, which had square-profile aluminium legs, featured a double-layer top enabling it to be used as a work surface with storage in the space underneath.

— RZ 60 / 606 Universal Shelving System

In the year following the commercial launch of the RZ 57, Dieter Rams came up with a wall-shelf system called the RZ 60. The main structural element was an alumin-
p.194 ium E-profile [+] that had been used for the sliding cupboard doors on the RZ 57. The profile, extruded into tracks of any length, could be screwed in a vertical position on to a wall, allowing shelves to be hung between pairs of tracks at various heights.
p.201 Shelves could be attached on both sides of the tracks [+] using pin supports, thanks to rows of holes perforating their entire length. The system was remarkably simple, lightweight and unobtrusive and, like the RZ 57, relied on the precision manufacture of a relatively small number of repeating components. The system was
p.204 also highly flexible [+] and could be adapted to a large number of interior situations.
p.202   In 1970 the RZ 60 was renamed the 606 Universal Shelving System. [+] Rams designed a free-standing version held in place by aluminium uprights compressed between wall and ceiling, or floor and ceiling. In addition to the shelves, Rams designed a whole range of elements that slotted into the system, including cabinets with sliding doors or fold-down doors, desk and table modules, and LP record racks and holders for the Braun 'audio 2' stereo-system components, including speakers. The shelves and cabinets were made of powder-coated steel or lac-quered wood, and could be finished in off-white, black or beech plywood. By 1980 the Vitsœ catalogue listed more than 150 different positions for the 606 system, which, since its design, has won numerous awards and has been added to the collection of many museums. It also became a bestseller for the company and the backbone of its collection.

[6]   Unlike that of the Braun products, the nomenclature for Dieter Rams's furniture systems is relatively easy to understand and in keeping with the intended anonymity of his designs. Up until 1969, when Otto Zapf left the company, all products were named with the prefix RZ ('Rams Zapf') and then a number indicating the year of the design. For example, 'RZ 57' stands for 'Rams Zapf 1957'. The model number is signified by an additional number, as can be seen in RZ 571 / 72. After 1969, the RZ prefix was dropped and a zero added to the number, so the 'RZ 57' then became simply '570'.

Of all Rams's products, the 606 Universal Shelving System is perhaps his most successful in fulfilling his own principles of good design. It is still in production today, some fifty years after its conception. The system is distinctive yet unobtrusive, and when the shelves and cabinets are filled, its slim profile allows it to fade quietly into the background. Its 'plainness' lends it a timeless quality that has transcended the vagaries of fashion like no other of Rams's designs. It was conceived in such a way as to optimize its function as simply and in as many different situations as possible, while still permitting upgrades and alterations without falling into obsolescence: all later adaptations and additions could still be integrated into the original structure and sizes. Thus a customer who bought a shelf unit in 1967, for example, was still able to add a cupboard, a shelf or a table unit or extend it with further shelves in 1977, or 2007. It is also very easy to understand and install.

'Fashion objects are not capable of being long-lived,' said Rams in 2007. 'We simply cannot afford this throw-away mentality anymore. Good design *has* to have in-built longevity. I have lived with nearly all my furniture designs since they were first produced and they have all aged well. With the 606 shelving system, for example, apart from small details, like the curve of the lip of the shelf, which we improved once a new metal folding technique became available, the design has basically remained unchanged over more than 40 years and it is still in production. I believe that the secret of the longevity of my furniture lies in its simplicity and restraint. Furniture should not dominate, it should be quiet, pleasant, understandable and durable.'[7]

RZ 60 / 601 / 602 Chair Programme

p.210 Ancillary to the RZ 60 programme was Dieter Rams's first chair [←] (later called the 601 / 602), which had similarities to Charles and Ray Eames' Aluminium Office Chair from 1959. Unlike the Eames chair, however, it had a number of variations that lent it a systemic quality. It had a low-volume, two-component format composed of a cast aluminium two-footed base and an ergonomically formed shell of polyester resin that could be upholstered in leather[8] or fabric with either a plain surface or horizontal bands of stitching. The RZ 60 chair programme had head-rest extensions, with and without an upholstered head cushion and a further element that could be a stool or a side table depending on whether its top was upholstered or plain lacquered resin.

[7]   Dieter Rams, in conversation with the author (August 2007)

[8]   Nearly all of the upholstery for Dieter Rams's seating was designed to be in black or brown leather, although customers could order fabric and even patterned fabric variations from suppliers.

—   RZ 61 / 610 Hall Stand

p.211   In 1961 Rams designed a hall stand system [+] suited to hallways, bathrooms, kitchens and offices. The main modules were 40 x 80 cm (approximately 16 in x 32 in)
sheets of grey powder-coated perforated steel with folded edges designed to
hang on the wall in various combinations, with a 15 mm (⅝ in) clearance. The perforations allowed the attachment of various fixtures such as hooks, coat-hangers,
umbrella stands and small shelves, as well as permitting ventilation to help
dry wet clothes and umbrellas. From 1970 the hall stand system was also available
in matt black and aluminium and renamed the 610 *Garderobenprogramm*
(Wall Panel System). Like the 606 shelving system, this model had a timeless,
functional aesthetic.

—   RZ 62 / 620 Lounge Chair Programme

p.212   The design of an ingenious lounge chair programme [+] in 1962 is another highlight
in what was a remarkably creative phase for Dieter Rams. It must be remembered
that at this time he was turning out not only one furniture system concept after
another (with all their respective components) but also televisions, radios, hi-fi
systems and other appliances for Braun. His creative productivity during this period
was extraordinary.

The RZ 62 system (later 620) is an armchair, a lounge chair, a sofa, a seating
ensemble, a stool, a storage box, a coffee table, as well as being several variations
in between. Each element is an attractive, stand-alone item of furniture yet still
manages to be part of a system without looking like it belongs in a conference
centre or an airport lounge. One of the most interesting features of this design is
its interesting fusion of puritanical restraint and luxurious comfort.

The body of the chair is a solid wooden sprung frame measuring 66 cm (26 in)
square. The back and side sections are covered in a shell that, in the prototype,
was constructed of lacquered metal but was made from lighter fibreglass-reinforced
polyester when the chair went into production in 1964. It was available in off-white
or black and contained a soft upholstered interior of leather or fabric that crum-
ples slightly with use, lending the chair an inviting aura of cosy comfort as well as
softening its rather strict form. Separate chair elements can be joined together
to make a multi-seat sofa and there are also low- and high-back variations. The base
of the chair can be supported on a swivel, castors or feet. All the individual components can be dismantled for cleaning or the replacement of parts should they
p.221   become damaged. The 621 nesting coffee tables [+] that accompany the system
are made of injection-moulded foamed polystyrol.

Like the 606 shelving system, the 620 armchair was a bestseller for Vitsœ + Zapf.
Between 1964 and 1975, the firm produced and sold 20,000 pieces at the substan-

606 system, detail of aluminium E Profile

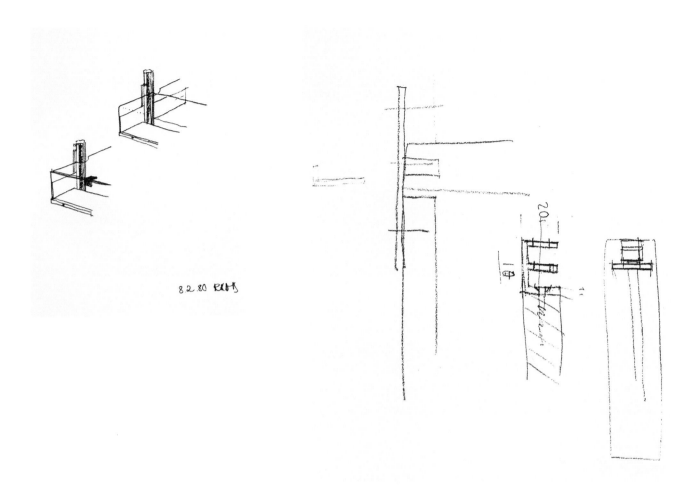

8 2.80 ℞℞ℬ

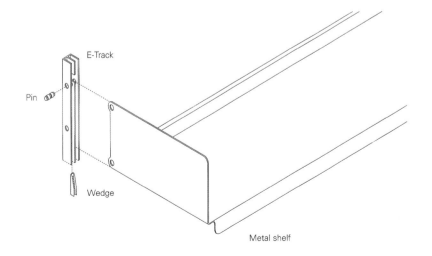

E-Track

Pin

Wedge

Metal shelf

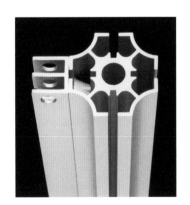

606 system, sketches and drawings of the aluminium E Profile

tial price of 2,194.50 deutschmarks for a standard leather-upholstered chair.[9] However, success brings imitation in the product world, and the company fought a six-year copyright battle against another firm, which had reproduced the 620 system without a licence. The result was that in 1973 the German Federal Court granted Rams's 620 system 'artistic copyright' as a paradigmatic 'object of applied art' – a legal status shared by very few design objects, even today. It rapidly became a design classic and, still in production, graces many modern interiors, including the German Federal Chancellor's office in Berlin, which was built in 2001 after the country's reunification.

p.215

p.214

Rams designed various other products for Vitsœ + Zapf in the 1960s, including a dining / conference chair programme (622), [+] which was similar to the 601 in styling but not nearly as elegant, and a compact folding-door system (690) for limited spaces. He also devised a rather stylish couch programme, the 680, [+] which ingeniously recycled the expanded polystyrene product packaging as part of the filling for the insulated mattress that came with it. The couch could be converted into a sofa through the addition of an upholstered backrest, and multiple seating modules arranged to form a lounge landscape.

p.219

All these products were sold from Otto Zapf's showroom in Eschborn and various retailers around Germany. Although sales were modest in comparison to those of an international company such as Braun, the firm's niche market resembled that of Braun's hi-fi appliances, appealing to primarily well-off individuals with an interest in architecture and design, and critical interest remained high. In 1964, the 601 / 602 armchair programme and the 606 shelving system were included in an industrial design exhibition at Documenta III. In 1966, the 620 was awarded the Rosenthal Studio prize and in 1967 Vitsœ + Zapf's graphic designer Wolfgang Schmidt received the highest honours with the Graphic Design Deutschland award for the Vitsœ + Zapf corporate identity. [+] As with Braun, the packaging, graphics and assembly instructions were considered to be an integral part of the products made by Vitsœ + Zapf and as such had to reflect the company's aims. As with Braun, the corporate identity was characterized by clean lines and a reduced, unfussy appearance with plenty of white space. It was, however, more playful than that of Braun, and Schmidt's use of a red hand as a logo and his strong typographic style, together with his and Rams's packaging concepts, such as the wrapping for the 621 side tables from 1962, [+] were experimental and quite avant-garde.

p.221

—

Wiese-Vitsœ

The prizes and exhibitions awarded to Dieter Rams and Vitsœ + Zapf continued throughout the 1960s with the 606 and the 620 systems being included in shows at the Stedelijk Museum in Amsterdam in 1969 and the Victoria and Albert

[9] 'Einrichtungstip des Monats', *Bauwelt* magazine no. 32 (1975)

Museum in London in 1970. Both furniture programmes won gold medals at the 4th. International *Wiener Möbelsalon* in Vienna in 1969. Rams himself was made an Honorary Royal Designer for Industry by the Royal Society of Arts in London in 1968 for his groundbreaking work in electric appliance and furniture design.

p.224

 It was a busy decade. Yet Rams found time to accommodate his parallel worlds: he would sometimes work all day at Braun then head off to Vitsœ + Zapf [*] in the evenings, or occasionally work from home in his own fully-equipped workshop. Dividing his time between being the sole designer at a small family-sized firm and a team member of what had now become a conglomerate seemed to satisfy him: 'Of course it was all quite stressful, but you are happy to take on hard work if it is enjoyable, it is part of what being a designer is about.'[10] In one environment he had whole teams of designers and technicians at his disposal; in the other, although he could make use of his experiences with technologies and materials at Braun, he was pretty much on his own. 'I had to do everything myself,' he says, 'but I was of course extremely interested in working that way because design and construction belong very much together for me.'[11] In 1961, however, Rams gave up his official partnership in the company Vitsœ + Zapf. He had just been made head of the design department at Braun and also become a member of the executive board. As such, it seemed inappropriate at the time to have conflicting loyalties. Nevertheless, he continued to design for Vitsœ + Zapf with as much freedom as before.

 Meanwhile, cracks were beginning to appear in the relationship between Niels Vitsœ and Otto Zapf and it became clear that the two remaining partners had different ideas about the direction that the company should take. In 1969, Vitsœ bought out Zapf's share of the firm for around a million deutschmarks, which was a considerable sum of money at the time. The name Zapf was removed from the company logo and the product labelling, and in 1970 the newly named 'Wiese-Vitsœ' opened a showroom and an office at Kaiserhofstrasse

p.226

no. 10 in Frankfurt. [*] The former physics student Zapf went on to become a highly successful designer of office furniture, notably creating the 'Zapf Office System' and the 'Office Chair Collection' for Knoll International, as well as the 'Management Office' later produced by Vitra.

 The Wiese-Vitsœ showroom was on the ground floor of a modern building. It had a tiled white floor and white walls and ceiling, and was entirely furnished with Dieter Rams's systems. His signature pale grey colour scheme dominated in the open-plan space, which included an office, seating areas and a bar. It was the perfect environment in which to display the integrative nature of Rams's furniture: everything was interconnected and worked together as a single family; the units were flexible, adaptable and expandable yet clearly remained the product of a single design approach. The showroom became a meeting place and venue for events,

[10] Dieter Rams, in conversation with the author (October 2008)

[11] Ibid.

especially during the annual autumn furniture fair in Frankfurt. Much to Rams's irritation there was pressure to show new pieces on these occasions. Rams hated the idea of treating furniture like fashion, with seasonal collections. 'The whole furniture industry is suffering from the same ailment. The something-for-everyone collections are to help lessen the risk. Today the designer in the furniture industry is often degraded to an idea machine,' he said way back in 1979.[12]

Rams and Plastics

Although he rejected pandering to fashion, Dieter Rams was keen to experiment and explore, especially in terms of using new technologies and materials. In an interview in 1969 he welcomed material innovations but bemoaned the lack of investment in methods and tools with which to process them in the German furniture industry: 'In Italy there are several very good examples, particularly in the command of synthetic materials … [which] are unbelievable in their methodology of material processing. I presume that they have had much more help there, probably from the big plastic raw materials manufacturers that are offering more support on the financial side'.[13]

Rams had always worked with synthetics and been interested in finding new uses for them in his products: the transparent acrylic lid of the SK 4 phonograph, for example, and the innovative combination of hard and soft plastics to improve the grip on the Braun electric razors. In particular he was interested in the possibility of using synthetics to lend products a precious quality in visual and haptic terms. He had already achieved this with his design team at Braun by giving products matt black plastic casings, for example, beautifully finished and with careful detailing, and mixing plastics with aluminium or steel. But furniture manufacture involved a different scale of implementation entirely. Casting, tooling and moulding plastics was a highly expensive business, as were the raw materials themselves. Although Rams was keen to explore the use of synthetics in his furniture, and despite having invaluable access to research facilities at Braun, Wiese-Vitsœ simply did not have the facilities or the funds available for the necessary research and tooling for their own products. Thus it was only in collaboration with plastic raw material producers such as Dynamit Nobel AG that Dieter Rams and Niels Vitsœ were able to pursue the incorporation of plastics into their furniture. In the 1960s, synthetics featured in various furniture elements: the 601, 602 and 620 chair programmes had glass-fibre reinforced shells, and vacuum-formed Polystyrol formed the components for the 610 wall panels, the 620 / 621 tables, and mouldings for the bases of the 680 and 681 bed and chair programmes. But it was in 1974 that Rams's

---

[12]   Rams, 'Zurück zum Einfachen' in *Design: Dieter Rams* & (English edition), 206 (208 in the German edition)

[13]   From a transcript of an interview with Johann Klöcker for 'Zeitgemäße Form', *Süddeutsche Zeitung* (1969), Vitsœ archive

p.215

plastic devotion reached its peak with the 720 / 21 *Rundoval* (round-oval) table system [+]. It was one of the largest ever furniture pieces made from foamed Polystyrol, using low-pressure moulding machines in a two-phase production process and was a considerable technical achievement. The table seated four comfortably and could be enlarged with an additional insert to accommodate eight or more.

— 740 Stacking Programme

p.230

Dieter Rams's first visit to Japan in 1968 marked the beginning of his particular love affair with the country, and also inspired a highly unusual outdoor furniture system: the *Stapelprogramm* (Stacking programme) 740 [+]. Made almost entirely of plastic, this collection of hollow stacking elements went into production in 1977, and was available in a light grey or dark brown finish. The elements could be stacked to create stools of varying heights, from a single unit that functioned as a simple cushion on the floor to standard chair level. With the addition of a tabletop, the stack became a mushroom-shaped table. Filling some of the bases with sand increased stability, and thus three stacked units could become a garden umbrella stand, or four units, with the addition of a backrest, became a chair.

— Stagnation

Despite the clever innovations and despite the extra subsidies from the plastics industry, however, nearly none of Dieter Rams's furniture designs in the 1970s were a success commercially. They were, as he later rather bluntly admits: 'total flops'. [14] Wiese-Vitsœ was not set up to produce furniture, particularly plastic furniture, on the mass scale that would have been required to make it financially viable. Manufacture was not centralized and difficulties with some of the materials in particular meant that components and furniture items had to undergo journeys between several locations before they even made it to the showrooms. For example, some of the plastic surfaces developed a static charge, which meant that they rapidly got covered in dirt and dust unless they were sent off after manufacture to undergo a costly lacquering process with anti-static paint. 'The whole thing was very uneconomical' recalls Rams, 'if it hadn't been for [sales of] the 570 and the 606, then it would have been hard'. [15] Because the company did not manage the balance between production volume and price, much of the later Wiese-Vitsœ furniture ended up being an unviable crossbreed between the handmade and industrially mass-produced. The plastic pieces in particular were expensive and the high visual and haptic quality for which Rams had strived failed to convince the buying public.

[14]   Dieter Rams, in conversation with the author (July 2009)

[15]   Ibid.

The company kept going through most of the 1980s predominantly due to sales of the early system designs, including the 620, the 606 and the 570, each of which had become good long-term sellers, but the firm was stagnating. In 1993, in the year that Niels Vitsœ turned eighty, the company Wiese-Vitsœ was in serious trouble and in 1995 it finally went into liquidation. With the exception of the 606 shelving system (in 1984, the Italian company de Padova had been granted a licence to produce an aluminium version, which was still going strong) it looked as though Rams and Vitsœ's furniture could come to the end of the line.

A Universal Shelving System

Dieter Rams had very specific aims when he started to design his furniture systems. In 1995 he wrote: 'Perhaps more directly than with the Braun products, my furniture arose from a belief in how the world should be 'furnished' and how man should live in this artificial environment. In this respect, each piece of furniture is also a design for a certain kind of world and way of living, they reflect a specific vision of mankind'.[16] In the same text he goes on to explain that his views as a young designer in the 1950s were shaped by his experience of war, dictatorship and destruction, and later by freedom and the 'first years of a new beginning'. As a result he wanted to make a new kind of furniture that was above all 'simple', not in terms of being sterile and empty, but as a 'liberation from the dominance of things'. Rams wanted to design a living environment that allowed for freedom of expression. In order to achieve this, his furniture first needed to be free from the superfluous and the fashionable. It needed to be quiet and almost introverted in form and colour, harmonious and well thought through right down to the last tiny detail. The second quality that Rams required of his furniture was flexibility of function, hence the systems and the components that permitted adaptation and change. Third, his furniture had to be of high quality in terms of design, materials and construction to allow for a long life: 'A Vitsœ furniture system is designed to survive decades of use, extension, alteration and relocation without damage, and it does'. But he adds: 'Unfortunately, this high quality led to prices that gave what should have been simple, uncomplicated and materially economical fuctional furniture a degree of exclusivity that was never intended.'[17]

It has been a source of great regret to Rams that due to the circumstances of their manufacture and technical limitations, his furniture designs have never benefited as many people as he would have wished, being confined to a somewhat elite niche market. Nevertheless, the thinking behind Rams's furniture and examples of his ideas can be said to have made an ideological contribution to the

[16]   Dieter Rams, 'Furniture', in *Less but better / Weniger, aber besser* (Hamburg, 1995), 128. Translation modified by the author

[17]   Ibid., 136–37. Translation modified by the author

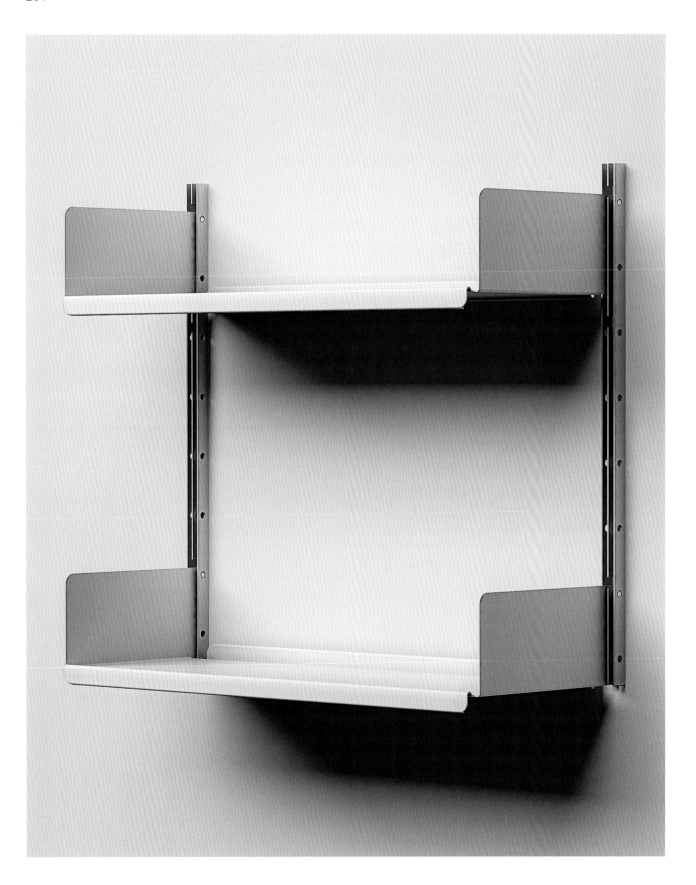

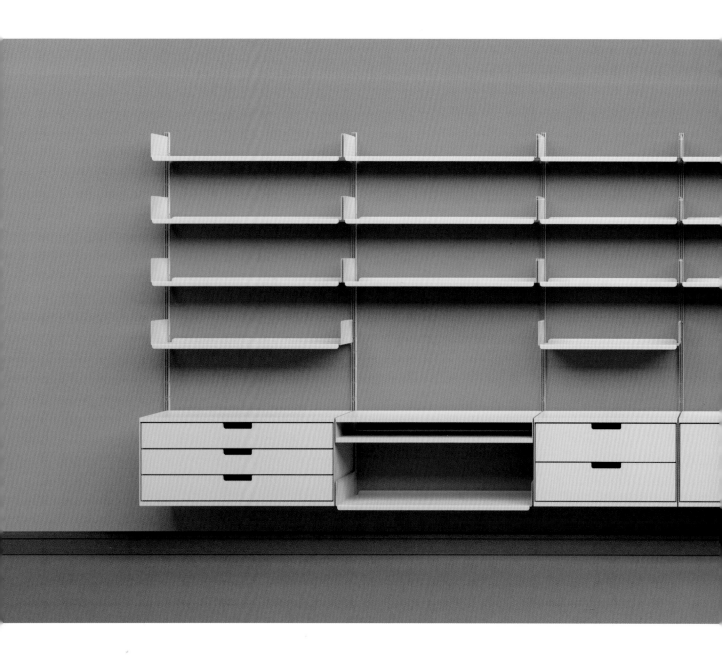

606 shelving system. Originally designed as the RZ 60, Dieter Rams, 1960

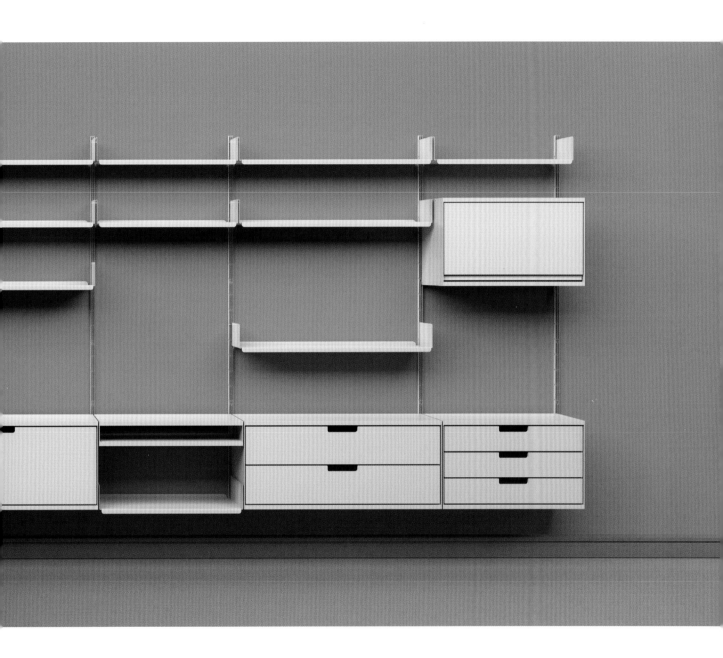

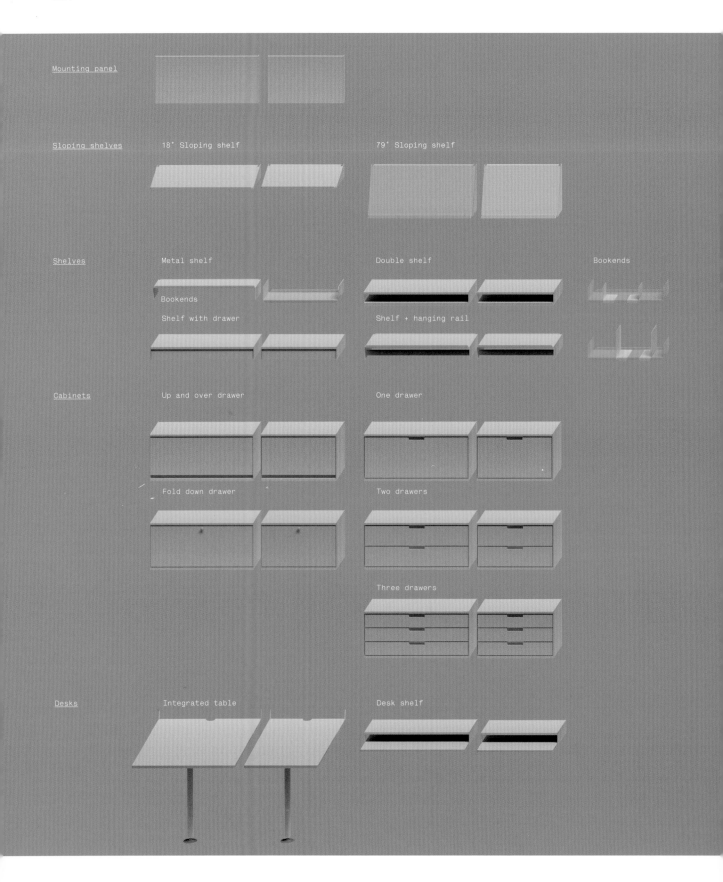

Mounting panel

Sloping shelves   18° Sloping shelf   79° Sloping shelf

Shelves   Metal shelf   Double shelf   Bookends

Bookends

Shelf with drawer   Shelf + hanging rail

Cabinets   Up and over drawer   One drawer

Fold down drawer   Two drawers

Three drawers

Desks   Integrated table   Desk shelf

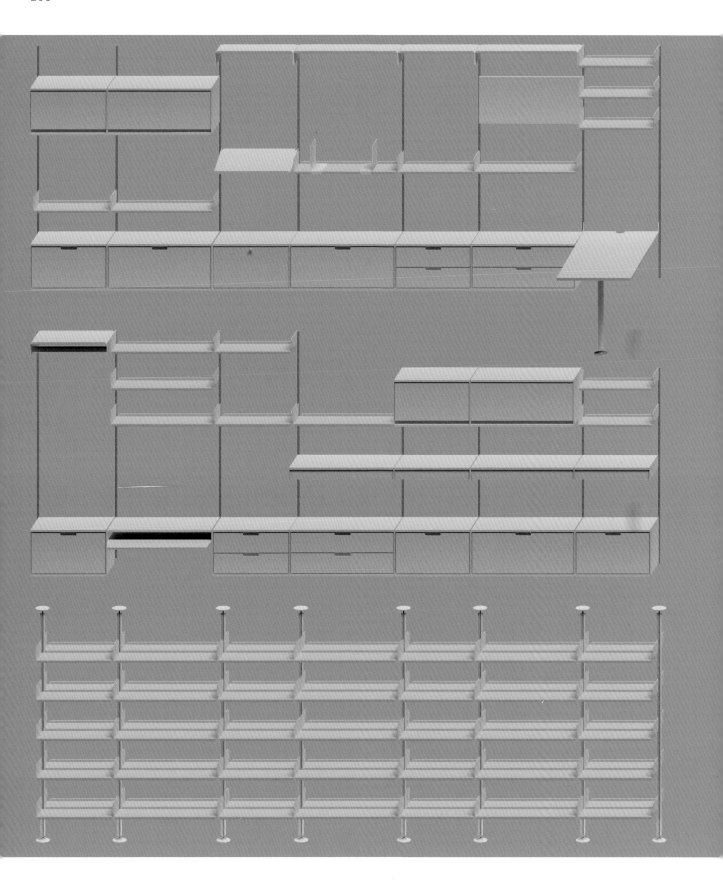

Endless configurations

RZ 57 furniture system, Dieter Rams, 1957.

RZ 57 furniture system. Dieter Rams's T 22 radio is on the shelf.

RZ 57 furniture system. Dieter Rams's TP 1
radio and record player is on the shelf.

RZ 57 furniture system

All images: 601 / 602 chair programme, originally designed
as the RZ 60, Dieter Rams, 1960. Top left: 601 chair, low back
Above left: 601 footrest with 601 / 602 tables

Above right: 601 chair, high back

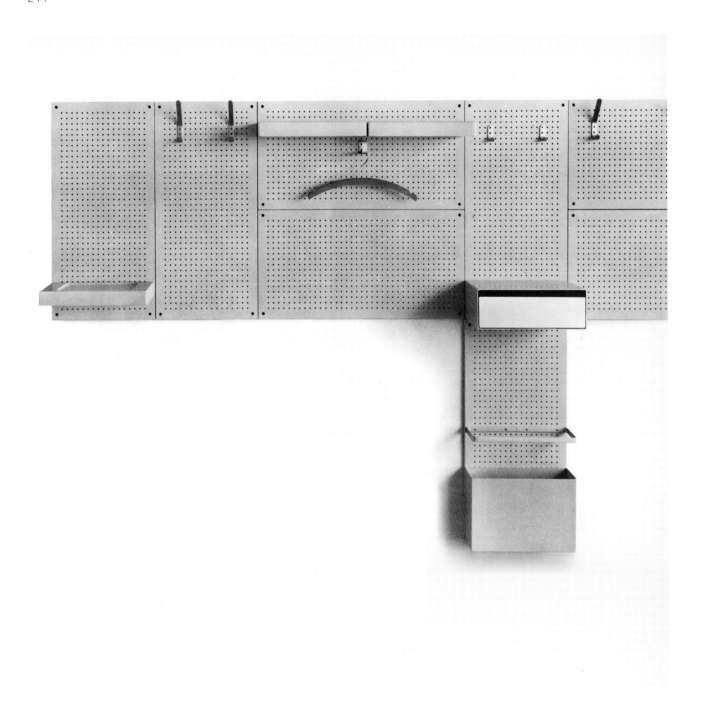

610 wall panel system, originally designed as
the RZ 61, Dieter Rams, 1961

620 chair programme, originally designed as the RZ 62,
Dieter Rams, 1962

681 chair programme, Dieter Rams, 1968

680 bed / couch programme, Dieter Rams, 1968

720 round-oval table (1972) and a plastic version of the 622 dining / conference chair (originally 1962),
both Dieter Rams

620 chair programme, seen here with the 621 nesting coffee
table and the 606 system in Vitsœ's Frankfurt showroom

world of contemporary furniture design. In 1992, he received an award from the
IKEA Foundation for the user-friendly clarity and timeless nature of his work at
Braun and with Vitsœ. This recognition from the world's largest furniture manufacturer, who pioneered flat-pack furniture at affordable prices, is certainly
appropriate. Although Rams may not agree with the overall standards of quality
and design achieved by IKEA, he acknowledges that they have succeeded at
a mass level, where his furniture designs have not: 'IKEA is the exception in the
furniture branch,' he said in 1979, 'Through clever marketing, it proved that a
furniture manufacturing and sales company can succeed in achieving broad effects
with a programme of partially acceptable designs at a low price … living in this
respect is seen here more in terms of being a creative process. "Do-it-yourself"
plays an important part in this programme and that, I think, is a positive thing.'[18]

sdr+

One highly successful aspect of many of the Rams-designed furniture systems
has been their longevity and therefore sustainability. After Wiese-Vitsœ folded in
1995, a group of German furniture dealers[19] gathered together, calling themselves
sdr+, and acquired the licence to continue making Rams's furniture bestsellers
in Germany. The name sdr+ stands for *Systemmöbel Dieter Rams* (System Furniture
Dieter Rams), and the plus sign represents the designer Thomas Merkel, who
took on developing the product line in collaboration with Rams, who was close to
retirement at the time.[20]

   The systems that sdr+ initially produced were the table programme 570 from
1957, the 606 shelving system from 1960, the 620 seating programme from 1962
and the 710 *korpusprogramme* (containers and cabinets) from 1971. The designs for
this furniture were between twenty-four and thirty-eight-years-old at the time,
but within a year of its foundation, sdr+ was making a profit selling in the Benelux
countries, Switzerland and Germany.

Mark Adams and the new Vitsœ

Back in 1993, as it became clear that Wiese-Vitsœ was going to fail, Vitsœ's
family invited a young man from London over to Germany to discuss the fate of
the business. Then thirty-three years old, Mark Adams had been successfully
marketing Vitsœ products in Great Britain since 1985 under the name Vitsœ UK.

[18]   Rams, 'Zurück zum Einfachen' in *Design: Dieter Rams* & (English edition), 209 (211 in the German
       edition). Translation modified by the author

[19]   Stoll in Cologne, Loeser in Hannover, Modus in Berlin, Burgor in Karlsruhe, Schroer in Krefeld and
       Frick in Frankfurt

[20]   Thomas Merkel designs his own furniture for sdr+, along with another design team called Dreiform.

His company had earned a loyal following among private customers and a young generation of British architects, particularly with respect to the 606 shelving system. After talks with the Vitsœ family, Adams took over the name Vitsœ and decided to concentrate on one product, the 606 system (joined later by the 620 lounge chair programme). For various reasons, he decided to move production to the UK in 1995 to cater to the local and international market. Together with Dieter Rams, he set about working on a continuous series of upgrades and improvements that would help reduce production costs (and thus end price) yet still allow the system to remain compatible with older components. Adams says he took on the challenge of producing the shelving system because of his 'total and utter belief in what the company stood for – the authenticity and integrity of the products and the solidity of the ethos behind them'[21] Since meeting Rams in 1985 and getting to know him well, Adams had become a great admirer of the designer, notably for his 'steely strength of character' and his sensitive aesthetic understanding. 'He understands beauty completely,' he says.

Although the strength of the product was beyond question, Adams was well aware that the big stumbling block to a broader buying public was the price. 'Dieter Rams design is expensive design, he says, 'because every last detail is thought about, so every step of the way for us since 1993 has been about trying to make it cheaper without affecting the quality.'[22] Adams also understood early on that because Rams's furniture systems reflect the designer's particular attitude to furniture and how it should fit into the user's way of life they are often bought by individuals who have a similar attitude. For many of his customers, the 606 system is not a single purchase, but a furniture decision that accompanies them throughout various life stages and living situations. They may buy it for its aesthetic quality of timeless, unobtrusive elegance but end up keeping it because it also fulfils its function so well and for so long. Therefore, unlike most other furniture dealers, today's Vitsœ has a long-term customer care approach that includes product care as well. 'Our company policy is to allow more people to live better with less that lasts longer,' says Adams. 'Around 50 per cent of our customers are existing customers who are adding to, installing or rearranging their furniture, which might have been bought as far back as 1960.' This is a valuable lesson in sustainable design that carries increasing resonance, more than half a century after Rams first started designing his 'less but better' furniture.

[21]   Mark Adams, in conversation with the author (June 2009)

[22]   Ibid.

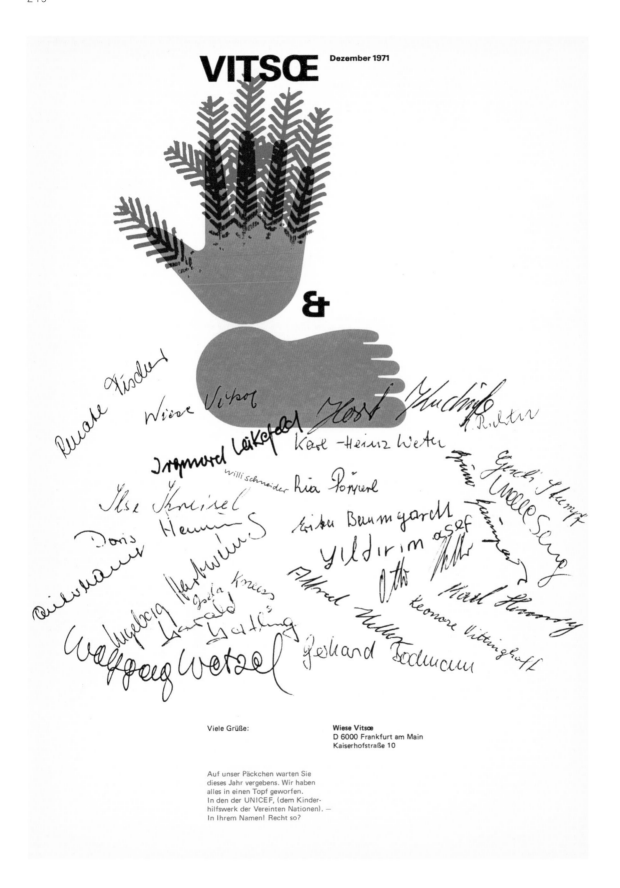

VITSŒ Dezember 1971

Viele Grüße:

Wiese Vitsœ
D 6000 Frankfurt am Main
Kaiserhofstraße 10

Auf unser Päckchen warten Sie
dieses Jahr vergebens. Wir haben
alles in einen Topf geworfen.
In den der UNICEF, (dem Kinder-
hilfswerk der Vereinten Nationen). —
In Ihrem Namen! Recht so?

1971 Vitsœ Christmas card

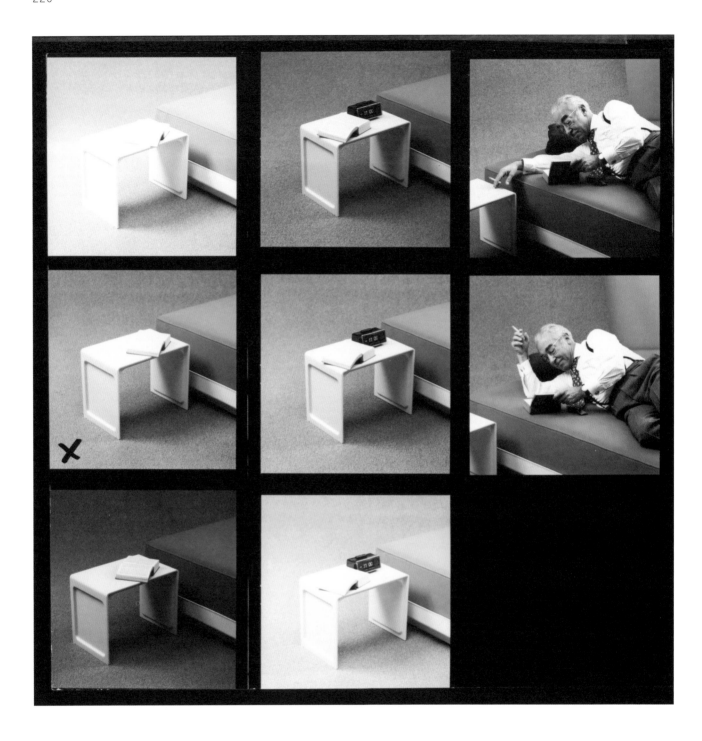

Niels Vitsœ, with the 680 bed and 621 coffee table

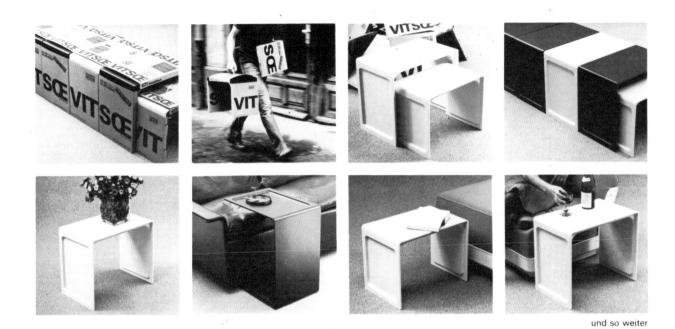

und so weiter

621 nesting coffee tables, Dieter Rams, 1962

Promotional postcard for 602 chair programme

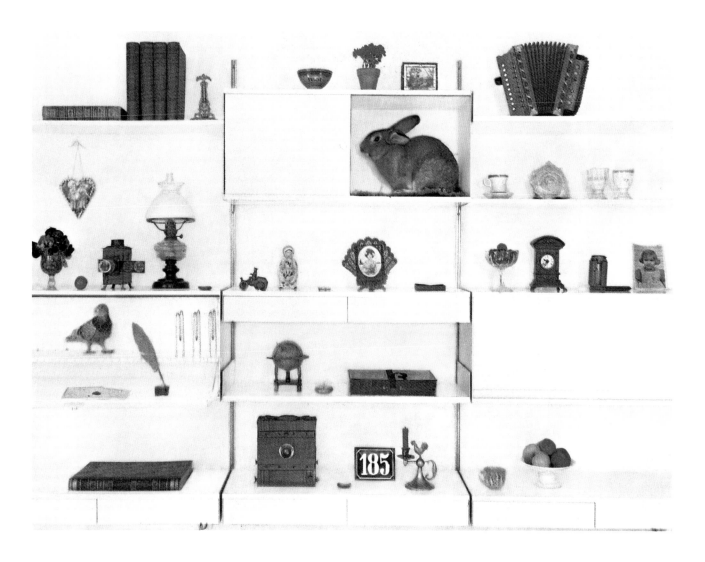

Promotional postcard for 606 universal shelving system

Dieter Rams (near right), Niels Vitsœ (far left) and colleagues
meeting at Vitsœ's Frankfurt showroom

All images: Dieter Rams, Niels Vitsœ and colleagues
at the Vitsœ showroom

Vitsœ showroom, Frankfurt, c.1970

Ingeborg Rams (left) and Dieter Rams (right) with the
606 system in Vitsœ's Frankfurt showroom, c. 1973

740 Stacking programme, Dieter Rams, 1977

Designing Details

'My heart belongs to the details.
I actually always found them to be more important
than the big picture. Nothing works without details.
They are everything, the baseline of quality'.[1]

Every good designer knows that 'God is in the details'.[2] Anyone can sketch an idea, but the approximation to perfection, the genius of inspiration *and* execution comes from the hard slog involved in making all the tiny curves and interfaces, angles, materials and technology work together in harmony. Details enable communication, aiding transparency and closing the gap between object and subject, user and product. It is appropriate that Dieter Rams's first great design success involved not only a detail, but a transparent one: the acrylic lid of the SK 4 super phonograph, nicknamed 'Snow White's Coffin'. This was an inspired idea that not only helped to ensure the great commercial and critical success of the SK 4 as a product but represents a defining moment in audio design: record players have transparent covers because Dieter Rams thought of it. That alone should be enough to earn him a place in the design history books.

'Truly functional design only comes from the most careful and intense attention to detail,'[3] says Rams. It could be argued that his greatest overall contribution to design has come from working in areas that most users are not consciously aware of. In his four decades as head of design at Braun, although he did not directly design all products and even had very little to do with some of them, he constantly encouraged tiny improvements that could make a good design better. This attention to detail ranged from the acuteness of angles in forms; the size, feel and distances between switches; the integration of handle fixings; the placement and nature of graphic elements on the products themselves and extended to product photography and packaging. Designing detail is about achieving a fine balance in all aspects and areas of the product, including those external to the object.

[1]   Dieter Rams, in conversation with Rido Busse (1980), reprinted in François Burkhardt and Inez Franksen, eds., *Design: Dieter Rams &* (English edition, Berlin, 1981), 195 (197 in the German edition). Translation modified by the author

[2]   Mies van der Rohe, quoted in *New York Times* (19 August 1969)

[3]   Rams, in conversation with Rido Busse, in *Design: Dieter Rams &*, 195 (197 in the German edition). Translation modified by the author

Detail at Braun

Between 1955 and 1995 Braun manufactured more than 1,200 products and Dieter Rams was directly involved in designing 514 of them.[4] In addition he kept the smaller company of Vitsœ + Zapf (later Vitsœ) supplied with entire furniture ranges including shelving, tables, armchairs, seating and storage systems. For an industrial designer working with relatively small teams his output was extraordinary – especially considering the depth and detail involved in his particular approach.

This chapter looks at the importance of detail in Rams's work and then goes on to examine a selection of appliances that he designed (or significantly co-designed) for Braun, with emphasis on the detailing that makes them worthy of note. In each case these products are distinguished by Rams's 'signature' or 'design vocabulary'.

Although the Braun style was initially developed before Rams joined the company, his pursuit of an industrial design based on a functionally oriented attitude that was proposed by Wilhelm Wagenfeld, nurtured by Erwin Braun and Fritz Eichler and furthered by other designers, notably Hans Gugelot and Herbert Hirche, was central to the firm's development. It was through Rams's design talent and his direction that this approach matured and refined Braun's product family into one of the most recognisable and successful of the twentieth century.

One would think that on the basis of his own principles and those of Braun, however, Rams's design should not be recognisable. 'Good design should be as little design as possible,' says Rams. Or in Wagenfeld's words, a product 'has to exist for itself … completely purged from the individual influences that let it come into being.'[5] Is not the whole point of Braun design that the form should be dictated by function, as an appliance in the hands of the user and as a part of the environment for which it is created? That the needs of the user should take precedence and the ego of the designer(s) should not be allowed to interfere with decorative flights of fancy? These products should do their job but be as neutral as possible. Thus Braun design is greatly reduced – stripped of all that is unnecessary. Nevertheless, there is a strong aesthetic characterized by balance, order and harmony. Unless placed in an environment that echoes that aesthetic, these appliances often stand out from the surrounding 'visual chaos'. However, much as Rams would like to put the quality of his design solely down to the application of a rigorous and disciplined approach, he does admit that his own aesthetic came into play at Braun: 'Self control is very important. Although my own taste is involved it always

[4]   Klaus Klemp et al., eds, *Less and More: The Design Ethos of Dieter Rams* (Osaka, 2008), 25

[5]   Wilhelm Wagenfeld, 'Kunstlerische Zusammenarbeit mit der Industrie' lecture at the 'Bund Deutscher Kunsterzieher' convention at the Technical University of Darmstadt (18 September 1954), reprinted in Hans Wichmann, *Mut zum Aufbruch: Erwin Braun, 1921–1992* (Munich, 1998), 178–80

has to be under control. Not suppressed though! Controlled!'[6] His is an aesthetic tempered by reason and careful consideration, with no selfish or wanton abandonment permitted.

The beauty and distinctiveness of Braun products created during Rams's time lie in their combination of simplicity, proportion and feel. They are indeed reduced, with simple and clean lines, but not for the sake of being minimal. They are not blank boxes. Close examination reveals that this reduction of form is the result of many hours of refinement, problem-solving and co-operation to create the right balance among a large number of variables including function, materials, electronics, mechanics and form. The topography of each object is primarily defined by these variables but what makes them so pleasing to the eye and the hand are the proportional aesthetics involved at the millimetre level. The value Rams attaches to proportion is evident in his sketches. The fact that he initiated an entire product graphics department within his very compact team is further evidence of this belief: product graphics provide the punctuation to the grammar of his design method.

You can recognize Rams's products not only by looking at them, but by feeling them as well. The tactile effect of operating elements such as gently rounded buttons on the calculators and hi-fis, the combination of soft and hard plastics for better grip on the Micron Vario 3 shaver, the indented, thumb-shaped switch of the 'cylindric' table lighters and the absolutely smooth transitions between different materials on many products are all details that were part of the long-term design attitude at Braun that was fostered by Rams. These products were not only made to last, but designed to be a pleasure to use as well as to look at; they were intended to be favourite tools that fit the hand and are intuitively understood.

'In questions of detail, Dieter was very fastidious,' says Dietrich Lubs, former head of product graphics and designer at Braun. 'He had a great talent for improving what was already a good solution with detail suggestions such as increasing or decreasing curve radii. Proportions too played a considerable role.'[7] This level of attention to detail is at the high-end of design; it requires a continuous pushing for perfection beyond the point when many would have said 'that will do'. Another great industrial designer, Naoto Fukasawa, says he was strongly influenced by Rams in this respect. 'Lately I have become occupied by edges and corners – tiny details that are simplified and smoothened in the millimetre realm to reach a simpler state. These are tiny details but they involve great effort … Industrial designers have to work on the tiniest points and edges to have meaning. Industrial design is a precise job – it took me thirty years to realize this.'[8]

[6]   Dieter Rams, advice to design students during a workshop in Osaka, Japan (16 November 2008)

[7]   Dietrich Lubs, in conversation with the author (2009)

[8]   Naoto Fukasawa, talk at the opening of the exhibition 'Less and More', Suntory Museum, Osaka, Japan (15 November 2008)

The Braun Method

From the start, the Braun style was not dictated by the latest fashion or consumer taste. The opposite is true; the company products were innovative for their time. In the early 1950s, the Braun brothers had to invest considerable amounts of money into convincing the buying public of the merits of their products. The foundations for the Braun style were in place before the customers began to realize that they wanted the products and later, particularly in the 1980s, that same style seemed to fly in the face of fashion. In the context of that decade's post-modern, 'anything goes', 'form follows fashion' mood, Braun appeared positively staid in its continuity: the firm did not change, it conveyed the same message and the product family line continued.

The main element that all Braun products from 1955 to 1995 share is the design team: they were designed by more or less the same people under the same head of department using the same methods. 'We have no idea what the appliances of tomorrow will look like,' said Rams in 1965, 'but if they resemble today's products in terms of style then this has nothing to do with a pre-planned pursuit of a particular style, rather that they will be designed by a group of people who have shared the same experiences and work with the same methods, who have grown together in their shared work because they have similar views and similar tastes'.[9] This was a prediction that was to hold true for another thirty years.

p. 242 Each new project began [+] with an in-depth look at every aspect relevant to the design: the market, available technology, the needs of potential users and so on. The first designs were made in soft pencil on rolls of tracing paper so that sheets could be overlapped and variations in detail explored. Many models were made, to check form and answer questions, such as how the product should feel in the hand, the best angles for grips, how best to accommodate motors and ventilation and where to place switches. All this was done in close collaboration with the technology department. The models were a key part of the design process – Rams calls them 'three-dimensional drawings' – and they were initially made in wood, plaster and clay, later using plastics as well. The workshop designers whose task it was to make products in 3D shared the same studio as the rest of the team. The models progressed in stages, from rough formal experiments to highly detailed prototypes that were then presented to the rest of the company before going on to production. The product details were also specified as technical drawings. This method was employed throughout Rams's time at Braun. Computers did not feature significantly in the design process for much of this time, nor were there artistically styled images or renderings, says Dietrich Lubs. 'We always worked with technical drawings, not renderings. It was very important, especially for communication

---

[9]   'Produktdesign bei Braun', *Form* vol. 1 (1965), reprinted in Uta Brandes, ed., *Dieter Rams Designer. Die Leise Ordnung der Dinge*, (Hannover, 1990), 38

with the technicians, that we didn't behave like artists'.[10] The emphasis was on clear and accurate engineering, so that the designers felt under no obligation to sell their ideas by dressing them up with pretty pictures.

Even after the take-over of the company by Gillette in 1967, this methodology remained essentially the same. Had the new owners been heavy-handed, they might easily have lost the essence of the 'Braun style' at this stage. 'The Gillette take-over was a shock for us', remembers Lubs, 'we thought we would have to work with American styling and renderings. But the Gillette president at the time said he had bought the company because of the design and he wanted that to continue'.[11] The influence that the design team wielded in the company was clearly understood from all sides. The team believed in themselves, their abilities, their methods and their products and Gillette wanted this successful format to continue. The products continued to sell, and the design team continued to hold sway. Or as Lubs puts it: 'we convinced them and they made an effort to understand'.

Using Colour

Few of the products designed at Braun between 1955 and 1995 could be described as colourful. The principal colours used for appliances and other products were white, pale grey, black or metallic and, of course, there was careful reasoning behind this palette. One of the key aspects of Braun philosophy at this time was that products should be what Erwin Braun called 'faithful servants'; they should accompany and serve an individual over a long period of time without hindering or disturbing through 'extravagant forms, loud colours or flashy proportions'.[12] Because Braun appliances were intended to form part of the domestic background, they needed to have a subdued and inconspicuous colouration. A product that is dressed in bright colours to seduce buyers from shop windows might seem 'young, jaunty and à la mode,' says Dieter Rams, 'But when it stands gaudily in the kitchen, day after day, its colour is disturbing. It adds to the colour chaos that most people today wreak in their living environments'.[13] He considered bright colours used for their own sake to be pure fashion, therefore fleeting and temporary: 'Too much money is invested in furniture, carpets, curtains and domestic appliances for them to be changed whenever the colours or colour combinations get on your nerves'.[14]

p. 308 Nevertheless there were a number of colourful appliances [+] produced by Braun, particularly from the late 1960s onwards, when plastics in bright primary colours became fashionable and available. The 'cassette' shaver from 1970, for

[10]   Dietrich Lubs, in conversation with the author (2009)

[11]   Ibid

[12]   Dieter Rams, 'Braun Design und Farbe' (c. 1985), Rams archive 1.1.1.3

[13]   Ibid.

[14]   Ibid.

example, had a version with a bright red housing and a plastic case in black and yellow, and the T 3 'domino' table lighter from 1973 was a clunky cube in the same yellow and black. Rams's own design of the KMM 2 Aromatic coffee grinder from 1969 was available in white, red or yellow versions and his HLD 4 hairdryer from 1970 came in red, yellow or blue with black detailing. Florian Seiffert's KF 20 Aromaster coffee machine was almost Pop in its form and colour range of white, yellow, orange, red, burgundy and olive. In the 1990s, the AromaSelect KF 145 coffee maker (1994) and the HT 95 pop-up toaster (1991) also had a number of colour variations.

When Rams's design team used colour in such a way, it was uncompromising in its intensity: loud and demanding. The highly reduced forms of the products that it clothed, which had gently rounded edges, smooth opaque surfaces and discrete (usually black) detailing only served to increase this intensity. 'The intention was to create product alternatives for people who wished for strong colour highlights in their living environments. This impulse came from marketing – not from design,'[15] says Rams, dissociating himself from this approach. This was one instance where marketing got the upper hand in the decision-making process and the design team had to bow to contemporary fashion. Indeed, there is a defiant aspect to these chromatic exceptions; they are not so much compromises as mutinous responses. Nevertheless, the resulting products are beautiful objects in their stand-alone way.

The rejection of colour as decoration and an antipathy to what he calls the 'abuse of colour' is something that Rams has always felt strongly about. Colour, in his opinion, 'has to fit the product: Some products, like things you put on a table are colour-capable, but tools and appliances – kitchen appliances – should not be coloured, they should stay in the background … you have to think very carefully about where colour is important and where it can be dangerous'.[16] This is not to say that he rejected colour per se; in fact he took it very seriously as a means of communication: 'using colour as a signal, I find, is often better than colouring the whole product'.[17] When not compelled to do otherwise, the Braun design team's use of colour in products was reduced to highly specific areas such as control switches. Restricting the use of colour to small points on an otherwise neutral object concentrates its effect, which is shifted away from decoration and towards function, especially when each colour is assigned a signal role such as green for 'on / off' switches, red for 'fm' and yellow for 'phono' on hi-fis or yellow for the second hand on clocks and watches.

This colour coding of operating details is a primary example of the self-explanatory nature of Braun products. One of Dieter Rams's principles of good design is that design should make a product easy to understand: 'I have always laid emphasis on the fact that a product can be brought to "speak" through good design. My aim

15   Ibid.

16   Dieter Rams, advice to design students during a workshop in Osaka, Japan (16 November 2008)

17   Ibid.

has always been to raise the self-explanatory aspect. I never trusted instruction manuals – we all know that most people don't read them. The information always came through how the product looked – with the colour-coding / labelling. Red is demanding, green is more restrained and so on.'[18]

Colouring details on products was a feature that belonged primarily to the area known as 'product graphics' at Braun. This was another field that Rams developed at the company and as a result distinguished Braun clearly from its competitors. 'Product graphics were particularly difficult because in the 1960s there was no one trained to do this,' he says, 'Graphic designers found it too mundane or weren't able to do it and the [industrial] designers didn't *want* to do it. I had to try and train people myself.'[19] Rams set up a special screen-printing department at Braun that dramatically improved the quality of the graphics on the products. Rams' care and attention to this, often overlooked, aspect of product design is another example of the thoroughness of his approach.

The Products

During his time at Braun, Dieter Rams designed some products almost single-handedly and concentrated on a range of fields with varying degrees of involvement at different stages of their development. His early main areas of interest lay with the pocket and portable radios. Then he focused on many of the hi-fi elements that were his 'babies', including amplifiers, tuners, cassette recorders and loudspeakers up until 1980 – later he collaborated with Peter Hartwein. He also worked a lot on the flashguns and slide projectors in the early years, before handing them on to Robert Oberheim. Rams took over the television sets from Herbert Hirche and the record players from Wilhem Wagenfeld, with Hans Gugelot and Gerd A Müller in the 1950s (the SK 4 and the PC 3), and was joined by Oberheim in 1972 and Hartwein in 1980). He also initiated designs on products such as the Nizo movie cameras before handing over to other designers, in this case Oberheim again and Peter Schneider. Clocks, watches, calculators and clock radios were developed in partnership with Dietrich Lubs, who later took over most work in this area. Cigarette lighters were also predominantly developed by Rams, first alone and then together with Reinhold Weiss, Jürgen Greubel and Florian Seiffert. In other areas Rams had little direct involvement (with a few notable exceptions mentioned below), particularly electric toothbrushes, hairdryers, kitchen appliances and irons. Nevertheless, as design director he was always involved in significant decisions and when detail issues needed discussion and solutions.

[18]   Dieter Rams, speech at a symposium during the opening of the exhibition 'Less and More', Suntory Museum, Osaka, Japan (15 November 2008)

[19]   Ibid.

— Portables

Portable radios had a tradition at Braun. Max Braun toyed with the concept in the 1930s but was somewhat limited by the hardware. Then in 1954 and 1955 companies in the United States and Japan brought out the first transistor radios. Transistors caused an absolute revolution in radio technology – they not only took up far less space than their vacuum tube predecessors, they also needed far less energy, which meant that battery-powered portables were suddenly a viable option for private use. Dieter Rams's first radio project was a new form of housing made of a plastic called thermo-plast for Braun's 'transistor' radio from 1956. It was simple in appearance, and its only 'decorative' elements were the beautifully proportioned sets of horizontal slits for the loudspeaker. Rams' ventilation patterns later became something of a trademark of his on a whole range of products.

p.247
The 'transistor' was a *'Kofferradio'*, which literally translates as a portable radio, but portable in the way that a briefcase is portable: [+] it had a leather carrying strap on the top and was not particularly lightweight. However, in the mid-1950s, a new kind of miniaturized portable began to appear on the market, one that was so small it could fit in your pocket (provided you had a relatively big pocket). The Regency TR-1 from a firm called Texas Instruments in the United States was released in 1954, and the Sony TR-55 in Japan and the Telefunken TR-1 in Germany were also pioneers in this field. Although Braun did not make the first pocket transistor radios, as always they were distinguished from the competition in their refined and attractive design. Designed by Rams in collaboration with the p.244 Hochschule für Gestaltung Ulm, the T 3 / T 31 pocket receiver [+] from 1958 had an entirely plastic, off-white housing. Instead of elongated speaker slits, it had circular perforations, and the channel dial, operated by finger touch, was completely flush with the casing, apart from having two small ridges to stop your finger slipping. Although several other early transistor radios had circular dials, including the Regency TR-1, none of them had the minimal simplicity and quality of interface supplied by the Braun models.

p.244
Rams designed several variations on the pocket receiver, such as the T 4 [+] from 1959, on which the perforations were arranged in a circular format and the channel dial was moved inside the housing – you could only peek at it through p.260 a little plexiglass window. In the T 41 version [+] (1962) this window was enlarged and shaped like a fan to reveal more of the dial beneath and echo the circular speaker element.

One of Rams's first system designs emerged from the pocket receiver models. p.245 The TP 1 / TP 2 [+] from 1959 was a radio-phonograph combination that was revolutionary at the time. It consisted of an aluminium bracket that joined the T 3 radio p.261 to the P 1 compact record player [+] (which played 45 rpm records via a spring-operated stylus concealed within the casing). The system came complete with leather strap and headphones so you could actually carry it around while it was playing. 'Retrospectively, I like to call it "the first Walkman",' says Rams. 'The radio reception was limited, but the sound quality wasn't at all bad – especially using the headphones.'[20]

The pocket radios were popular but the sound quality and reception was relatively poor. Thus the larger, more powerful Braun portables were still widely used in the 1960s, especially as car radios, which were not standard at that time. The

p.258

T 52, [+] for example, designed by Dieter Rams in 1961, was able to receive VHF, medium and long-wave transmissions. The operating elements were all located at the top of the device, which became the 'front' when it was laid on its side (a more practical position for when driving in a car, for example). The metal carrying handle could then be folded under the radio to act as a prop.

The pinnacle of Braun portable radio design was also the last portable it ever made: the renowned T 1000 from 1963. [+] It was known as the 'Weltempfänger', or

p.262

'world receiver' because it was able to receive all wavelengths, and particularly excelled with short-wave transmissions. The T 1000 was a great piece of technology that is still highly popular with radio buffs, long after production has ceased. Dieter Rams's design (developed together with the Braun technicians Joachim Fahrendholz and Harald Haupenberger) in anodized aluminium with a black scale, concave push buttons and precision typography is not only lovely to look at, but makes a highly complex and difficult piece of professional technology surprisingly easy to understand and operate. For transport, the aluminium casing, containing a bulky operation manual, could be closed to insulate the dials. It could also be fitted with a direction-finding adaptor, extra antenna and compass, which turned it into a piece of navigation equipment. Despite being expensive at the time (around 1,500 deutschmarks), the T 1000 sold well and 25,000 sets were made. This helped Braun to realize there was a sizeable high-end, high-tech niche market waiting to be explored and most likely encouraged them on the path to their high-fidelity system era that was developing at the time.

—   Audio

One other stand-alone radio designed by Rams requires a special mention. In 1961

p.264

the 'Tischsuper' VHF and medium-wave radio RT 20 [+] came on the market. Like the SK 4 phonograph, its design is a cross-over between the technical-looking modules that Rams was already designing and the warmer, more domestic audio 'furniture' that had come before. Like a piece of furniture, the RT 20 was available in two different finishes: a pear wood body with a flush, graphite-coloured sheet-steel front, pale grey knobs and white graphics, and a beechwood housing with an off-white front, green-grey knobs and black graphics. From the front, the RT 20

[20]   Dieter Rams, in conversation with the author (November 2007)

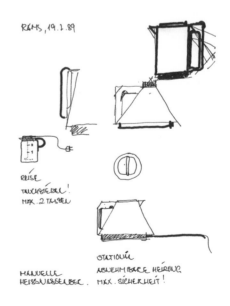

Top: Dieter Rams, 1989   Above: Sketch for a kettle, Dieter Rams, 1989

243

Model for a kettle, Dieter Rams and
Jürgen Greubel, 1967 / 77

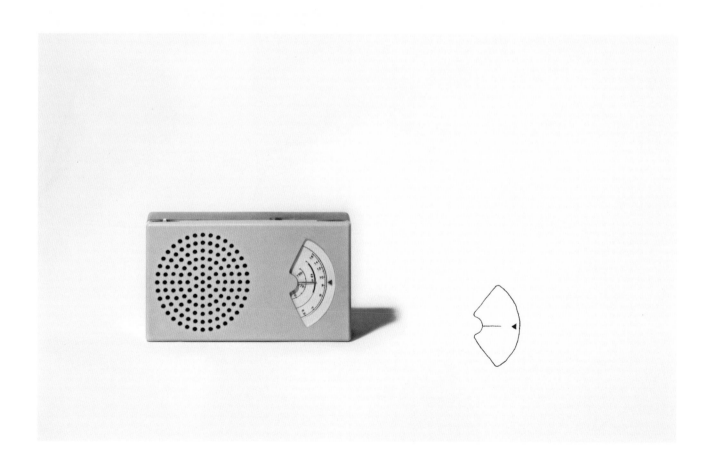

Top: T 4 radio, 1959 (left) and T 3 radio,
1958 (right), both Dieter Rams

Above: T 41 radio,
Dieter Rams, 1962

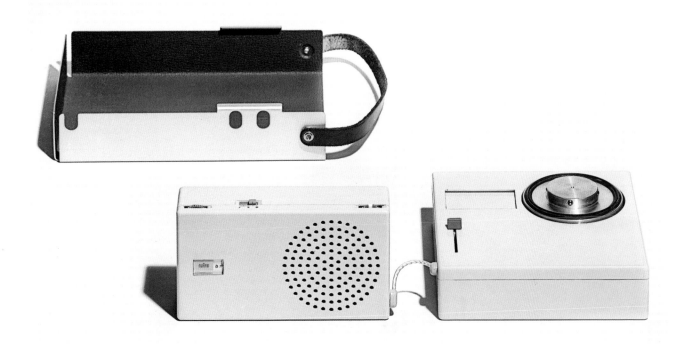

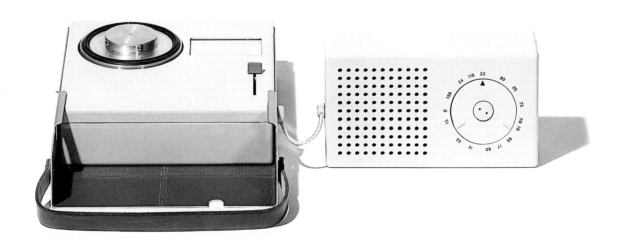

P 1 record player, Dieter Rams, 1958, with the T 4 radio (top) and T 3
radio (above) and bracket for the TP 1 radio / phonograph (both)

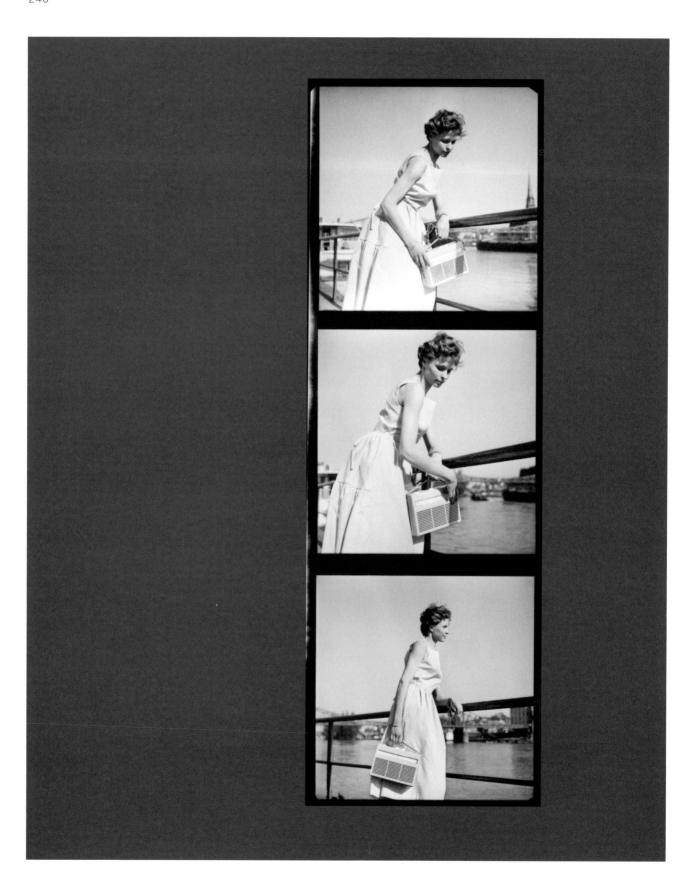

Promotional images for the T 22 radio,
Dieter Rams, 1960

Promotional images for the T 22 radio,
Dieter Rams, 1960

Promotional images for the TP 1 radio and record player,
Dieter Rams, 1959

resembled the T 4 pocket radio with its perforated, circular loudspeaker vent, but instead of circular holes, Rams returned to the slit pattern found on the SK 4 that he designed with Hans Gugelot. This seems to have been a purely aesthetic decision based on scale; slits on a larger surface work better than dots. The RT 20, like the SK 4, is distinguished by its honest beauty, devoid of decoration, which stems from a balance between function, materials and proportion – the two products had many similar features. Rams is justly proud of this design: 'This has often been called "the definitive radio",' he says. 'In terms of design, it represents a return to the essence … This is something that I have striven for all my life: an aesthetic quality that is freed from ballast and therefore lighter … It is a return to simplicity. Aesthetic does not mean, as so many tend to think, the addition of some kind of ornamentation that once played a role somewhere'.[21]

Modular Audio Systems

p.266

Although radio-phonograph combinations remained popular and appliances such as the SK 4 had a number of successors – notably the steel and elmwood clad 'atelier 1' and its accompanying L 1 speakers [+] from 1957 – the era of the chunky audio appliance was coming to an end. In the 1950s, the generic term 'hi-fi' also began to usurp the old-fashioned phonograph, radiogram or simple record player and heralded a demand for high-quality, high-end sound reproduction.

Towards the end of the 1950s, the development of high-fidelity technology was already well established in Great Britain and the United States, but Braun began pioneering the modular audio system in Germany. Designed to give high quality sound reproduction, the Braun hi-fi system was a series of units that fitted together like building blocks. Thus a customer could buy parts of the system, later adding to it and updating it according to their budget and needs. It also offered the designers and technicians a way to accommodate complex and sometimes bulky technology (at first they still had to use valves because the new transistors were still too expensive) into a reduced and more compact format. The appearance of these systems was severely functional: technological-looking yet minimal, clad in steel and aluminium. They sat well with the angular, slim lines of the Knoll International furniture in the showrooms where they were displayed and hence, by implication, the contemporary interior of the time. This appearance also reflected the fact that these appliances were intended to be at the high end of sound technology for the normal user. They appeared as practically scientific devices, rather masculine and authoritatively 'tech', yet in the showrooms they could be seen to comfortably share the living room with coffee tables, upholstered furniture and the odd vase of flowers.

21   Ibid.

Another important factor in this development was that both the Braun brothers and the core creative team were big jazz fans. They went to concerts, listened to jazz regularly, and they were eager to hear recordings and broadcasts on equipment with high fidelity and the cleanest sound possible – so there was a considerable personal incentive involved in producing equipment that met their own requirements. This somewhat idiosyncratic passion inspired the Braun brothers to give their technology and design departments *carte blanche* at the time to come up with the very best and most advanced hi-fi equipment possible.

The design of the early Braun modular hi-fi systems belonged almost exclusively to Dieter Rams. He was already producing modular living room furniture at Vitsœ at this time and the flexibility of his system principles lent themselves perfectly to the domestic audio realm. His first hi-fi system – in fact one of the first hi-fi modular systems ever designed – was the CS 11 control unit, the CV 11 amplifier and the CE 11 tuner, which together were known as 'studio 2' from 1959. [•]

p.278

p.274,
275, 276

Around the same time Rams designed three highly distinctive new kinds of loudspeakers: the L 2 [•] (1958), the L 01 [•] (1959) and the LE 1 [•] (1959). The L 2 was made to augment the sound quality of the 'atelier 1' radiogram. It was a large but lightened in appearance by a slim tubular steel stand, and contained a stack of low, medium and high-frequency diaphragms that later became models for standard loudspeaker formats. Although the L 2 had a wooden frame, like the 'atelier 1' and the SK 4, its partner speaker, the L 01 auxiliary tweeter, was quite different. It had a remarkably delicate construction: a white lacquered square box with a slim profile mounted on an equally slim tubular steel rod and a round base. It had an aesthetic that was way ahead of its time. 'People were listening to a lot of jazz and baroque music at the time,' explains Rams, presumably referring to his own immediate audio environment, 'music with crystalline tones that were accentuated by the materials we used, such as perforated aluminium instead of the usual fabric for the fronts'.[22]

The LE 1 was a large but very slim loudspeaker that housed an electrostatic technology licensed by Braun from the British company Quad. The product was state-of-the-art at the time and had a particularly clear sound quality thanks to large lightweight membranes that could follow impulses better than the usual cone-shaped membranes of dynamic speakers. However, it was not as good with bass tones and the sound was very directional. The LE 1 was an attractive piece of furniture: the thin flat body with a black perforated metal front floated just above floor level on two metal feet and was tilted upwards to direct the sound into the centre of room. It was also very expensive and Braun made only 500 pairs up until 1966. Nevertheless, like the equally expensive T 1000 radio receiver, the LE 1 is a highly prized item for its looks and its performance, and rare examples command high prices on the collectors market. An internally

[22]   Ibid.

updated version of the speaker has been re-issued and is still in production today by the German company Quad Musikwiedergabe for the princely sum of 6,000 euros per pair.

Rams's somewhat less expensive L 40 loudspeaker from 1961 combined the slim profile of the L 01 with the stacked membranes of the L 2. It was a simple rectangular box that could be stood upright or laid on its side and had a uniform textured front of woven aluminium. The narrow radius of the side edges contributed greatly to its elegant design. It can be seen as the epitome of hi-fi speakers and was followed by many updates, including the L 60, the L 80 and the L 450.

Along with the modular hi-fi units, Rams continued to design compact stereo systems and variations in-between. The 1962 successor to the SK 4 was the

p.271

'audio 1' [+] . Thanks to sound quality improvements in transistor technology, at 11 cm (4 in) high this horizontally aligned amplifier-radio-phonograph combination was considerably slimmer than its predecessor. But the 'audio 1' was not an autonomous entity like the SK 4. Rams produced a number of studies that

p.268

included a selection of companion elements [+], ranging from tape recorders to televisions, which could be combined in various ways. They could be stacked, arranged in a row on a shelf (the product was devised to be compatible with Rams's 606 shelf system for Vitsœ + Zapf and those of Knoll), on a specially designed aluminium base or even hung on the wall. Not all the designs went into

p.268

production, but those that did included the TS 45 [+] receiver, the TG 60 reel

p.268

to reel tape recorder, [+] the TS 40 tuner amplifier and the L 45, L 50, L 60, L 61 and L450 loudspeakers.

Particularly noticeable in the 'audio 1' is the attention paid to the grid patterns that defined the placement of the control elements. Both Braun and Rams believed that products needed to be easy to understand. An asymmetric switch on the TS 45, for example, points clearly to the current mode of operation. The dark grey plastic knobs controlling volume, balance, bass and treble were unmistakably marked with thin white lines to indicate levels. The graphics too were reduced and unfussy as in the case of other new Braun audio appliances: the wavelengths of the various radio frequencies, for example, were marked in Megahertz and Kilohertz rather than names of radio channels as with other manufacturers. A lower case script was used for simplicity and cleaner lines and tiny amounts of colour began to make an appearance as a form of signal to the user. The 'audio 2', which came out two years later, had a green on / off button that was to become a feature on all Braun hi-fi products right up to the last 'atelier' systems. Successive

p.270

'audio' models up until the 300 [+], made in 1969, were all designed by Rams and all shared a high-tech utilitarian aesthetic in white lacquered steel with aluminium faces, transparent acrylic lids and clearly visible retainer screws. The audio range was to be a product system that defined Braun hi-fi: its high-tech, high-quality and distinct visual language put the company at the forefront of the German audio industry – just as it had hoped.

As with other Braun products of this era, attention to detail meant not only designing products from the 'inside out', giving priority to the user and coordinating materials, photography and packaging; the design approach was also applied to a careful selection of accessories. One of Rams's most charming and sophisticated designs at this time was a small, simple scale for balancing the pick-up

p.284

on the record players. [+] Designed in 1962, it came in a plain grey box and cost a mere 4.50 deutschmarks.

High End High Fidelity

Although it was never to be an economically successful area for them, Erwin and Artur Braun gave their technical department considerable funds to research and improve hi-fi performance. As a result, the sound quality of products steadily increased as did complexity and price. In 1965 Braun introduced Rams's top-of-the-

p.279

range 'studio 1000' stereo system. [+] It had the most powerful amp on the German market and a range of impressive technological features. The bodies of all the components in the series were lacquered in black with rounded aluminium fronts and concealed screws for a more elegant appearance. With the 'studio 1000', Dieter Rams yet again defined the look of audio equipment not just for Braun, but for the competition too, for years to come. This was an elite system for wealthy hi-fi buffs – retailing at 15,000 deutschmarks, it cost as much as a luxury car at the time. A later, more economical range, the 'studio 500' retained many of the characteristics of the 1000 and the PS 500 turntable, which was considered by many to be *the* component of any top-of-the-range system, and remained in production until the mid-1970s.

In the early 1970s, the next big system designed by Rams to make its mark was the 'regie' series, which is his masterpiece in this area. It was the first completely

p.280

black hi-fi system and the 'regie 550' [+] from 1976 featured convex rather than the usual concave switches – two more world-leading innovations. Increasingly colour began to appear in the form of light diode indicators when the device was in operation. Furthermore, colour replaced certain words on the control: the 'phono' switch, for example, was now represented by yellow alone. By this time the Braun design studio had started to expand and Peter Hartwein, who joined the team in 1970, began to work together with Rams on the hi-fis. He collaborated initially on the 'studio' system before eventually taking over most of the hi-fi section towards the end of the 1970s.

The last hi-fi system to be produced by Braun before the company capitulated to the cheaper and faster Japanese industry entirely was the 'atelier' line in 1980–84. [+] This was designed by Rams and Hartwein together in Frankfurt

p.282

and manufactured in the Far East. Different components were produced in different factories in different countries for later assembly, and the whole process became a logistical nightmare.

The 'atelier' system could be stacked vertically or horizontally and it featured receding 45-degree edges at the top and bottom of each component, which gave them an exceedingly slim appearance. The entire system could be operated by remote control and comprised a wide range of elements including a television. Of special importance was the fact that all the 'atelier' components manufactured over the ten-year production period could be combined optically and technically with any of the others: they all shared the same dimensions and could communicate with one another despite technological updates, which meant they could be upgraded over time right up until the last edition in 1990.

— Televisions

p.286 Herbert Hirche designed the first definitive television for Braun, the HF 1 [+] from 1958. A striking appliance that marries Braun design to Bauhaus ideals, if you don't count the retail price of a hefty 950 deutschmarks. The HF 1 had such a smooth appearance and was so far removed from the usual polished wood cabinets of the time (the casing had a blue-grey matt lacquered surface) that it must have looked like a piece of technology from outer space when it first entered the market. The operating controls, apart from the on / off switch at the front, were hidden under a flush panel at the top of the device.

p.285 The loveliest television that Dieter Rams designed was one that never went into production. It was the FS 1000 TV-Portal [+] from 1962, which was intended to be part of the T 1000 'world receiver' family but sadly failed to get past the early model stage. The model was vertically aligned, with a handle at the top and a very light, brushed aluminium cover that opened at the front like a door. Even the bulky tube was reduced to the minimum possible size at the back. Frequently in the 1960s, 1970s and 1980s, Braun was way ahead in terms of technology; they were sometimes even too far ahead of the market itself (or the courage of the marketing department) and many great technical achievements got left on the shelf.

p.287
p.288 One of the TV set models designed by Rams that did make it into production was the FS 80 [+] from 1964, which stood on a single leg like a bird's foot. This was followed by his designs for the FS 600 from 1965, the FS 1000 [+] from 1967 and the FS 1010 from 1968. Later came other television sets like the TV 3 from 1986, designed together with Peter Hartwein. However, the TV 3 was no stand-alone piece of living-room furniture. It was little more than a monitor in appearance and intended to be a module supplement to the 'atelier' hi-fi range as part of a home entertainment system. It came in a matt black or matt off-white plastic housing, which curved into a soft, thin frame around the glass screen from the front and p.256 stood on a tiny base. This concept was based on a study for a TV component [+] of the 'audio 2' system back in the early 1960s – a rather avant-garde, white-framed screen that hovered above the module containing its control elements, mounted on a single, slender metal tube. Although it could also function separately on its

own metal bipod base, the FS 600 was designed to function as a component of the 'audio 2' system in 1965. Today, when we have had a couple of decades to get used to the aesthetics of the home computer, the image of a rather large monitor together with several 'hardware' units is not so surprising, but at the time these system ideas were sensationally 'modern'.

Cigarette Lighters

The story of the development of the cigarette lighters is a rather classic Braun tale of design, technology and function, and one of Dieter Rams's favourites. He begins as follows: 'A member of the Braun board came to me one day and asked if we could design cigarette lighters and I replied, "only if we design our own technology to go inside them".'[23] Many lighters back in the mid-1960s still operated using stone-age technology, with a flint and a striking wheel. The Braun technicians came across an electromagnetic induction system that they could use as a starting point – but it had previously been used only in larger objects and therefore required considerable adaptation. 'It needed quite a bit of pressure to ignite – the technology came from the motorbike kick-start mechanism,' recalls Rams. Thus the form of their first, rather clunky, tabletop lighter, the TFG 1 from 1966 by Reinhold Weiss, was somewhat dictated by the requirements of the ignition system (and looked not dissimilar to Weiss' HT 2 toaster design from 1963).

p.290 However, the second lighter design, the cylindric TFG 2 / T2 [←] by Rams from 1968, took this operational requirement and adjusted it to fit comfortably into the human hand. The lighter is cylindrical in shape with a large indented pressure switch at the side: 'So when you pick it up,' says Rams, 'you automatically put your strongest digit, your thumb, on to the button to press it'. By then, the technical department had also managed to miniaturize the electromagnetic mechanism, which allowed Rams the freedom to shape the lighter towards the needs of the user rather than the specifications of the apparatus inside.

The cylindric T 2 lighter may well have been a high-tech apparatus at the time of its introduction on to the market, but it was also one of the simplest of all Braun devices in terms of form and function. It is a tool to create fire to light cigarettes; that is the extent of its purpose. The only other role that it played was a decorative one, because it was intended to occupy the centre of attention like a little tabletop sculpture. Therefore it is one of the few Braun products that was permitted by the company's design department to be explicitly decorative. A whole spectrum of colours and surface finishes were produced, from a shiny ridged metallic casing to brushed matt metal, all-black plastic versions and a variety of coloured plastic finishes. The Braun team even produced a transparent model, which for them was dangerously close to frivolous. A later piezoelectric ignition

[23]   Dieter Rams, in conversation with the author (August 2007)

Prototype for the FS-1000 TV-Portal,
Dieter Rams, 1962

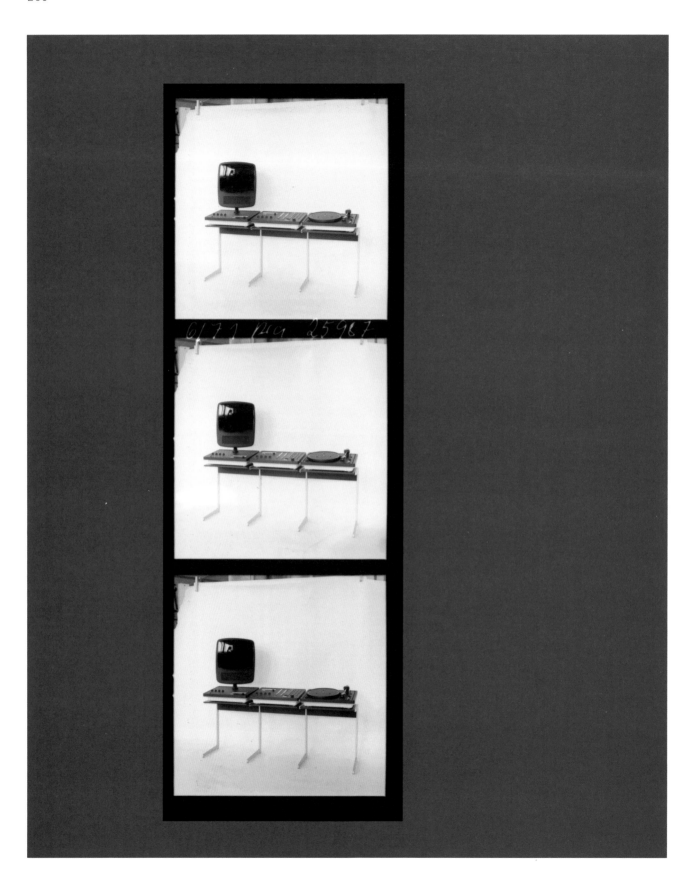

Study for a TV component to the 'audio' system, c.1968

T 22 radio,
Dieter Rams, 1960

T 52 radio,
Dieter Rams, 1961

T 41 radio, Dieter Rams, 1962

TP 1 radio / phonograph with T 4 radio and
P1 record player, Dieter Rams, 1959

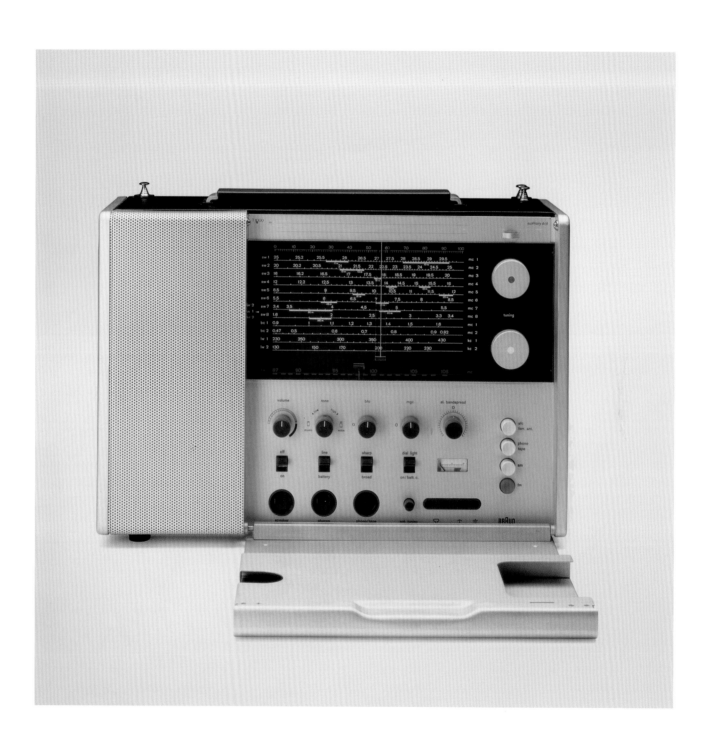

T 1000 radio,
Dieter Rams, 1963

RT 20 radio,
Dieter Rams, 1961

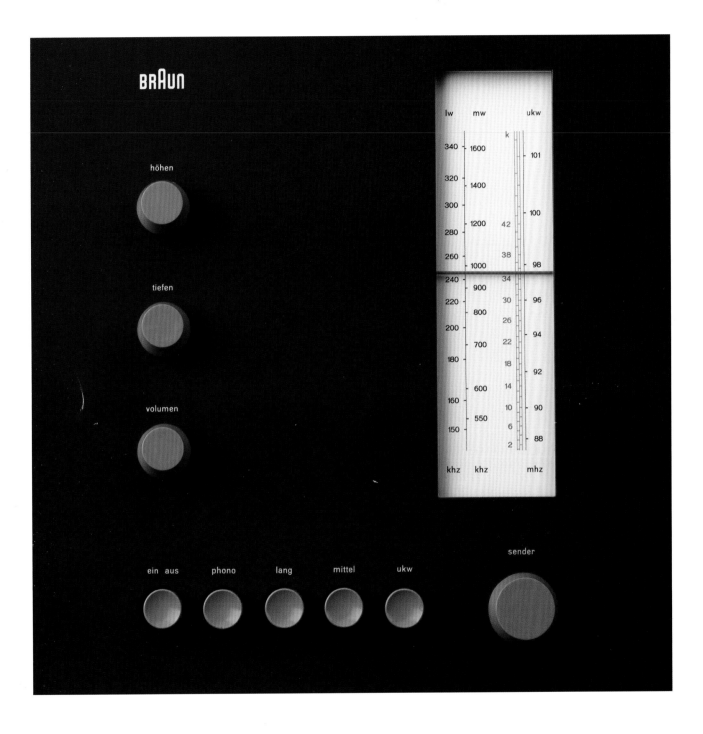

'atelier 1' radio and record player and L 1 speaker,
Dieter Rams, both 1957

TS 45 control unit, 1964, TG 60 tape recorder, 1965 and L 450
speakers, 1965, all Dieter Rams.

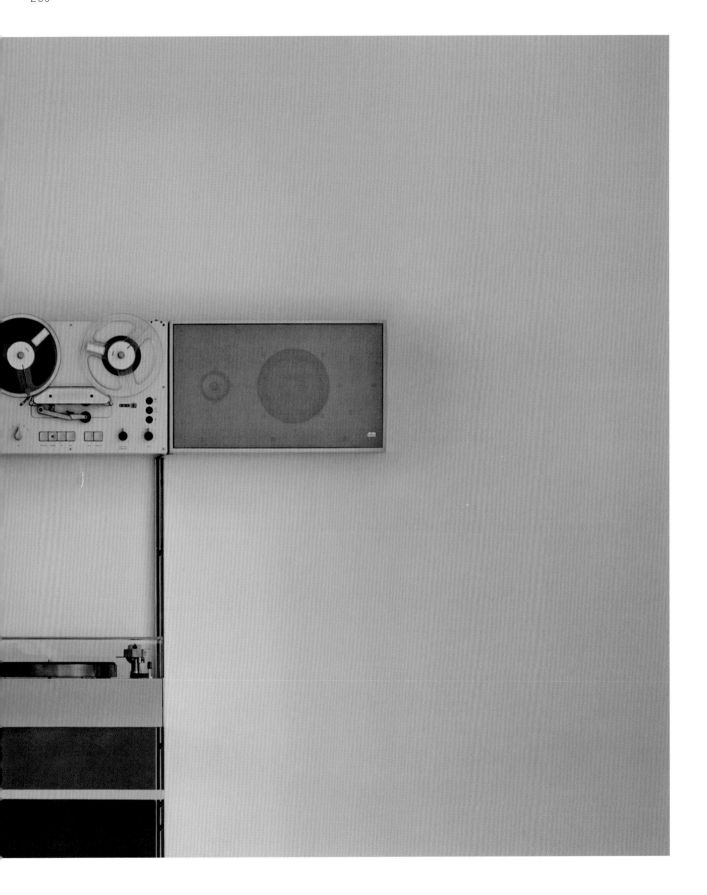

'audio 300' compact system, Dieter Rams, 1969

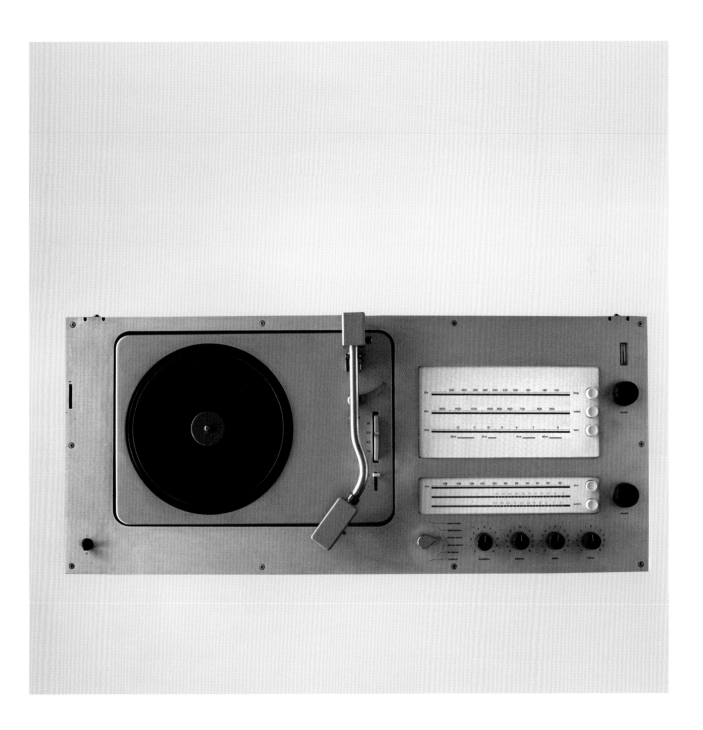

'audio 1' compact system, Dieter Rams, 1962

'audio 308' compact system, Dieter Rams, 1973

'audio 400' compact system, Dieter Rams, 1973

L 2 speaker,
Dieter Rams, 1958

L 01 speaker,
Dieter Rams, 1959

LE 1 speaker,
Dieter Rams, 1959

'studio 2' system, Dieter Rams, 1959. This configuration includes the
CS 11 control unit and record player, CE 11 receiver and CV 11 amplifier.

'studio 1000' system, Dieter Rams, 1965.

'regie 550',
Dieter Rams, 1976

Detail of the 'regie 350',
Dieter Rams, 1976

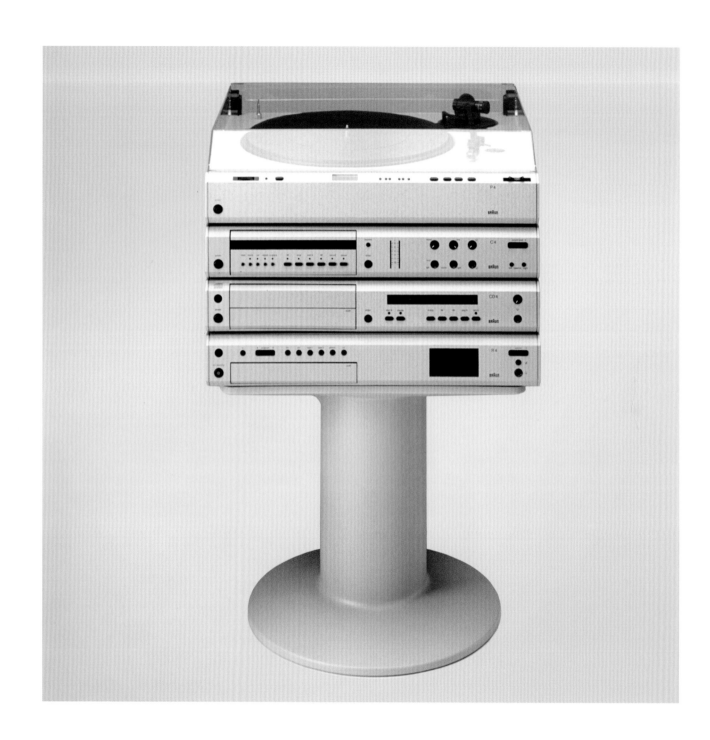

'atelier' system, Peter Hartwein, 1980-87

Scale for balancing record player pick-up,
Dieter Rams, 1962

Top left and right: Prototype for a TV component
to the 'audio' system, Dieter Rams, c.1970

Above left and right: Prototype for the
FS-1000 TV-Portal, Dieter Rams, 1962

HF 1 TV,
Herbert Hirche, 1958

FS 80 TV,
Dieter Rams, 1964

FS 1000 TV,
Dieter Rams, 1967

version of the Cylindric T 2 allowed the lighter to be more economical and the final 1974 version was even solar-powered. Another 'fashionable' tabletop lighter, designed by Rams in 1970, was the rounded cube-shaped Domino, which came in a variety of rather 'pop' colours and had a set of plastic ashtrays to match.

p.291

The Braun pocket lighters, on the other hand, were sleek and elegant, usually finished in matt silver, black or a combination of both. Between 1971 and 1981, a number of very successful models were designed and produced by Dieter Rams, Florian Seiffert and Jürgen Greubel and by external designers, such as the Gugelot Institute. Of particular note is Rams's own design, the Mactron F 1 [→] linear from 1971, a gas-powered lighter with an innovative mechanism, where the lid flips and swivels to ignite a flame.

—   Photography and Film

p.57

The first product that Dieter Rams designed completely on his own for Braun was a slide projector called the PA 1 [→] in 1956. Although relatively boxy in form, the edges and corners were softer than those of most other Braun appliances at that time, and the oblique slanting front gave the appliance a flow and a balance of proportion that made it very pleasing to the eye. The detailing on the PA 1 is reduced to the clear essentials. The textured grey finish on the cast metal casing gives the appearance of a neutral-looking projector with few additional elements: a black ventilator grill and a silver brushed-metal lens casing with black plastic detailing. The four chunky mechanical operating buttons are arranged in a row along the side, clearly marked in a strong signal red and etched in relief with symbols indicating their functions.

Braun developed an interesting niche in the photography and film market. The company's slide projectors, electronic flashguns and high quality Super-8 movie cameras for committed amateurs proved to be successful product ranges during the years when these technologies were at their peak, but its attempts to compete with Agfa and Kodak in the compact camera market were something of a flop. The company only manufactured one stills camera, the Nizo 1000 designed by Robert Oberheim and Karl-Heinz Lange, which was on the market between 1968 and 1971.

p.298

However, Braun flashguns, [→] which were nearly all designed by Dieter Rams from 1958 until 1972, when Oberheim took them over, were a huge success and there was a wide selection of models, including a professional range (the F 80 and F 800 professional) by Richard Fischer. What made them successful were their technical achievements in miniaturisation and the use of transistors; their high-quality plastic housing that provided stability and safety; their ease of use and, of course, their compact and modern design. Braun excelled in these areas of high-tech consumer products, such as hi-fis, where technicians and designers needed to work closely with one another, and this was in no small part due to Rams's early cultivation of goodwill and team spirit between their respective sectors of the company. He realized early on that to produce successful industrial design solutions,

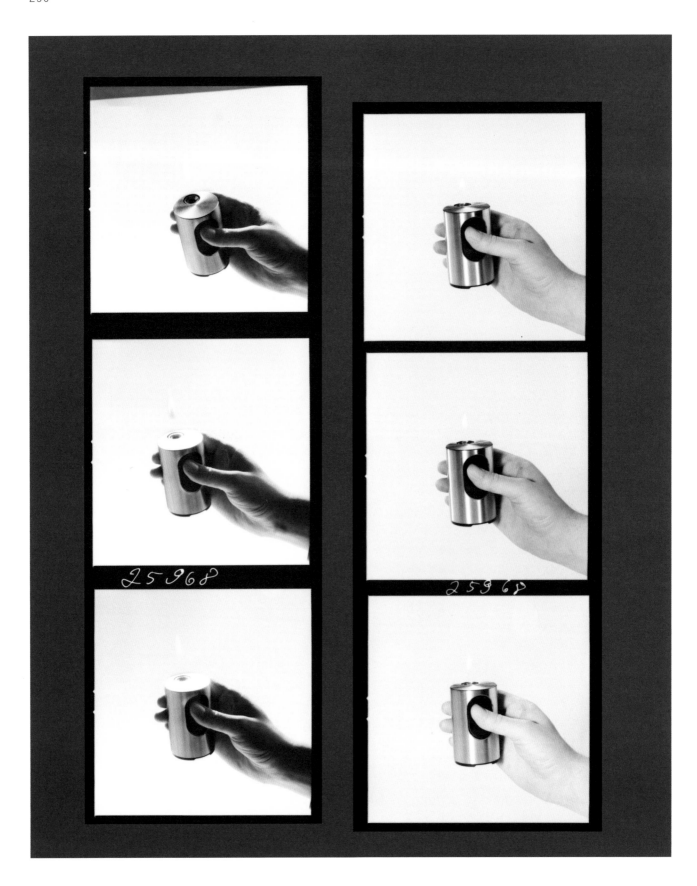

Promotional images for the T 2 lighter,
Dieter Rams, 1968

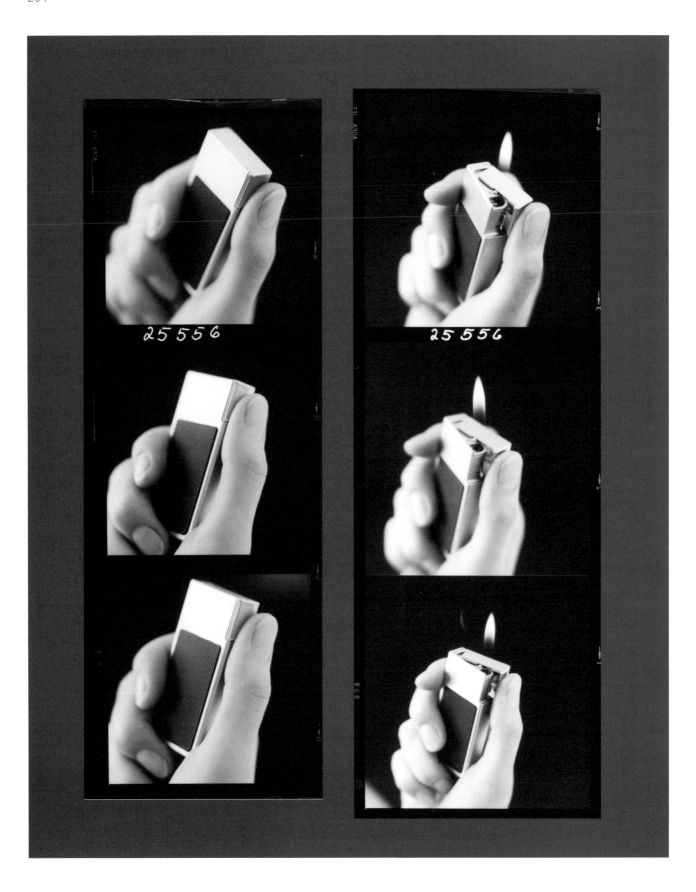

Promotional images for the F 1 lighter,
Dieter Rams, 1971

designers and technicians should not work in competition or in ignorance of the activities of one another, but in partnership. The practice at Braun of working at an early stage in the development process with detailed, 1:1 models was vital in this respect.

Like their flashguns, the Braun Super-8 cameras were innovative and good quality with a high capacity and easy operation, which made them world leaders in their day. The first Nizo movie camera by Braun in 1963 was the FA 3, designed by Dieter Rams, Richard Fischer and Robert Oberheim. It was a very technical-looking device, almost fussy-looking by Braun standards. The 1964 EA 1 [+] by Rams and Fischer was a more streamlined affair, with a folding handle that allowed it to fit into a compact leather travelling case. In terms of functionality, it set the standard for later models. From then onwards, Robert Oberheim took over the design of the Super-8 cameras. His Nizo S 8 [+] from 1965 was a tough, technological master-piece that gained an international reputation. It had an eloxy aluminium casing, and all its switches, which were recognisable by sight and touch, were located on the left-hand side for ease of access while filming with the right hand. It remained in production for eighteen years. Subsequent models were updated with new technologies; they included smaller, more compact versions, easier, more ergo-nomic switches, sound recording facilities, low-light recording, and so on.

In the mid 1970s came the first sound cameras, which had bigger and heavier cartridges and needed more space for the sound recording elements. Peter Schneider designed the first of these, the silver and black 2056 'sound' from 1976. After much experimentation, the best and most compact solution for the location of the microphone was to place it underneath the body as part of a forward-slanting handle. There was also a foldable shoulder support, like those found on professional cameras. Other notable sound camera designs by Schneider were the 'integral' series from 1979–1981.

In 1981 the entire film and photographic technology segment, which also included film and slide projectors, was passed on in a staged handover to Robert Bosch Photokino, and production in this area ceased completely at Braun in 1985.[24] With the advent of a new technology in the form of video camcorders, the Super-8 film market ceased to be viable.

Household Appliances

Kitchen appliances were another big market for Braun, but not an area where Dieter Rams designed a lot himself. The well-known Braun food processor, the KM 3, was one of the first semi-professional appliances on the market in the 1950s. Designed by Gerd A Müller, it was perfectly geared towards the convenience

p.73

p.73

[24]   See Günter Staeffler, 'Braun Elektronenblitz-Geräte: Künstliches Licht formschön verpakt', *Design + Design* no. 44 (August 1998), 3–9

of the user and had the clean Braun lines but was far curvier than Rams's style. The 1963 black and chrome HT 2 single-slit toaster by Reinhold Weiss was another Braun classic; it even received a Pop-art accolade from the artist Richard Hamilton, who mistakenly attributed it to Rams when he said that Rams's consumer products 'have come to occupy a place in my heart and consciousness that the Mont Sainte Victoire did in Cézanne's'. Authorship is a tricky issue in product design.

p.305 However, Rams did have a hand in another successful kitchen appliance, the MPZ 2 / 21 / 22 citromatic juicer [+] from 1972, which he devised together with Jürgen Greubel and the Spanish designer and engineer Gabriel Lluelles. In 1962 Braun acquired a factory near Barcelona and began to produce appliances for the Spanish market there. The citromatic is a superbly simple electric citrus press. You just gently push down half an orange on the top, which then rotates underneath the orange, place a glass at the side next to the spout and collect the juice. When the glass is full you can click up the spout to prevent further drips. It is robust, the components are easy to clean and it takes up little space. In addition, it has a Perspex lid, an echo of the SK 4 phonograph. It was not long before this home kitchen appliance made its way on to seemingly every bar top in Barcelona, successfully making the jump from the domestic to the commercial. Dieter Rams is justifiably proud of the 'usefulness' of the citromatic. It is perhaps one of the most perfect of Braun designs in that it fulfils its job so well that is still in production today, almost 40 years after it first came on to the market.

The Braun Aromaster filter coffee machines that initially appeared in 1972 with the KF 20 by Florian Seiffert were based on a design principle that was novel for such an appliance: the various elements were stacked on top of one another in a compact cylindrical format. Many versions were produced by various Braun designers, the epitome of which was the L-shaped model, the KF 40 by Hartwig Kahlke from 1984, which had two cylinders, one to hold the water and another to filter and then hold the coffee. The advantage of this form was that only one heating element was required to heat the water and then keep the coffee warm, which reduced production costs. Rams's contribution to the coffee machine range p.308 was a coffee grinder, the KMM 2 Aromatic [+] from 1969, which was also cylindrical in shape. The KMM 2 was one of Rams's rare 'colourful' designs; its plastic housing elements were available in white, deep red, yellow or black. It also had a clear Perspex lid and indented, flattened sides at the base, allowing it to be easily grasped with one hand.

p.308 One year later in 1970, Rams designed his one and only hairdryer, the HLD 4 [+] (a follow-up to the HLD 2 by Reinhold Weiss). It too was available in a range of colours (red, blue and yellow) and had the same rocker switch developed for the KMM 2 Aromatic, which could easily be operated with the thumb, this time with a white dot representing the 'on' position. The hairdryer had a rather clever tangential fan that made it very compact and good for travelling, but its lack of a handle created a risk that the user would cover the air intake vent with their hand, causing the appliance to overheat. Braun later returned to hairdryers with handles and the introduction of the angled handle for a better grip was to become an industry standard.

— Clocks

Electric clocks, clock radios and pocket calculators were a branch of product design at Braun that belonged almost exclusively to Dietrich Lubs (often working in collaboration with Rams). As a young designer who worked his way up through product graphics to become responsible for a whole product range, Lubs' eye for graphic detail and talent for balancing 2D with 3D design made him the ideal team member to tackle both digital and analogue interfaces where he was often working in the realm of micro-millimetres. Initial models such as the 'functional' [+] alarm clock from 1975 had digital displays, but it was the analogue clock faces such as the ABW wall clock [+] from 1981, the AW10 wristwatch [+] and the compact alarm clocks such as the 'phase 3' from 1972 and the AB 20 [+] designed together with Dieter Rams in 1975 that won the hearts and minds of customers.

p. 79

p. 301, 80

p. 311

The analogue clocks may have appeared basic but their simple appearance concealed a significant amount of engineering and new technology. The delicate transition between sleeping and waking was the subject of much research by the design team. Some of the many experiments with different buttons and switches included infra-red sensors that reacted to a wave of the hand, which Braun called reflex control, and voice control, so that the alarms turned off when the user shouted at them. Many of the clock switches were simply colour-coded with a thin green stripe or dot on the switch to signify 'alarm on', for example, or had a Braille-like ridge on one side so the user could locate the switch position by feel alone. These were particularly easy to operate – another concession to the rather vulnerable and unfocused state of the sleepy user.

— Pocket Calculators

The first Braun pocket calculator, the ET 11, designed by Dieter Rams and Dietrich Lubs in 1975, was a lumpy affair due to the imported Japanese technology inside. Lubs recalls debating how to improve it with Rams in his office: 'We discussed the form, that the new version should be tighter with smaller radii and that we needed to improve the keypad.'[25] Thus the follow-on models, in particular the ET 22 from 1976 and the ET 33 from 1977, were much flatter and had a colour-coding of brown, red yellow, green and black that had proved effective with the Braun hi-fi systems. In addition, the designers added innovative convex buttons, which Lubs had tried out

[25]   Dietrich Lubs, in conversation with the author (June 2009)

with his 'functional' alarm clock from 1975 and were also seen in the 'regie' 550 from 1976. 'Psychological functionality is essential in the detail of a product,' says Rams. 'The old mechanical buttons had a concave form because of the pressure needed to push them. But we made the electronic buttons [of the ET calculators] convex, because hitting the right point had become more important than pressure. We got the graphic design details so right that although the technology changed, the design of these calculators remained the same for 20 years.'[26]

Shavers

Electric shavers had been a core product area at Braun ever since Max and Artur Braun brought out their first electric razor in 1950, complete with a patented foil and cutter head, known as the S 50. In fact, the huge revenue generated by licensing a later model to Ronson in the United States provided most of the funding for the experimental design developments initiated by Erwin Braun. Right up until the present day, Braun foil electric shavers continue to be world market leaders. Over the years the designs have been updated with new technological developments to keep ahead of the competition. Many different designers, technicians and material experts have worked on the Braun razors, making adjustments that included tiny changes to the motor and casing to switches and surface form, in order to increase performance and ensure they are easier to hold, use and clean. As a successful product area, they illustrate the flexibility and cohesiveness of the design approach at Braun.

p. 74

Following Hans Gugelot and Gerd Alfred Müller, Dieter Rams was particularly involved in the 'sixtant' shaver range, first produced in 1962 (the SM 31 'sixtant' by Hans Gugelot was the first shaver with a black housing). He co-designed the 'sixtant' 8008 [+] from 1973, together with Robert Oberheim and Florian Seiffert and the 'sixtant' 4004 from 1979 with Oberheim and Roland Ullmann. Both razors had black, lightly structured plastic surfaces for good grip combined with a brushed metal finish and white product graphics. 'The most important area for the design [of the shavers] is without doubt the surface feel of the appliance, how it sits in the hand during use, when putting it down as well as mobile and non-mobile placement,' says Rams.[27] In 1985 the Micron Vario 3, designed by Ullmann, came on the market. It was to be an innovative descendant of the successful 'sixtant' series. The 'micron plus' was some ten years in development – an indication of how much attention was paid to getting the design 'just right'. Two key details in this model were the long hair-cutter at the top of the shaver and the highly innovative surface structure. The shaver grip was made from a combination of soft (Desmopan) and hard (Makrolon) plastics that had a comfortable, non-slip surface

[26]   Dieter Rams, in conversation with the author (August 2007)

[27]   '"Technologie" Design', *Design Report* no. 12 (1989), reprinted in Brandes, ed., *Dieter Rams, Designer,* 199

with an attractive-looking knobbly structure manufactured using a specially developed double-injection procedure. 'Our aim,' says Rams, 'was for a surface that feels good, which is pleasant to touch, which is easy to clean. A soft material seemed more appropriate to us than a hard one or even a sleek cold metal. This is why we started a search for a new surface structure.'[28] The resulting soft / hard surface was developed exclusively by the technicians and designers at Braun in close collaboration with the plastic manufacturer Bayer and was later used for other equipment.

—   External Commissions

Rams designed a few products with significant details for other companies and sister firms in the Gillette group. In the mid-1970s, Dieter Rams, Dietrich Lubs, Hartwig Kahlcke and Klaus Zimmermann designed two pen ranges [+] for the writing instrument company Paper Mate, which belonged to Gillette. As one would expect, every detail of the pen programmes, which included propelling pencils, ballpoint and felt-tipped pens, was carefully thought through, ranging from the mechanisms to the bodies, packaging and graphics. In one version of the pencil, the leads were pushed forwards from the top, in another via a twist mechanism in the centre. The snug-fitting clips on top of the pens opened with the application of gentle pressure, allowing the user to easily clip them on to a pocket. The materials considered were plastic, black chrome-plated metal, aluminium and steel. The range did not make it into production.

p. 302

p. 304

p. 304

In 1985 Dieter Rams was asked, along with a number of other well-known international designers to submit designs for a range of door fittings [+] for the German metal-fitting manufacturer FSB. Rams came up with a selection of matt silver and black door handles made from a combination of aluminium and thermoplastic. Despite the rather severe aesthetic of the designs, they are surprisingly ergonomic, with curves and bumps that allow for good grip and hand or finger pressure in the appropriate places. The resulting rgs[29] programme, [+] which later included twenty-six elements such as window handles and door stoppers, are examples of Rams's consideration for 'feel' and his method of setting tactile aesthetics on a par with the visual. The rgs series, in particular the rgs 1, was a particular success and some elements are still in production today.

[28]   Dieter Rams, speech manuscript (27 March 1980), Dieter Rams archive 1.1.2.11

[29]   rgs stands for 'Rams *grau schwarz*' ('Rams grey black')

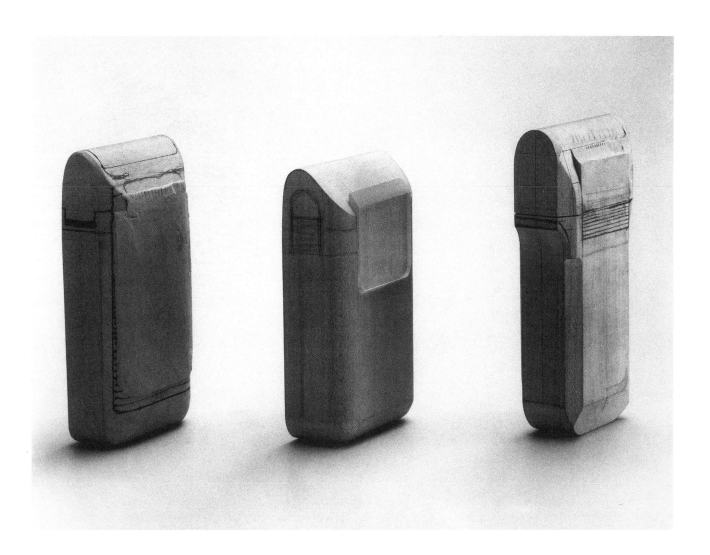

Shaver models, Roland Ullman

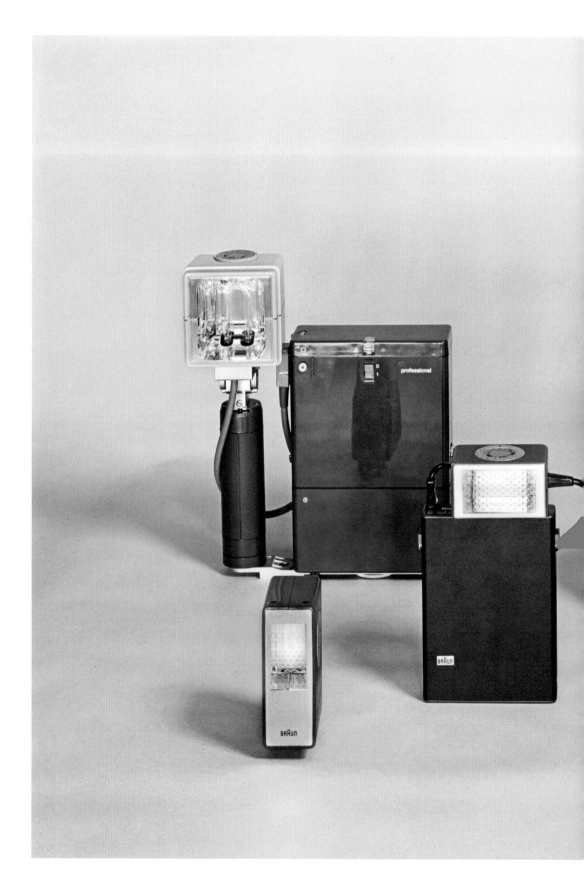

Braun flash range, c.1970

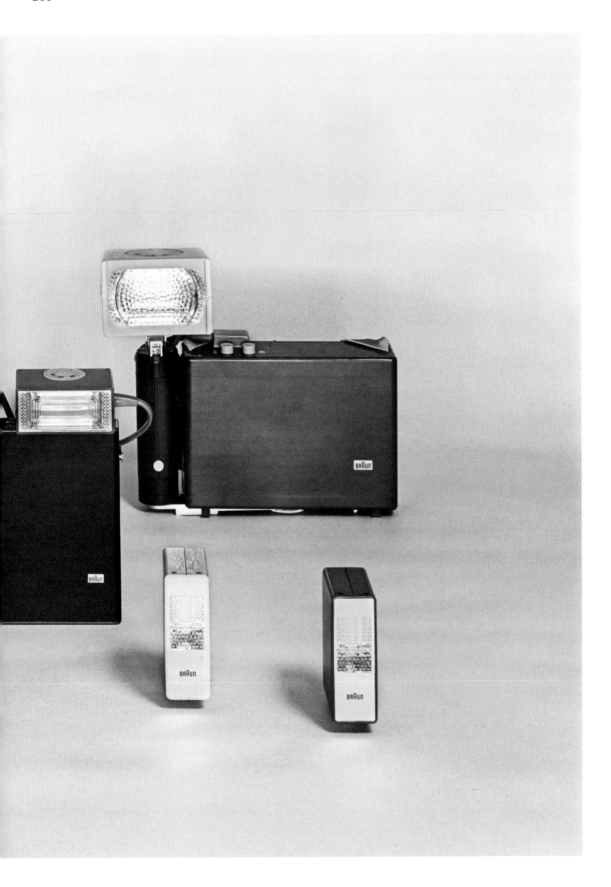

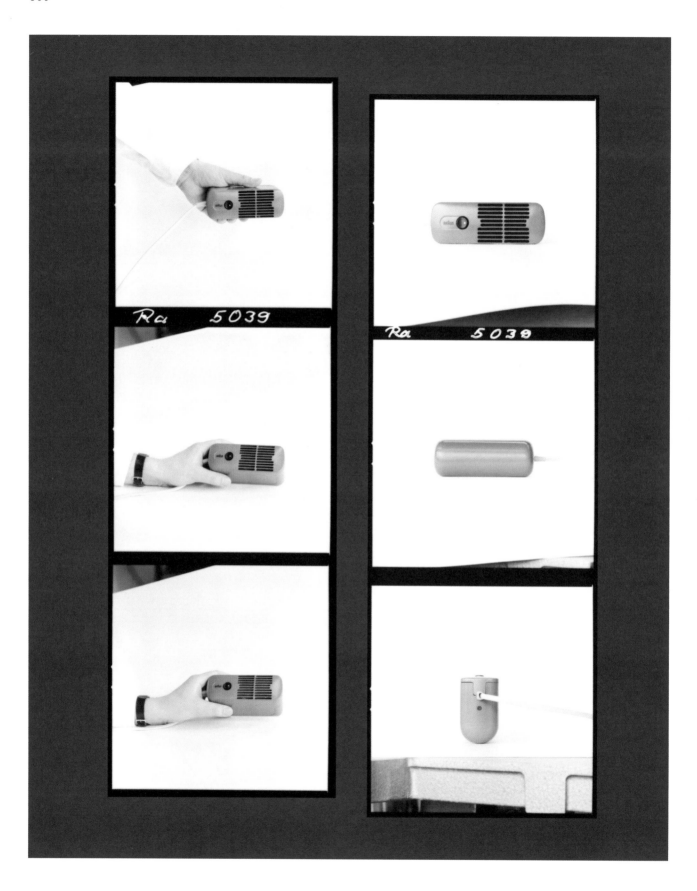

Promotional images for the HLD 4 hairdryer, 1970

Work on the ABW 41 clock,
Dietrich Lubs, 1981

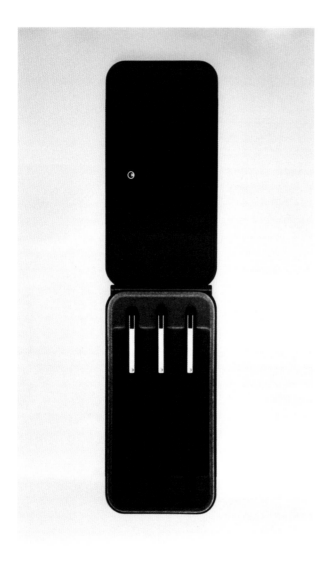

Study for Gilette Papermate pens, Dieter Rams, Dietrich Lubs,
Hartwig Kahlcke and Klaus Zimmermann, c.1975

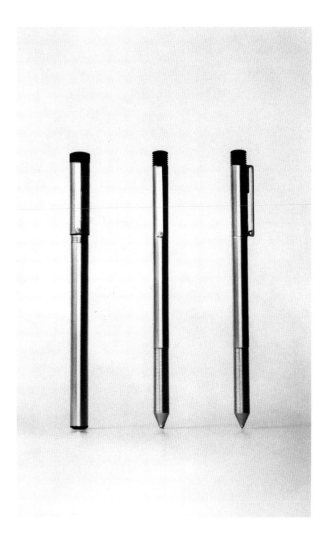

Study for Gilette Papermate pens, Dieter Rams, Dietrich Lubs,
Hartwig Kahlcke and Klaus Zimmermann, c.1975

FSB door handles, Dieter Rams, 1985

MPZ 2 'citromatic' juicer,
Dieter Rams and Jurgen Greübel, 1972

T 2 lighter, Dieter Rams, 1968

Top left: KMM 2 coffee grinder, Dieter Rams, 1969
Bottom and centre left: HLD 4 hairdryer, Dieter Rams, 1970

Top and above: KSM 1 coffee grinder, Reinhold Weiss, 1967

Top and centre: cassett shaver, Florian Sieffert, 1970   KF 20 coffee maker, Florian Sieffert, 1972
Bottom: T 3 'domino' lighter, Dieter Rams, 1973

AB 1 alarm clock, Dietrich Lubs, 1987

Top left: AB 20 tb, Dietrich Lubs and Dieter Rams, 1975   Above: ABR 313, Dietrich Lubs, 1990
Top right: AB 20 sl, Dietrich Lubs, 1979

'micron' shaver,
Roland Ullmann , 1976

4004 'sixtant' shaver, Dieter Rams, Robert Oberheim,
Roland Ullmann, 1979

The following photographs were taken in the Braun archive.
All products are by Braun.

1	L 1 speaker perforations
2	T 1000 radio dial
3	T 1000 radio typography
4	HLD 6 hairdryer switches
5	AB 1 and phase 1 clock faces
6	PA 1 slide projector buttons
7	KMM 2 coffee grinder bowl
8-9	T 52 radio buttons
10	RT 20 radio dial and buttons
11	CSV 12 receiver switch
12	T 41 radio dial
13	PCS 5 record player arm
14	TG 550 reel-to-reel tape recorder buttons
15	RT 20 speaker slots
16	F 1 lighter
17	EF 300 flash exposure dial
18	T 4 radio tuning dial
19	regie 350 receiver buttons
20	TG 550 reel-to-reel tape recorder buttons
21	HLD 4 hairdryer switches
22	L 1 speaker perforations

BRAUN

höhen

tiefen

volumen

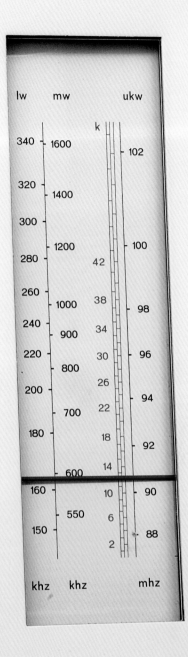

lw	mw		ukw
		k	
340	1600		102
320	1400		
300			
280	1200	42	100
260	1000	38	98
240	900	34	
220	800	30	96
200		26	
	700	22	94
180		18	92
	600	14	
160		10	90
	550	6	88
150		2	
khz	khz		mhz

sender

ein aus   phono   lang   mittel   ukw

netz

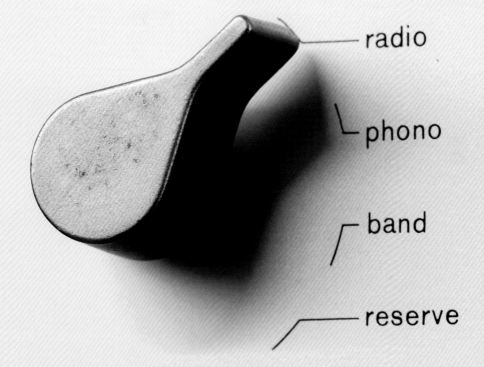

radio

phono

band

reserve

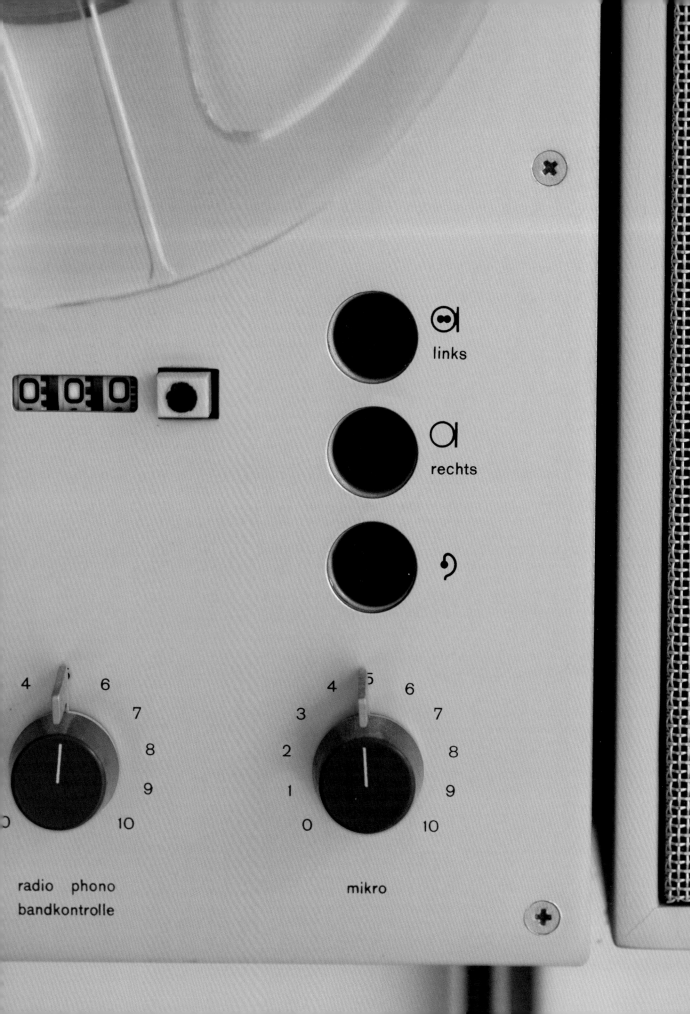

links

rechts

4   6
     7
      8
      9
    10

5
4   6
3   7
2   8
1   9
0   10

radio   phono   mikro
bandkontrolle

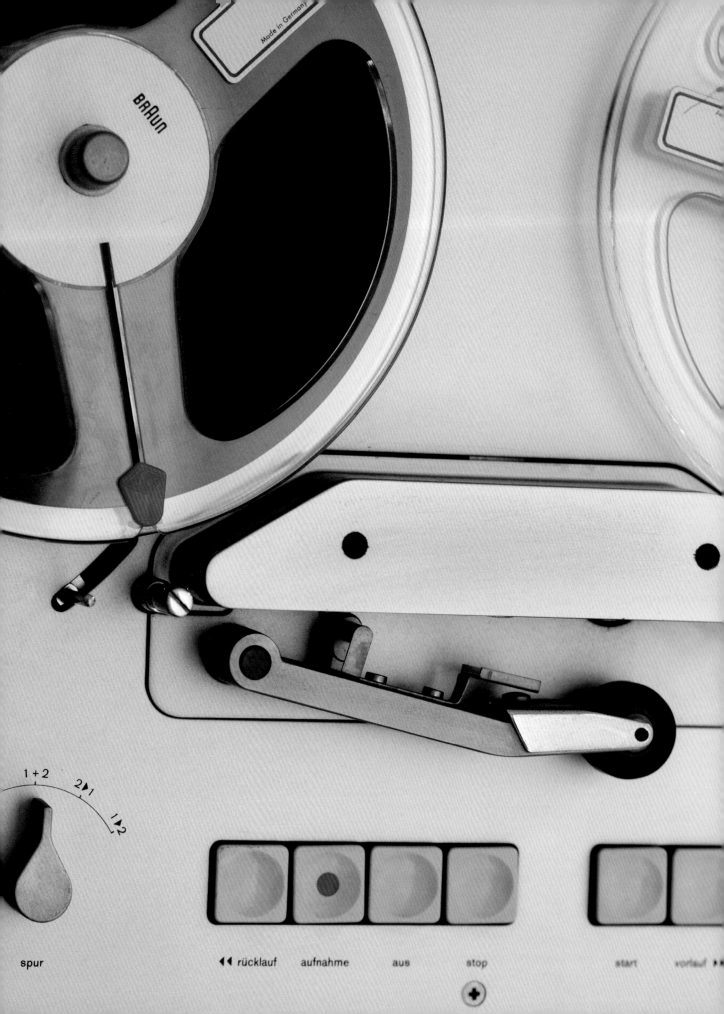

Less But Better

One of the most striking and impressive aspects of Dieter Rams as a person and as a designer is the extraordinary completeness and consistency of his vision. His work, his home (which he designed himself), his life, his thinking, and even his appearance are all interconnecting expressions of a clear set of ethical values. Every element has its place. There is no evidence of flashy ephemera. No loud neck-ties, no frivolous souvenirs or bric-a-brac on the shelves, no garish, short-lived annuals in the garden. If you look at the many hundreds of objects he has designed and co-designed for Braun, Vitsoe and – very occasionally – others, you never see any obvious form of ornament that does not turn out to have a function. Colours are only there if they need to be, primarily as visual aids for the user. You will most certainly not find evidence of any conscious excursions into the world of art. Although some of his sketches, with their reduced balance, could easily hold their own in an art gallery, their intended function is to aid the realisation of tools for living – nothing more. His is an aesthetic of simplicity and utility and it is almost impossible to find exceptions to this in his products, his person, his environment and his statements.

Despite the fact that his working career spanned the entire second half of the twentieth century, a time of great and rapid change in all respects, his approach, his method, his principles and even his style remained essentially unchanged. While keeping pace with technological innovations as they became available in a highly technical product field, Rams has steadfastly resisted the temptations of novelty, fashion, trends and caprice in all its forms, and followed his own path with a rare strength of conviction. This dogged commitment is clearly evident in the speeches, lectures, interviews and seminars that Rams has given over the years in the name of Braun, in his own right as a designer, and later as President of the Rat für Formgebung (German Design Council), as a board member of International Council of Societies of Industrial Design (ICSID) and as Professor of Industrial Design at the Hochschule für bildende Künste (University of the Fine Arts), Hamburg.

This chapter looks at the design and cultural heritage that Rams entered into at the beginning of his career; his thoughts and writings on industrial design and designers; his ideas on the roles, values, requirements and responsibilities of designers and his views on how design has an important role to fulfil in shaping our future existence on this planet. These ideas, which Rams first developed as a way to commuicate within Braun, have evolved over a lifetime of intense involvement with his *metier*. The thoughts that Rams revisits again and again, which he has refined and adapted over several decades. They are his credo, the rules that he lives and works by; distilled over time into a set of themes that became his, now famous, ten principles, commandments or theses of good design.

—

Context

When Dieter Rams first came to work at Braun in 1955 as an architect and interior designer he had already been exposed to modern ideas about an industrial approach through his college and while working for the architect Otto Apel. At Braun, Rams encountered a company galvanized by creative excitement and adventure. The goal was to bring practical, modern and attractive electrical products to a buying public, which traced a direct line of inheritance from the German architects Gottfried Semper and Hermann Muthesius via the functionalist principles of Louis Sullivan and Adolf Loos to the Bauhaus. These principles hinged on the idea of considering the needs of society and then creating the most functional solutions possible to fulfil those needs.

Ornament and decoration were proscribed for their own sake. The design of products in the industrial age left the domain of the artisan almost entirely and was submitted to the rules of mass production. This meant that a twentieth-century designer not only had to design for the needs of ordinary people but also for the demands of industrial production in regard to raw materials, technique and execution. A whole new range of skills was required to design these products, and this meant new kinds of education: The transition that the Bauhaus itself made, from its 1919 founding in Weimar as an Arts and Crafts College (Kunstgewerbeschule) with rather esoteric leanings to a Design School with University status (Hochschule für Gestaltung) at Dessau in 1926, was an early example of the growing need to train industrial designers as opposed to artisans, and even artists. The courses on offer changed too, from those that developed artisanal skills such as textile-making, woodcarving and bookbinding, to a more systematic and scientific training that included subjects like psychology, photography and even architecture. By the time the Bauhaus closed down and many of the staff emigrated in the face of National Socialism in Germany in 1933, it had already set a standard for a new kind of teaching for architects and designers.

After the World War II, Otl Aicher and Inge Scholl founded the Design College (Hochschule für Gestaltung (HfG) Ulm, picking up German design education where the Bauhaus left off. Teachers such as Hans Gugelot and Tomás Maldonado concentrated on bringing design, science and technology closer together under the mantle of their own interpretation of functionalism. The Ulm approach to design was one of engineering rather than that of an art form. Although the HfG Ulm only existed for 15 years (it closed in 1968), like the Bauhaus it was to have a vast influence on industrial design thinking and practices of its time, and for years to come.

When Erwin and Artur Braun started to reshape their father's company in the 1950s, they turned to former Bauhaus designer Wilhelm Wagenfeld and to Hans Gugelot and Otl Aicher, then at the HfG Ulm, in search of a new language of form for their products. Although these designers were not in full-time employment at Braun, the young Dieter Rams was naturally exposed to their presence and thinking, and to the effect they had on the Braun brothers. Rams had not studied at Ulm, but at a *Werkkunstschule* (Applied Arts College), a sympathetic institution in Wiesbaden, and by the time he became a product designer for the company in 1956, he had already shown that he had not only assimilated functionally orientated ideas and an engineering approach, but was able to help shape what was to become the basis for the Braun image and modus operandi. The company marketed its new products under the slogan 'Gute Form' ('Good Form'), which became synonymous with 'Good Design' and, thanks in large part to Braun, post-war German industrial design gained an international reputation for excellence. By 1958, Dieter Rams was already proving to be the company's key designer and had played a role in the design of all five Braun products included in the permanent collection of The Museum of Modern Art (MoMA) in New York.

It is important to note that a manufacturing firm where design and the design department form a powerful component – a design-driven company – was, and still is, a highly unusual entity. As such, it was necessary for the design department at Braun, which was effectively led by Rams from 1961 right up until his promotion to the board as member responsible for Corporate Identity Affairs in 1995, to continually justify and maintain its position in the company. This was especially the case after the US company Gillette became the major shareholder in 1967. Therefore the establishment of rational and defendable thinking positions was indispensable for Braun's design department.

On good design and function

'Good design is as little design as possible' is one of Dieter Rams's most famous and favourite phrases. He means this in the sense that a well-designed product should be so good that it is barely noticeable. By omitting the unnecessary, says Rams, the essential factors come to the fore: the products become 'quiet, pleasing, comprehensible and long-lasting'.[1] However to arrive at products with this quality the designer has to travel a very long and difficult path filled with questions, trials, discussion and experimentation. The product may be simple but the path taken to create it is highly complex for the 'true' product designer. Rams explains: 'Product design is the organisation of the product in its entirety so that it fulfils its respective function as well as possible. At the same time, this design must meet the factual terms and conditions under which the product can be brought on to the market. Designers that confront this task have nothing to do with those who may also call themselves designers, but only concern themselves with a retrospective clothing of products purely according to criteria of taste.'[2]

[1]   Dieter Rams, speech to the Braun International Marketing Meeting (Feb. 1976), Dieter Rams archive 1.1.2.5

[2]   Dieter Rams, 'Die Rolle des Designers im Industrieunternehmen', talk given at *Deutscher Designer-Tag* (German Designers' Day) in Karlsruhe (4 October 1977), Dieter Rams archive 1.1.2.2

Rams has a resolutely rational understanding of the term 'design' – all formal decisions need to be 'substantiatable, verifiable and understandable'. He believes the criteria by which good design can be measured, beyond woolly notions along the lines of 'I like that' or 'that looks attractive', are useability or 'functional quality', 'feasibility' and 'aesthetic quality'. The useability of a product is a direct result of the designer's ability to anticipate the needs of its user. The design has to be such that the product can meet all the demands that the user places on it (under normal conditions) as well as possible. The better the designer has anticipated the needs of the user and the better the product meets these needs, the better the design. 'Useable design has to be worked out right from the beginning. One has to get to know the use-reality of the product. One has to understand the wishes and expectations of the user. One must know the limitations of the technology and the production. One has to understand the market and understand what is best left alone and what would be plain fraud,' he says.

The feasibility of a product is its capacity to be produced within limitations, including cost, materials, production technology, time and competition. 'When a designer is "strong" – imaginative, competent, patient, hard-working and optimistic – then he can of course do a lot to change and improve the conditions involved ... but generally one needs to be able to move within a strictly defined framework – the framework of what is feasible,' he explains. The aesthetic quality is something that Rams finds harder to define: for most individuals, in his view, it comes down to a superficial question of taste and is therefore a debatable variable. But to the eye of a well-trained designer, who is able to appreciate the complexity of interconnecting elements involved in the creation of a product, the aesthetic value can be judged, if not quantified.

Good design is, for Rams, also about careful and intensive research. In a talk from 1980 on the role of the designer in an industrial concern,[3] Rams outlined fifteen questions that a designer should ask of a product or product-to-be in order to produce a well-designed result. They provide an insight into the level and breadth of critical enquiry employed by himself and his design team, as well as the strongly user-oriented values that shaped their product design. They are as follows:

1   The first question is not if one should be designing something but how.
2   Is the product that we are designing really necessary? Are there not already other, similar, tried and tested appliances that people have got used to and are good and functional? Is innovation in this instance really necessary?
3   Will it really enrich people's lives or does it just appeal to their covetousness, possessive-ness or ideas of status? Or does it wake desire because it is offering something new?
4   Is it conceived for the short- or long-term, does it just help increase the speed of the cycle of throwaway goods or does it help slow it down?

[3]   See Dieter Rams's, 'Die Rolle des Designers im Unternehmen', speech (18 January 1980), Dieter Rams archive 1.1.2.10

5   Can it be simply repaired or does it rely on an expensive customer service facility? Can it in fact be repaired at all or is the whole appliance rendered redundant when just one part of it breaks?

6   Does it exhibit fashionable and therefore aesthetically short-lived design elements?

7   Does it help people or incapacitate them? Does it make them more free or more dependent?

8   Is it so accomplished and perfect that it perhaps incapacitates or humiliates you?

9   Which previous human activity does it replace and can that really be called progress?

10 What possibilities for change, what scope does the product offer people?

11 Can the product be used in other, perhaps playful, ways?

12 Does the product really offer convenience or does it encourage passivity?

13 What does the expected improvement look like in a broader context?

14 Does it make an action or activity on the whole more complicated or simpler, is it easy to operate or do you have to learn how to use it?

15 Does it arouse curiosity and the imagination? Does it encourage desire to use it, understand it and even to change it?

All these considerations about a product's design are related to its function, and this would be a good point at which to clarify Rams's view of functionality. When we consider functionalism and functionalists we think first of architects such as Mies van der Rohe or Walter Gropius. Often conflated with 'lack of ornament', functionalism began as a reaction against historicism, turned into a dictum ('form follows function') and an ideal that was at times almost dictatorial ('a house is a machine for living in'), and ended up being criticized as an aesthetic style like all the others that came before it. Although function plays a central role in Rams's ideas about design, he does not perceive it as a decorative attribute nor as a straightjacket: 'Strict functionality has fallen into disrepute in recent years. Perhaps rightly so in a way, since the functions that a product had to fulfil were often too narrowly, too puritanically determined. Human needs are more diverse than many designers are sometimes ready to admit or, perhaps, capable of knowing. For me the territory that the term "function" covers is constantly expanding. One is simply forced to keep learning how complex and manifold the functions of a product are.'[4] These include psychological, social and aesthetic functions as well as just usability. Rams is always at pains to stress that the duty of industrial design is first and foremost to users and the users are, generally, human beings, with all their complexities, habits, ideas and idiosyncrasies: 'Indifference towards people and the reality in which they live is actually the one and only cardinal sin in design. Function-orientated design is the fruit of intense, comprehensive, patient and contemplative reflection on reality, on life, on the needs, desires and feelings of people.'[5]

[4]   Rams, 'Die Rolle des Designers im Industrieunternehmen'

[5]   Dieter Rams, 'Functional design: A Challenge for the Future', lecture (1987), Rams archive 1.1.3.1

—

On what makes a good designer

Dieter Rams's experience of design is that of someone who worked predominantly for one company throughout his career. It therefore comes as little surprise that he does not view the role of the industrial designer as an autonomous presence but as an element within a larger system. He understands design to be an integrated process within the 'whole', but nevertheless one with a large measure of importance. Therefore the basic qualities that a good designer needs to have, in his view, show many parallels with those of any other well-qualified individuals within the company system: 'A designer needs to be intelligent and quick on the uptake … He should have a grasp of technology. He should be critical, reasonable and realistic. He should have a talent for teamwork.… He must also be patient, optimistic and persistent… and finally he should have the capacity for better ideas, a sense of proportion and colour, sensitivity and, last but not least, a foundation in handcraft and aptitude'.[6]

Being a product designer, insists Rams, has nothing to do with being an 'artist' or a 'decorator'. It is more about being a 'Gestalt-Ingenieur', an 'engineer of form' or 'technically orientated designer'. Rams explains: 'He synthesizes the concrete product from given specifications laid down by technology, production and the market. His work is predominantly rational in the sense that the formal decisions are substantiatable, verifiable and understandable'.[7] It is a hard and uncompromising viewpoint that leaves little room for the softer, more artistic sensibilities involved in design, but this too can be seen as the result of a need to establish and maintain an authoritative position in a complex hierarchical workplace.

This rather strict view of a designer's work is not the whole definition, however, a designer must also take notice of cultural and social values and developments in society, as well as thinking of individual users, and integrate them into their designs. 'The designer who wants to develop a function-appropriate product must think / feel himself into the role of the user… the designer is the user's advocate within the company,'[8] says Rams. Thus he or she needs to be rational but sensitive and empathic at the same time.[9]

As if that was not enough, a designer in a manufacturing company must also understand everyone else's position and needs (especially the customer's) and communicate with them all through the products he or she designs. This means that an industrial designer is perhaps above all a communicator, someone who is fluent in a variety of expressive languages, ranging from words, modelling, drawing and technical specifications to the ergonomics of form.

[6]   Rams, 'Die Rolle des Designers im Industrieunternehmen'

[7]   Dieter Rams, 'Design ist Eine Verantwortliche Aufgabe der Industrie', speech (1977), Dieter Rams archive 1.1.2.8

[8]   Dieter Rams, presentation at the AT (27 March 1980), Dieter Rams archive 1.1.2.11

[9]   This is a consideration that parallels the ideas of Tomás Maldonado, an influential design theorist at the Hochschule für Gestaltung Ulm between 1954 and 1966.

In summary, a good designer is a person who can feel, listen and understand, analyze precisely and quantifiably in detail, then share and communicate the results of that analysis using appropriate media to manufacture a product that, in turn, communicates with the user and fulfils their needs. Finally, a good designer has to produce 'good design'; they must be innovative in the best sense of the word. In the end, says Rams, a designer needs to ask themselves: 'Have I succeeded in improving things? Making them better than others did? Is my design good design?'[10]

On the role of design within a company

'The industrial designer is dependent on the business goals of the company he works for' said the German industrial design theorist Bernd Löbach in 1976.[11] This is certainly true, but a significant conflict of interest can easily arise between a good designer's first duty to the user and a company's concern for other priorities. It is quite possible that we would never have heard of the name Dieter Rams had it not been for the decision in 1955 by Erwin and Artur Braun, encouraged by Fritz Eichler and others, to make Braun a design-driven company. 'Design cannot just be about speculative leering towards better sales opportunities,' says Rams. 'It is a far more comprehensive task that can only be realized through a candidly and confidently implemented overall concept. Once a firm has set itself this goal, it affects the entire enterprise, its standpoint and its objectives'.[12] The safest way to make new products is to look at the market, see what sells well and make something similar. This 'me too' approach is conservative and market-driven. It does not encourage innovation nor user-orientated design.

However, coming up with new designs that are outside of the established system is a risk. It is also time-consuming and expensive to research and develop good products. The commitment in the company needs to be across the board. 'The decision to try to generate good design must therefore be a company-wide decision,' says Rams. 'That means it cannot be the design department that imposes it and who are made ultimately responsible. It has to be an integral part of the fundamental objectives of the company and finally it must be underpinned by a specific organisation and decision-making structure.'[13] It is the role of the company to give their designers the space within which to make good design, he adds, and it is the role of the designers to come up with designs and then repeatedly defend them. Finally, says Rams, the commitment to design must also reach into every aspect of the

[10]   Dieter Rams, speech in Boston (October 1984), Dieter Rams archive 1.1.5.1

[11]   Bernd Löbach, *Industrial Design: Grundlagen d. Industrie Produktdesign* (Thiemig, 1976), 187

[12]   Dieter Rams, introductory lecture to the exhibition 'Form – Nicht Konform 20 Jahre Braun-Design' at the Haus Industrieform, Essen (1976), Dieter Rams archive 1.1.2.3

[13]   Dieter Rams, 'The Designer's Contribution to Company Success', lecture given as part of the Canadian government's Industrial Design Assistance Program (22 September 1975), Dieter Rams archive 1.1.2.1

company and also its products: 'In the development of a design, the entire product world, from product concept – way before starting the actual design – to product graphics, instruction manual, packaging, advertising, marketing and presentation, has to be understood, thought through and resolved as part of the design process.'[14]

This need to defend design innovations and decisions, combined with the complexity of considerations involved in developing new products, encouraged Rams, the Braun design team and the communication department to outline an in-house order system or set of guidelines for good design – what Rams called the 'grammar' of Braun design. These guidelines provided the backbone of the design-driven brand identity by outlining two related design strategies: suggesting how the company's products could belong to a characteristic family and aiding company members to stay in touch with priorities as products were developed. 'Good design is not only a part, but to an ever-increasing degree the nucleus of what is today considered to be "corporate identity", and this is ultimately expressed by the products themselves which are offered to the public,'[15] says Rams. This constantly evolving set of guidelines, which covered innovation, quality, utility, aesthetics, modesty, honesty, comprehensibility, consistency, ecology and longevity, was also the inspiration for Rams's ten principles for good design developed in the 1970s and 1980s. 'Based on these principles, design is a product benefit that contributes towards profitable and lasting market performance, and at the same time facilitates getting a foothold in new markets,'[16] says Rams. It is certainly true that the company flourished and continued to innovate for much of his time there. In 1955 Braun had some 2,000 employees and a turnover of 50.5 million deutschmarks; by 1975 it had 9,000 employees and a turnover of more than 700 million deutschmarks.[17]

On aesthetics

Rams is often reluctant to talk about aesthetics, not least because of the subjectivity of the issue ('beauty is in the eye of the beholder') and just about everyone, qualified or otherwise, has an opinion on the subject. For him the design of an industrial product is 'aesthetic if it is honest, balanced, simple, careful and unobtrusively neutral'.[18] In other words, the aesthetic appearance of a product does and should

[14]   Dieter Rams 'Braun Design Philosophie', lecture at the Internationales Design Zentrum, Berlin (August 1989), Dieter Rams archive 1.1.5.3

[15]   Dieter Rams, speech at the opening of a Braun design exhibition at the Victoria and Albert Museum's Boilerhouse project, London (29 June 1982), Dieter Rams archive 1.1.2.13

[16]   Dieter Rams, 'Market Performance with "Technology" Design', speech (July 1988), Dieter Rams archive 1.1.4.2.

[17]   Dieter Rams, 'Kann Design zum Erfolg eines Unternehmens Beitragen?', lecture (October 1975), Dieter Rams archive 1.1.2.1

[18]   Rams, 'The Designer's Contribution to Company Success'

not play a primary role: 'design is not merely and certainly not exclusively there to feast the eye like a work of art or to be decorative'.[19] For an object to be beautiful, says Rams, it must also do its job properly. When products are well – that means usefully – designed, they have a kind of beauty that is inextricably related to their function, 'like a tool or the exterior of an aeroplane'. Thus the aesthetic beauty of an industrial product is bound to its utility.

Rams does admit that there are aesthetic criteria that go beyond the functional, but they are difficult to articulate in many cases due either to lack of measurable definitions or lack of training. 'It is hard to discuss aesthetic quality, he says. 'For two reasons: firstly, it is difficult to talk about anything visual since words have a different meaning for different people. Secondly, aesthetic quality deals with details, subtle shades, harmony and the equilibrium of a whole variety of visual elements. A good eye is required, schooled by years and years of experience, in order to be able to draw the right conclusions.'[20] He is clearly more at home talking about the rational world – a world of quiet, quantifiable order. In his view, the human need for beauty lies in opposition to the status quo of a world filled with visual pollution: 'It is difficult, strenuous, energy-consuming to live with objects, to be surrounded by objects which are off-balance, obtrusive, confusingly complicated or dishonest'.[21] This is the closest Rams comes to admitting his own artistic nature. His designs are a visceral response to a world that distresses him – he cannot help but want to tidy it up.

Beauty, for Rams, comes with simplicity and a certain humility: 'I believe that the product should play a secondary role in the relationship with the user, that it should not permanently vie for attention, that it should leave the user freedom and leeway for his own self-assertion as an individual.'[22] The designer's conviction underpins the Braun design approach: 'This is why we do our utmost to give Braun products this austere beauty which remains appealing for years. We are convinced that a well-balanced, quiet, clear, neutral and simple design corresponds best to the real needs of the users.'[23] That is not to say that Rams's concept of beauty did not have its opponents at Braun or elsewhere. He often had to fight for a product's right to be plain and inconspicuous: 'The labile tastes of certain decision-makers in a company are often a great burden for designers. Too many feel themselves qualified to pass judgement. And how insensitive, how superficial [these judgements] often are.'[24] Taste, believes Rams, is something that needs to be trained, since the aesthetic decisions at this level in product design are intrinsically bound to the entire form and function of the object. It would be unimaginable, for example, that

[19]   Ibid.

[20]   'Master and Commandments', *Wallpaper** magazine, no.103 (October 2007), 317–339

[21]   Rams, 'The Designer's Contribution to Company Success'

[22]   Rams, 'Die Rolle des Designers im Industrieunternehmen'

[23]   Rams, presentation at the AT

[24]   Rams, 'Die Rolle des Designers im Industrieunternehmen'

the management of an aerospace company would ask the designers of a new plane to shorten the wings because they think it would make it look prettier.

Rams's trust in the taste of consumers is not much better. 'The labile tastes of the buyer are a great temptation to many companies – there is little that can be exploited as easily and as profitably as bad taste. The design of many products is unmistakably determined by speculating upon the weaknesses of the buyer.'[25] This may be profitable in the short term, says Rams, but it brings no success: 'For it cannot be in our own interest to live and work in a society that is based upon the cynical exploitation of the weaknesses of others.'[26] Striving for aesthetic quality and convincing people that understated neutrality is neither a shortcoming, nor an end in itself, he adds, is something that designers always have to do both for themselves and their own companies.

On superficiality and chaos

Dieter Rams's biggest dislike is 'visual pollution'. It distresses him. For him, visual chaos places an equally disruptive and restrictive burden on our quality of life as the pollution of air water and the earth. He finds the man-made world an ugly and confusing place. Much of his approach to design can be traced from a personal need for calm and order: 'I wanted to clean up, to get rid of the chaos,' he says of himself at the beginning of his career, 'But the chaos has got worse since then. Chaos from products, noise and pollution. We are not really in control of anything. In those days I just wanted to tidy up people's immediate environment. Now we have to clean up a whole world.'[27] He blames much of this chaos and pollution on misplaced priorities on the part of producers, consumers, designers and governments, as well as a lack of properly thought-through design in everyday culture. It is designers, he believes, that can help relieve us from this pollution: 'Our culture is our home. Especially the everyday culture expressed in the objects for which I, as a designer, am responsible. It would help us a lot if we could feel more at home in this "everyday" culture. If the alienation, confusion and overload would lessen.'[28] We have too many things, he says. Our world is filled with too many products with superficial attractions and little or no real use. We have been indiscriminate and greedy. The term 'design' has been exploited and abused in the name of commercialism.

Rams has long seen that rampant consumerism is not viable and began predicting the end of the era of Dingkultur (object culture) in the 1970s. This was at a time when the Club of Rome report, 'Limits to Growth', published shortly before

[25]   Ibid.

[26]   Ibid.

[27]   Dieter Rams 'Ich habe einen Traum, Das Chaos beseitigen', *Zeit Magazin Leben* no.14 (27 March 2008), 49

[28]   Braun Design Department, 'Design Philosophy – the importance of good design' (1987), Dieter Rams Archive 1.1.5.4

the first oil crisis of 1973, did much to raise awareness about the environmental impact of human activity by predicting severe repercussions in the forseeable future should the rate of consumption of global natural resources not be controlled. He was very much aware of the activities of the Club of Rome, and he travelled increasingly in the 1970s to conferences and seminars around the world (such as the famous Aspen Talks, which he first started to attend in 1971 to hear the likes of Richard Buckminster Füller and George Nelson). He was party to many discussions and debates on the shortfalls of consumer culture, which struck a chord for him in his quest for restraint and quality in design. For Rams, good design is the world's strongest weapon in the war against visual chaos and thus product pollution. His design is a weapon of humble, yet determined resistance – one that serves and subsumes itself to the needs of society and the user. It is always about 'sensitive, disciplined simplicity and restraint'.[29] Simplicity for Rams is the stripping away of all that is unnecessary: 'Our one and only chance is to return to simplicity … one of the most important (for society, perhaps the most important) duties of designers today is to help clear up the chaos in which we live'.[30] Discipline is involved in having the will to consistently see it through and restraint is the control of the ego in the process. Rams saw no contradiction in the fact that he spent most of his life designing yet more consumer goods for the bloated market. Companies like Braun, he felt, were leading the way to simpler, better design. Quality, not quantity was his goal, and his conviction has always been that fewer products, better designed and longer lasting will limit environmental damage.

On poor design

Rams's rejection of visual pollution is synonymous with his rejection of 'poor design'. For him, poor design is the 'cynical exploitation of human weaknesses' that tries to appeal to the covetous nature, vanity or status concerns of individuals. Poor design is also 'showy and creates illusions'; it 'puts the designer in the spotlight instead of the product's functions' and results in products that make 'promises they are unable to keep' under conditions of daily use. Poor design, he says, is 'dull and unexciting'.[31] This is a direct response to those who criticize simple shapes and formally reduced ('good') design for being boring. In his view, individuals who have been desensitized by visual excess have become blinded to the beauty of restrained, function-orientated design. '[This design] is never commonplace,' he explains, 'on the contrary … you sense the energy of the mind, the intense creative work that was necessary to arrive at the formal reduction.'[32] Therefore, as someone

[29]   Ibid.

[30]   Ibid.

[31]   Dieter Rams, undated speech fragment (c. 1990), Dieter Rams archive 1.1.5.10

[32]   Dieter Rams, undated speech fragment (c. 1987), Dieter Rams archive 1.1.5.10

who understands the intellectual and physical effort that goes into good functional design, he finds that egoistic, garish and overcomplicated products are tedious in their lack of discipline and rigour.

On users and consumers

Rams makes an interesting semantic distinction between users and consumers when he talks about the people at whom his products are aimed. The general term for consumer in German is Verbraucher, which can literally be translated as 'one who uses things up' or 'consumes' things. However, Rams prefers to use the term Gebraucher, which translates as 'one who makes use of something' – the user. This distinction is related to his belief that a product has to be designed to last. If it is good design and does its job well, if it is a useful tool, then it needs to last as long as possible. Rams's approach has always been to persuade his company's customers to be users, and it has worked: Braun customers choose the brand and often pay more for a product because they expect it to fulfil its function well and to last a long time; they expect quality. People who, on the other hand, choose products predominantly for their interesting shapes or their fashionable colours, for example, are consumers in Rams's eyes. They are satisfying short-term desires at a superficial level or making aesthetic decisions that are not primarily driven by functional requirements. Braun products in Rams's time were aimed at 'intelligent, sophisticated, critical Gebraucher – users that consciously select products that they can utilize'.[33] For Rams, the term consumer (Verbraucher) is negative, implying someone who is wasteful, unthinking and impulse-driven.

On sustainability and the environment

Concern for the environment has been a continuous theme in Rams's talks and writings. It grew from a revulsion towards consumer excess, the over-abundance and 'chaos' of cheap, bad design and the resulting pollution, in both visual and material terms. It infuriates him that so many badly designed products are made and sold. Although they stimulate the desire for possession, they turn out to be useless so are discarded and then replaced in an ever-increasing cycle of waste. If these products were better designed we would need less of them and the cycle could be slowed or even changed completely: 'People of subsequent centuries will get the shivers when they look at the thoughtlessness with which we today litter our apartments, our cities, our landscape with a chaos of junk of every description. What fatalistic indifference we have towards the impact of things. Think of all the impositions we endure of which we are only half aware,' said Rams in 1975.[34]

[33]   Rams, introductory lecture to the exhibition 'Form – Nicht Konform 20 Jahre Braun-Design'

[34]   Dieter Rams, 'Kann Design zum Erfolg eines Unternehmens Beitragen?', talk (October 1975), Dieter Rams archive 1.1.2.1

Design can and must be a 'motor for change', he says. We all know that 'our technical / industrial civilisation is threatening the existence of life on earth'[35] and that 'radical change is unavoidable'. In 1999 Rams renewed his call for a 'new ethic of design'. The value of design in the future, he predicts, will lie in its contribution to the survival of life on earth as a whole. Design is in a position to dramatically improve the immediate material and ecological qualities of products. Design too must instigate a sustainable reduction in the quantities of products in favour of increased quality: 'Design will play a key role in the redesign of our consumer culture. It must work towards optimal functionality and the best possible user-quality, and facilitate long-term and economical use. It must also co-operate in creating new production and distribution structures.'[36]

Dieter Rams's well-known catchphrase 'Weniger aber besser' ('Less but Better'), is at once an exhortation to reduce individual products to the best of what is essential and a clarion call to change consumer culture. Our acquisitive habits must be replaced by 'an aesthetic that supports economical, long-term use of products'. He sets little store in just appealing to the goodwill of customers and proposes radical changes in the system. His most far-reaching suggestion is a leasing system whereby manufacturers no longer sell household appliances to customers. The products would remain the property of the manufacturer and the user pays to use them. When they have finished using the product or it needs repairing, it would go back to the manufacturer who updates it, repairs it or recycles it. This system, he believes, would dramatically reduce quantity and improve quality since it is everyone's interest that the appliances work well and last longer. Another aspect of design that needs developing in this context, says Rams, is what he calls 're-design'. By this he means we also need to escape our addiction to novelty and set about optimizing and improving what we already have: 'I am sure that even so-called trivial products of daily use such as door knobs, can-openers, paper punches, staplers, let alone cars ... can still improve greatly'.[37]

On the future

'The times for unimaginative design that could only flourish under an unimaginative production for an unimaginative consumption are drawing to an end,' said Dieter Rams in 1975. He was well aware that uncontrolled growth, increasing pollution and resource shortages were not the only issues that designers would need to confront

[35]   Dieter Rams, 'Designed in Germany – Ökologie und Design', opening speech for an exhibition organized by the German Design Council, Herbstmesse, Frankfurt am Main (21–25 August 1993) Dieter Rams archive 1.1.6.2

[36]   Dieter Rams, speech given at 'Bundespreis Produktdesign' award ceremony, Frankfurt am Main, Germany (27 August 1994)

[37]   Dieter Rams, speech on market performance with technology design (July 1988), Dieter Rams archive 1.1.4.2

in the future. Globalization and the 'increasing and irreversible compounding of all systems,' he predicted, would also have a greater role to play in the approach to design. As it becomes more and more apparent that there can be no discrete individual actions, that nothing can be isolated, that everything is enmeshed and interdependent, we must engage in a more thorough and broader consideration about what we do, why we do it and how we do it: 'Unless we want to risk the collapse of the entire system, none of the blunders that we might get away with for single products in individual use may be allowed to occur.'[38]

By 1990 this prediction had solidified into a vision of how design and the role of the designer will need to adapt themselves to future challenges in a system-orientated, rather than object-orientated world: 'Design in the future will become more of a managerial strategy – of planning and conceiving comprehensive production processes, of economising, rationalising and controlling them, regardless of whether "industrial" or "cultural" products are concerned. However, as interrelationships and work flow processes in highly complex industrial societies become increasingly impenetrable and obscure, unfaltering belief in polytechnical solutions is starting to disrupt. We will probably only be able to "manage" many design problems [that] we would quite well be able to define, but no longer be able to solve convention-ally.' He had by then acknowledged the steadily growing level of complexity and stretched his principles to encompass a changing understanding of industrial design that moves away from the individual object or product.

Rams had also begun to reassess the definitions of 'functional' and 'rational' design, but without diluting their value: 'In view of this aspect of complex interde-pendencies, design as we understand it today – namely giving shape to tangible objects primarily under aesthetic criteria – will fall back to second place. None-theless, there is certainly plenty to do there too. Enlarging the functionalistic concept would be desirable, in that a rigid shape canon should no longer be misused to glorify economic restraints, asserting, as it were, that design has come into its own through functionalism. Even if it should cede some of its absolute author-itative leadership and influence in society, rationality, the foundation on which it is built, need not and should not be given up. Preserving functional constants (simplicity, understandability, utility, long, useful life) certainly permits opening up and managing new shapes and their possible combinations. Although they will, to an ever-greater extent, be compulsorily determined by the standards set by industrial production, the designer should not be tempted to think exclusively in technocratic categories, which tend to end in unwearied positivism. They should keep in mind that their most important potentials – creativity and innovation – are rooted in the arts as well, and that their focus should therefore be to marry the virtues of technology and the arts.'[39]

---

[38]   Rams, 'The Designer's Contribution to Company Success'

[39]   Dieter Rams, 'Designed in Germany', keynote speech at the opening of the German Design
      Council exhibition at the Pacific Design Center, Los Angeles (1990), Rams archive 1.1.6.1

The Ten Principles of Good Design

From the 1970s onwards, Dieter Rams began condensing and formulating his ideas about design into a set of rules to explain to the world at large the values and issues related to what makes a good product. They first appeared in his lectures and writings around 1975, particularly in a design seminar that he delivered in Canada as part of the Canadian government's Industrial Design Assistance Program (IDAP) where he said: 'Three general rules govern every Braun design – a rule of order, a rule of harmony and a rule of economy.'[40] By 1976, at an International Marketing Meeting, this had grown to six design principles:

1   The function for us is the starting point and the target of every design
2   Experience with design is experience with people
3   Only orderliness makes design useful to us
4   Our design attempts to bring all individual elements into their proper proportions
5   Good design means to us: as little design as possible
6   Our design is innovative because the behaviour patterns of people change'.

At talks in 1983 and 1984 he summarized various speeches with six pared-down principles:

1   Good design is innovative
2   Good design renders utility to a product
3   Good design is aesthetic design
4   Good design makes a product easy to understand
5   Good design is unobtrusive
6   Good design is honest.[41]

The principles had grown to ten by the time he gave a lecture during the 1985 ICSID Congress in Washington and with slight variations in wording have remained in that format ever since. In German they tend to go under the heading: 'Zehn Thesen zum Design' (Ten Theses on Design) but somewhere along the line a rather grandiloquent translator seems to have come up with the phrase: 'Ten Commandments of Good Design', which is not Dieter Rams's style at all – they are not intended to be set in stone, pompous, inflexible and intransigent – so here we shall stick to the term 'Principles'. He introduced the principles of good design as follows: 'Some fundamental reflections on the – all things considered – essence of design which determined me and my fellow designers was summed up in ten simple statements a few years ago. They are helpful a means for orientation and understanding. They are not binding. Good design is in a constant state of redevelopment – just like technology and culture.'[42]

[40]   Rams, 'The Designer's Contribution to Company Success'

[41]   Rams, speech in Boston

[42]   Dieter Rams, Ten Principles of Good Design, June 1987/July 1991, amended March 2003, Dieter Rams archive

1   Good design is innovative

The possibilities for innovation are not, by any means, exhausted. Technological development is always offering new opportunities for innovative design. But innovative design always develops in tandem with innovative technology, and can never be an end in itself.

2   Good design makes a product useful

A product is bought to be used. It has to satisfy certain criteria, not only functional, but also psychological and aesthetic. Good design emphasises the usefulness of a product whilst disregarding anything that could possibly detract from it.

3   Good design is aesthetic

The aesthetic quality of a product is integral to its usefulness because products we use every day affect our person and our well-being. But only well-executed objects can be beautiful.

4   Good design makes a product understandable

It clarifies the product's structure. Better still, it can make the product talk. At best, it is self-explanatory.

5   Good design is honest

It does not make a product more innovative, powerful or valuable than it really is. It does not attempt to manipulate the consumer with promises that cannot be kept.

**6   Good design
is unobtrusive**

Products fulfilling a purpose are like tools. They are neither decorative objects nor works of art. Their design should therefore be both neutral and restrained, to leave room for the user's self-expression.

**7   Good design
is long-lasting**

It avoids being fashionable and therefore never appears antiquated. Unlike fashionable design, it lasts many years - even in today's throwaway society.

**8   Good design
is thorough down
to the last detail**

Nothing must be arbitrary or left to chance. Care and accuracy in the design process show respect towards the consumer.

**9   Good design
is environmentally
friendly**

Good design makes an important contribution to the preservation of the environment. It conserves resources and minimises physical and visual pollution throughout the lifecycle of the product.

**10   Good design
is as little design
as possible**

Less but better - because it concentrates on the essential aspects, and the products are not burdened with inessentials. Back to purity, back to simplicity!'

¹   Ibid.

— Less but Better

Finally, 'Less but Better' has become Dieter Ram's ultimate motto for change.
It is consciously similar to the minimalist dictum 'Less is More', which is generally
accredited to the German-American architect Ludwig Mies van der Rohe, but
was apparently coined by his former teacher, the German architect and designer
Peter Behrens. Behrens had an enormous influence on twentieth-century industrial design and architecture. He taught Le Corbusier and Walter Gropius (who later
became the first director of the Bauhaus), as well as Mies van der Rohe, and can
be credited with being one of the founding fathers of industrial design. He designed
groundbreaking buildings in brick, steel and glass, including the 1910 AEG turbine
factory in Berlin. In 1907 he was a co-founder of the influential German Werkbund, an
organisation of designers and companies committed to improving the design
of everyday objects and products. He was also a pioneer in the concept of corporate identity, designing everything for AEG in 1907, from products to graphics
and advertising.

Behrens had an influence on many companies and individuals, not least of
which was Max Braun, the father of Artur and Erwin. Although he came from two
generations before Dieter Rams, his functionalist dictum about improvement
through reduction is a fitting choice for Rams to have improved and adapted himself.
By all means reduce, says Rams, but only in the service of utility and the user –
not for the sake of aesthetic reasons alone. Reduce quantity, superficiality, greed,
waste and excess and at the same time increase: increase humility, quality and
the effort to achieve better products, better design and thereby a better world: 'There
must be millions less of things, less words, less gestures, less of everything. But
every word and every gesture will become more valuable. If we can put it all into
perspective we will need less things as a result'.[43]

Rams's convictions, born out of the nascent years of industrial design, have
formed a bridge into our contemporary world despite all the technological, social
and political changes and innovations in between. Maybe that is what makes him
so fascinating as a designer. He has applied exacting, rational conditions to the broad
and comprehensive world of design and distilled a set of rules that still appear
to hold true. Reducing, testing and condensing again until his whole philosophy could
be summed up in just three words: 'Less but Better' which, like his sketches and
products, have a beauty about them that fulfils and transcends the functional and
rational position that he has always aimed to reach.

[43]   Dieter Rams, 'Statement' (July 1994), Dieter Rams archive 1.1.2.29

Dieter Rams's Legacy

During the latter part of his career, Dieter Rams increasingly turned his attention towards design education and improving quality and sustainability in product design. He used, and still uses, every opportunity when speaking publicly and conducting interviews to hammer home his message: 'Less but Better' in all its ram(s)ifications. Between 1988 and 1998, for example, he was president of the *Rat für Formgebung* (German Design Council), a government-backed organisation founded in 1953, which was aimed at promoting and improving design in Germany, with particular respect to its economic benefits. During his time there, he was at pains to propagate his message and encourage designers, politicians, business and the public to question 'unlimited quantitative growth' and be 'brave, open and competent enough to orientate ourselves anew in order to massively redesign our lifestyles and with them our future on this planet'.[1]

Rams is highly critical of the 'post-modern' approach to design that emerged in the 1980s and 1990s and which has led, in his view, to the increasing predominance of an egocentric, hedonistic attitude among designers in recent years. He considers the 'anything goes' material culture to be the triumph of arbitrariness. Allowing emotional and visual stimuli and the allure of novelty to override any system of ethical values demonstrates, for him, extreme irresponsibility towards the future of the environment and design, not to mention the user. 'In my experience, things which are different simply to be different are seldom better,' he said at an international design congress in Aspen in 1993, 'but that which is better is almost always different'.[2]

Although Rams has been preaching more or less the same message for the last fifty years, he is well aware that this has been a half-century of extraordinary change, and his missionary zeal does not simply call for a return to 'good old values'. In a speech that he gave in Tokyo in 2009, he acknowledges that the designers of today and tomorrow have a much harder task ahead of them than he had. Furthermore, he recognizes that the world has become a much more complex and interconnected place, in which the designer increasingly finds him or herself acting as a go-between between technology and the user. When he was working for Braun and Vitsœ, Rams and his colleagues believed in helping to design a better world, one with products that prove themselves through useability as well as aesthetic quality. For future designers, says Rams, it is not only the product, but 'new structures within which to interact with the product' that are vital. The systemic nature of products and their connections to the world, which Rams always understood so well, needs further investigation. 'The epoch of the industrial designers,' he suggests, 'could be followed by the epoch of the design moderators, who will bring a new harmony between man, nature and technology. If this were so, the concept

[1]   Dieter Rams, speech given at the opening of the 'Rat für Formgebung' exhibition '40 Jahre' (19 September 1993), Dieter Rams archive 1.1.6.6

[2]   Dieter Rams, 'The Future of Design', lecture at the International Designer Congress, Aspen (1993)

of technological and economic progress would be to stand by a new idea of equilibrium: a balance of tradition and future, of globality and home (*Heimat*), which comes from the needs of the human being as an individual and as part of the community.'[3]

On Education

In 1995, two years before he retired from Braun, Dieter Rams spoke of his intent to concentrate on design education. In an address to the International Council of Societies of Industrial Design (ICSID)[4] Congress that year, he declared, 'In the years that remain to me, I want to make education my theme and concentrate on improving the education of designers.'[5] By that time he had been teaching as a professor at the Academy of Fine Arts in Hamburg for fifteen years and had had ample opportunity to study and experience design education in Germany and to assess its relationship to the 'real world' of industry.

Based on his premise that the role of design should be that of a motor for change towards a sustainable product culture, he recommended a number of improvements to design education that would facilitate this responsibility. First, he pointed out that industrial design is all about technology: 'It is as much an art form as medicine, mechanical engineering or law.'[6] By this he meant that the depth and complexity of the areas involved in contemporary product design required a strong technical background to be able to make the right choices and communicate with technicians at an adequate level. Rams also called for a closer collaboration with industry to develop a more practice-orientated education. In addition, he suggested reducing the number of design schools considerably (particularly in Germany) to concentrate the financial means and facilities to deliver a meaningful level of quality. It was a viewpoint that has not made him many friends in the design education community, but Rams has never been particularly concerned about what people thought of him.

The Dieter und Ingeborg Rams Foundation

Throughout his working life, Dieter Rams has campaigned for the general improvement of our product world. Even today he is busy travelling all over the globe lecturing,

[3]   Dieter Rams, 'Tokyo Manifest', speech at the opening of the 'Less and More' exhibition, Fuchu Art Museum, Tokyo (May 2009)

[4]   The International Council of Societies of Industrial Design (ICSID) is a global non-profit organisation to promote better design around the world with over 150 member organisations from 50 countries. Dieter Rams was a member of the board from 1991 to 1995. He was also involved in the VDID (German Industrial Designer Association) and the Deutscher Werkbund (German Work Federation).

[5]   Dieter Rams, speech to the ICSID (1995)

[6]   Ibid.

advising, debating and writing on the subject. He formulated his ten principles of good design in the 1970s and 1980s based on his own long-term experience in the field of product design. These principles were initially for the benefit of his own design team, but today serve to help young designers in particular find new approaches and new solutions. Design for Dieter Rams means not only a rational and common-sense approach to our living environment but also an aesthetic one in every sense of the word. He is also deeply committed to a socially-oriented approach to design; one which highlights products and communication processes that serve a democratic society that takes responsibility for all its individual members.

In December 1994 Dieter Rams used the prize money awarded to him as part of the IKEA Design Prize two years earlier as well as some of his own personal funds to initiate a foundation that would further these commitments: the *Dieter und Ingeborg Rams Stiftung* (Dieter and Ingeborg Rams Foundation). Although his principles and approach towards 'good design' are central to the aims of the foundation, it is also specifically intended to encourage and provide a platform for debate as well as and assist new generations of designers to find new methods and new solutions in the pursuit of a better product environment for us all.[7]

Sustainable Design

That Dieter Rams is one of the most influential designers of his age is almost beyond question, but his most significant legacy may not be his products, but his articulation of the necessity for design to contribute to a sustainable culture. 'Dieter Rams stands for integrity in design,' says critic Hugh Pearman. 'He stands for true functionalism. He is anti-styling, anti-waste. He is against the throwaway society.'[8] Rams introduced the idea of sustainable development into his designs in the 1970s. Many of his products, particularly his furniture for Vitsœ + Zapf (later Vitsœ) were created as flexible systems that could be adapted to fit changing circumstances by their owners: it was possible to expand or reduce, add to and partially replace them if they broke or wore out. As a result, trade in these products relies on the manufacturer maintaining a close and long-term relationship with the customer, servicing, repairing and adjusting products when necessary. Vitsœ today manufactures just two product systems: the 606 Universal Shelving System

[7]   As interest in Rams's work and approach has grown, particularly in recent years, the foundation is increasingly called upon to furnish information and material. Therefore as of 2010, the Dieter and Ingeborg Rams Foundation and the Museum für Angewandte Kunst (Museum of Applied Arts) in Frankfurt am Main, Germany is expanding, digitalizing and setting up access to Rams's private archive for the purpose of international design research. Their collaboration will also result in a programme of seminars, publications, congresses and exhibitions for the communication of a 'functional, aesthetic and society-orientated' approach to design.

[8]   Hugh Pearman, 'Simply Successful', *Blueprint* (1 June 2002), 32–35

and the 620 Chair Programme. Because so little has changed in these products since Rams designed them in the early 1960s, and because nearly all of the changes have been small improvements in detailing as new materials or tooling became available, a 606 shelving system from the 1960s can still be updated with components from the 2008 version. One result of this longevity is an unusually loyal consumer base. Customers expect their Vitsœ products to last a lifetime and the better that product serves them, the less likely they are to ever buy anything else to replace it. 'Fifty per cent of our orders come from existing customers,' says managing director Mark Adams, with considerable pride. 'I manage a company where we want more people to buy less of our furniture,' he adds, 'Vitsœ is not primarily run for profit, because if we make the right decisions, we will make a profit'.[9]

     This kind of business model only works for products that are as perfect as possible, tools for living that are harmonious and timeless in appearance: less but better. Through his example, Rams has demonstrated that this approach can work. 'Designers and the businesses which produce good design have quite a task ahead,' he tells us, 'the task of changing our world where today it is ugly, irritating and confusing, into something better, from small everyday items to our great cities.'[10] It is up to manufacturers, designers and us, the buying public, to help meet that task.

The Designer's Designer

Where is design going? What is design today? We are in a dynamic phase of innovation, exploration and re-evaluation and there is a strong need for discourse and per-haps even guidelines if progress is not to drown in a confusion of overabundance and complexity. Most importantly, now that design permeates so many aspects of life, is so bound to technological development and attracts the increasing awareness of consumers, it occupies an increasingly responsible position. 'Good design' is no longer defined solely by the creation of useful and easy-to-use products, but requires sustainable products that result from forward-thinking and careful consideration for their entire lifespans and for the environment.

     Designers are in a unique position to influence the nature of our product-saturated world, but for that they need clear direction, awareness, understanding and an ethical framework. It is no accident that today's designers are looking with ever-increasing interest towards Dieter Rams as someone who has devoted his entire working life to responsible design. It is not just his pioneering work in defining an elegant, rigorous and legible visual language for products that facilitates the interface between user and technology, or his consideration for their place

[9]   Dieter Rams, 'Less but Better: A Return to Common Sense', RSA address at Glasgow's Light-house design centre (13 November 2007)

[10]   Dieter Rams, 'The Responsibility of Design in the Future', RSA Student Design Awards 75th anniversary lecture at Glasgow's Lighthouse design centre (4 November 1999)

in the environment that strikes a chord, but also his ethical consistency. His *Ten Principles of Good Design*," first published in the 1980s, could not be more relevant today, and his maxim 'Less but Better' has never seemed more necessary in a fatigued world of chaotic, wasteful excess that is on the edge of ecological disaster.

Dieter Rams has always been a designer's designer. The products that he and his design team created for Braun developed out of a way of thinking that came from the Bauhaus, Hochschule für Gestaltung Ulm school and others as they strove to bring a marriage of form and function to the modern, industrialized world. His principles are part of a continuing process of design theory refined by over fifty years of practical experience and hundreds of products. Many of today's leading industrial designers cite Rams as an inspiration and a role model, and although technology, materials and manufacturing techniques have developed enormously since Rams's heyday, there still seems to be much that can be learned from his approach.

Naoto Fukasawa

The Japanese designer Naoto Fukasawa was born in 1956 – a year after Dieter Rams started working for Braun. He is now one of the world's leading designers, connected most notably with the Japanese company Muji and ±0, which manufactures household appliances. Fukasawa calls Rams 'one of the few figures that I consider to be mentors'[12] and, like Rams, his own work is characterized by an almost obsessive attention to detail and thus a desire to strive towards perfection right down to the last fraction of a millimetre. He first encountered Braun products when he was at college and from then on Braun products and Dieter Rams design 'existed as a single image' in his mind. It was the methodology that interested him then. 'I learned about a number of elements pertaining to a product, such as arranging ventilation, switches and operation display characters along a grid, from Rams's designs at Braun,' he says. 'I remember that I was not only attracted to the precise, functional designs, but also to the human softness, the tenderness in them – the fact that they were functional and simple but not cold.'

In the 1980s, Fukasawa acknowledges that he was swept away on the wave of 'emotional design' around at the time. The market was demanding 'meaningless' and 'unnecessary' forms, he says, but by the mid-1990s he had tired of this direction. 'I wavered and it felt like I was continually searching for the right path to take,' he explains. When I finally discovered the answer – "Could it be this?" – Braun products and the work that Rams did were there ... His work was so very inevitable, the

[11]   The 'Ten Principles of Good Design' from Dieter Rams are as follows: Good design is innovative; makes a product useful; is aesthetic; helps us to understand a product; is unobtrusive; is honest; is durable; is consequent to the last detail; is concerned with the environment; is as little design as possible.

[12]   All Naoto Fukasawa quotes in this chapter are from an interview with the author in May 2009, unless otherwise noted.

results that I determined for myself were linked to his answer. Perhaps it was simply that I was looking at the cliff face while making my way to the top of the cliff and just before I reached the summit, I lifted my head and there he was.'

Fukasawa admires Rams's 'discerning willpower', the fact that his work resisted the urge to be fashionable, attention-seeking or innovative for its own sake: 'This is a temptation that is hard to ignore for designers; even if it is just a single dial or knob, they try to include some element of individuality.' He believes that Rams's designs come from the 'inevitable essence' of the objects themselves rather than the designer's ego. This is 'correct design' and inevitable in that it is close to how the objects ultimately *need* to be. Thus products such as the Phonotransistor TP 1 or the 606 Universal Shelving System show us that 'we don't need anything more than this … they stem desire and show us that this is enough,' he says.

'Good quality normality' – making what we already have better – is, in Fukasawa's view, an essential aim to strive for as a designer, especially in the light of today's surfeit of possessions. 'The time for exploring and experimentation has ended. I believe there should be no more hesitation in devoting oneself to the functions of life or to beautiful, modest, tranquil implements,' he believes. 'Adapting good things to our current lives and modifying them bit by bit, rather than making great leaps and creating different stimuli is what is important – this is what Dieter Rams has verified in a practical manner. I believe that no other design answer is necessary.'

Jasper Morrison

The highly respected British designer Jasper Morrison is also an outspoken admirer of Dieter Rams's approach. Morrison has created technical pieces for a number of companies, such as Sony, Olivetti and Samsung, but it was when he came to design a series of appliances for the German manufacturer Rowenta in 2004 that his respect for Rams's achievements at Braun doubled. 'To have controlled that company to the level at which he did, to have achieved those results so consistently,' he says, was a great feat. 'The Braun way seemed special. It was a design-led company back then. In every company there is a balance between marketing and design. The marketing strategy is usually "what's selling well now is the model for what we should do next". This cannibalistic process leads to total banality and bad design.'[13]

Morrison grew up with the SK 4 phonograph. It had been passed down in his family from his grandfather, to his parents and finally to him when he was sixteen. 'Even as a young boy something about that machine seemed impressive to me,' he says, 'the transparent lid was so modern at the time and the layout of the dials, the aluminium arm.'[14] It is very much the aesthetic aspect of Rams's design that

[13]   Interview with Jasper Morrison by Gerrit Terstiege, *Form* magazine, no. 195 (March/April 2004), 70

[14]   All Jasper Morrison quotes in this chapter are from an interview with the author in May 2009, unless otherwise noted.

appeals to Morrison. 'He's much more creative in an aesthetic sense than he likes to admit,' he says, arguing that Rams's spoken emphasis on the rational and functional sometimes goes a little too far. 'But,' he adds, 'repressing the creative urge is the right approach, and allowing it to emerge as a result of analysing the technical parameters was his speciality.'

As with Fukasawa, for Morrison it is the correctness of Rams's approach that is so inspirational: 'He serves design best now as a reminder of how it should be done.' It is both the elegance of the composition and the degree of perfection that Rams attained in his designs that Morrison most admires. He finds products such as the 606 Universal Shelving System, which he has in his office, show a refined approach. 'It is the endgame of shelving systems. There's no point in trying to design another one.' Morrison sees a degree of harmony in a highly complex work that is exemplary. 'I don't think anyone ever cared so much about getting it right and had the skill to do it,' he concludes. 'For me he still points the way to a better future for design'.

Sam Hecht

Another well-known British designer, Sam Hecht, born in 1969, grew up with a number of Braun household products in his parents' suburban home. He describes his house as being typically English and aesthetically uncoordinated but 'for some reason my Mum and Dad always bought Braun products'.[15] He thinks that part of the reason was that they were 'made in Germany, which was still a badge of excellence, reliability and quality', but this itself was at least in part because Braun spearheaded these qualities in domestic appliances at the time. 'These things lasted,' says Hecht. 'They were kind of repairable in that their "putting-together" was designed and not simply engineered.' They shaped his expectations as a designer and consumer in the years to come.

Hecht's career includes being employed by the big US industrial design company IDEO and setting up his own company, Industrial Facility, with his partner Kim Colin in 2002. As well as designing a wide range of products from furniture to toasters, they are also both creative advisors for Muji and Herman Miller. Hecht understands all too well the pressures of designing within the confines of a large organisation. Working in the United States in the 1990s, designing devices such as telephones and computers, he realized that 'something was awry' and, like Morrison, became very dissatisfied with the way that design had increasingly become the tool of marketing. He started to read again the writings of Otl Aicher and Hans Gugelot, and then about Rams because he felt there was not much interest in that design-driven approach at the time: 'Nobody looked at Braun then; it was totally off the radar in terms of any appreciation, if I am brutally honest. But the quality

[15]   All Sam Hecht quotes in this chapter are from an interview with the author in May 2009, unless otherwise noted.

was still there in terms of its functional reliability.' Hecht says he had many conversations with his then colleague Naoto Fukasawa and they both realized 'something needed to change'.

As a relatively new discipline, industrial design has only a limited amount of historical reference points, says Hecht, and in the 1990s these were sorely missing. 'With literature, for example, you have a sense of continuity in quoting previous writers, who had valuable things to say, but design didn't really have that,' Hecht says. He felt there were things to be learned from the work and ideas of Aicher, Gugelot and Rams, particularly with regard to the responsibility of designers within a company and towards their work. Good design boils down to making a set of correct decisions, he says, 'and the bigger the company or corporation you work with, the more complicated these decisions become'. A designer has to understand every step of the design process, from engineering down to a microchip level, graphics, typefaces and materials. If they lose control of the design process or do not pay attention to a particular aspect of it, and the resulting product is not satisfying, then according to Hecht they only have themselves to blame.

For Hecht, the great contributions that Rams has made to industrial design are the systemic quality and the continuity of his work. 'In understanding that what you produce as a company has an impact not only in the shop, but in the environment in which it is used ... Braun and Rams were complete pioneers in this context,' he says. This systemic quality is visible not only in the relationships among the Braun products and between the Braun and Vitsoe product ranges, but also within individual appliances. 'When you design a hairdryer, for example, you are not just designing it for the hand or the hair, but you are also designing how it is plugged in, how the cord is wired up and stored, what it looks like when it just sits in a room, where you keep it and whether it is offensive – this foreground / background throttle, as we call it,' he explains. Designing in this way gives the designer far greater power and allows for better products, 'but it is very long-term, not short-term, and you need a brilliant mind to spearhead it,' says Hecht.

Rams not only made great products, he also realized that the role of the designer goes beyond the product. 'There is a responsibility to the environment in terms of where these things are going, how they are being used, and how they connect with all life and the struggles that we have. I feel that to be able to do both of those things, which are in some ways often at odds with modern marketing techniques, is an incredible achievement,' concludes Hecht.

—
Michael DiTullo

Michael DiTullo, the design director at Converse, which is now part of the Nike group, grew up in the United States on the other side of the Atlantic from Hecht and works within a highly marketing-driven design environment. He too first came into contact with Braun products during his childhood and feels he has learned a great deal from Rams's example. For DiTullo, it was his grandparents' open-plan, post-World War II, modernist home that inspired his own early appreciation of design and thus, his own youthful purchases of a Braun travel alarm clock and an electric razor. 'When I first experienced Dieter Rams's work, I didn't have the design vocabulary to explain what drew me to it,'[16] he says, 'but instinctively I knew it to be right.'

As he pursued his career as a designer, DiTullo says he continued to experience Rams's work in new ways. 'I began to appreciate the functionality of it, how complex objects were made approachable by reducing their interface with the user to the simplest possible solution through a topically simple, but actually complex use of form, colour and material.' At the next level, he experienced the minimalism of Rams's pieces, their 'economy of form' and how they 'eloquently responded to their surroundings', regardless of the style of the interior. His Braun travel alarm clock, for example, has a design that he describes as 'comfortable with itself. It is the manifestation of an alarm clock in its most simple state, so it fits anywhere'. As a designer who has been through the process himself, he appreciates that the reduced nature of Rams's work and the Braun products is never something that just happens of its own accord. 'I know each product was laboured over, each design decision a battle, but as a consumer this comes across as being so effortless that the products look as though they have not been designed at all,' says DiTullo. It is this lack of 'fashion whimsy' that makes the products immune to the passing of time, and therefore still relevant.

A third feature that has affected DiTullo as a designer is how the Braun products 'talk to one another' as a family, how they individually and collectively came to represent the very best of Braun: 'Each individual piece is strong, but together the impact is enormous'. As the design director of a classic sports shoe brand, he thinks a lot about this idea, as well as the 'timelessness' of Braun appliances, in respect to his own work. 'The work is not just simple, it is selectively reductive, and I think that is what makes it relevant in any situation at any time.'

There is no 'perfect product' and 'industrial designers can only make the best solution that satisfies the highest possible number of people for the longest possible time,' says DiTullo. 'Objects need to be designed to be flexible, misused and imprinted with their users' emotions and values.' In this latter respect, Dieter Rams was a great designer. 'He did an exemplary job of boiling forms down to their most relatable and rational roots, which resonated with a broad audience. The forms are malleable in the way that individuals can interpret them,' he explains. 'Rams didn't look for the lowest common denominator, instead he looked to what I call the highest common denominator. The work does not pander, it aspires.' A further interesting point that DiTullo makes about the value of Rams's work lies in an approach that points to what he believes to be a healthier kind of material-

[16]   All Michael DiTullo quotes in this chapter are from an interview with the author in May 2009, unless otherwise noted.

materialism. 'We are taught that material things cannot make us happy, that the stuff of this world is trivial and temporary. Rams's work proves that wrong,' he says. 'It shows that material things do matter and that we should respect what we make, what we buy and what we use. It reveals that a simple functional object can do its job while conveying joy, optimism and democracy. Owning objects of this nature communicates that we get it, that we agree, that we also strive to do the best we can with our limited means, that we have a hope for tomorrow and equality.' Therefore by spending their money on 'good design', consumers are not only buying better products that last longer, they are also identifying themselves with a particular viewpoint or set of principles.

DiTullo has a significant amount of experience of working in the particularly aggressive marketplace of global fashion brands. He is highly critical of the cycle that exists where consumers are constantly fed with the 'new' and where 'better' products have 'more features, greater personal expression and a lower cost', or a combination of all three characteristics. 'The bald truth is that most of these things are worse, not better, and we know it, but this is the reality we design in,' he says. 'Our consumer-based economy needs to sell new things to people. This pressure leads to them seeking cheaper products and a very bad cycle that trivializes design and the products themselves.' The solution, he says, lies in the hands of designers. 'Designers can be agents for change in their own organisations and in a measured way lay the seeds for a return to Rams's way of thinking. I believe that we can convince the companies and the people who we design for to value more principled products through the type of design that Rams did. This will be neo-materialism, which I define as a respect for the physical world, meaning we stop spending on things we don't value and start investing in things we cherish.'

Konstantin Grcic

Konstantin Grcic, one of Germany's most prominent contemporary industrial designers, was born in 1965 and brought up in Germany. For him, Braun products were 'part of a very common product culture'[17] in the 1970s and 1980s. Although he appreciated the quality of Braun appliances, they also represented the past, something that he felt the need to move on from. As a student he began to learn about Dieter Rams, who he viewed as 'a very dogmatic figure, someone who had his rules about what good design is and should be. I didn't like this at all at the time'. During the 1980s, Grcic was most inspired by the works of Italian designers including Ettore Sottsass. Their approach and the whole design culture around them was, for Grcic, 'the opposite to the negative, off-putting idea of German design represented by Braun and Rams's.

[17]   All Konstantin Grcic quotes in this chapter are from an interview with the author in July 2009, unless otherwise noted.

In 1995 Grcic met Rams for the first time while on the organising committee for a big German design conference entitled 'Gestalt: Visions of German Design' in Aspen the following year. The meeting did not go well. 'He fulfilled all my prejudices about him,' recalls Grcic. 'We got into an argument about an exhibition I had been given to plan, showing a cross-section of German design. He had such rigid ideas about how this should be and I felt I could not communicate with the man.' But a few years later Grcic was to change his opinion completely. He had been invited to join a podium discussion together with Rams and was regretting his decision to accept until he found himself sitting in a quiet foyer area with his former antagonist, waiting to be called onstage, and they started talking. 'He began telling me little anecdotes about his time at Braun in such a nice, normal way that he somehow destroyed this whole myth about himself and the company's regime with these pure industrial products,' remembers Grcic. 'It all became so human; the scale became so beautiful. Suddenly for me, the keys on his calculators became Smarties rather than an ergonomic colour scheme. It was like there was a different man in front of me. So you could say I discovered Dieter Rams very late in my career.'

Grcic's conversation with Rams helped him to understand the man and designer behind the products, and he got a rare glimpse of Rams's passion for his work and his strong artistic sense, which he so rarely talks about. 'When you reassess Dieter Rams's work you could say that he was never as dogmatic as he pretended to be. That was what was so beautiful about these anecdotes he was telling me – they were all so casual and a lot of them were very subjective – emotional decisions were involved. Of course there was a successor to him at Braun but it was never the same. In the end his feel, his inspiration and the artistic touch, that he definitely has, made all the difference'.

Jonathan Ive

Perhaps the most famous and outspoken admirer of Dieter Rams's oeuvre is Jonathan Ive, Senior Vice President of Industrial design at Apple Inc, and the company's chief designer. Ive's designs for Apple, with their clean lines, reduced forms, user-friendly interfaces and intuitive controls, are among the most iconic of our age and freely trace their ancestry to Rams's signature style and the Braun tradition.

This can be seen in the visual similarity of the Apple iPod to the Braun T3 pocket radio from 1958, and the calculator keyboard of the first iPhone operating system to the 1978 ET44 pocket calculator. The forms of these products are a combination of natural evolution, a minimal philosophy and an insider's wink. Like Rams, Ive has paid close attention to the 'Less but Better' credo and his products follow many (but not all) of Rams's ten principles of good design. Apple's iPhone, introduced in 2007, is remarkable not only for its innovative technology and revolutionary interface, but for the fact that it comes with no instruction manual – and does not need one – which proves quite clearly that 'good design helps us to understand a product'.

It is hardly surprising that with similar goals, designers reach similar solutions, especially when they need to be as reduced as possible. But given the decades of time as well as the monumental leaps in technological development that separate Braun products of the Rams period from Apple's today, their close formal relationship is truly remarkable, and demonstrates how perceptive and forward-thinking some of the Braun designs were. It is important to note too that Apple, like Braun, is that rare example of a design-driven company where the design team has a strong and significant say in the output and identity of the firm. 'At Braun they were always willing to take a risk,' says Rams. 'We as designers cannot work in a vacuum,' he went on to say. 'The entrepreneur has to want it; the people at the top of the company have to want it.'[18] In another interview he continued, 'We need people who are prepared to take risks, to think long-term and not make everything dependent on short-term financial success ... Design is not marketing, even when ever more companies behave as if it is. We have to completely dedicate ourselves to design and technology. Both have to mesh with one another'.[19]

Loyalty on the part of a manufacturing company to their designer(s) and knowing how to nurture rather than stifle creative brilliance is a very uncommon phenomenon, especially at the multi-national level where millions of dollars are at stake. Hence a frequent comparison is drawn between Braun and Apple. In each case the name of the designer has become almost inseparable from the brand. Dieter Rams enjoyed a high level of trust at Braun over a long period of time and was given a lot of authority as a result. 'Braun believed in Rams,' says Konstantin Grcic. 'That is so good, and as we know today, so rare. Apple believes in Jonathan Ive, and that is rare too'.

Rams Today and Tomorrow

While researching this book I spoke to many designers and other individuals about Dieter Rams, not only those whose comments are listed above. I found out how they viewed his work, whether they distinguished between his design and 'Braun design', the relevance of his approach today, despite the technical obsolescence of many of the products he designed, and whether they felt themselves to have been influenced by his work and / or his thinking. The responses were often fascinating. Many people I spoke to who were not professionally concerned with design had never heard of Rams, but when I described some of the Braun products that he designed, their eyes inevitably lit up in recognition. Rams's designs and the Braun products made while he was there play an important role in the collective memory of the thousands of people who lived and grew up with them; those 'reliable

[18]   Marcus Fairs 'Dieter Rams', *icon* magazine no.10 (February 2004), 60–68

[19]   Dieter Rams, 'Dieter Rams Der Apple-Inspirator' (Interview with Mirjam Hecking) *manager-magazin.de* (October 2007) <http://www.manager-magazin.de/life/technik/0,2828,511925,00.html>

servants' that fulfilled their roles so well often became much-loved or fondly remembered companions.

As demonstrated by Konstantin Grcic, however, among the design community in Germany, the appreciation of Rams is mixed with other emotions. Although almost no one has a bad word to say about his products, Rams is still regarded by certain German designers as part of the dogmatic and rather dull 'old guard' from the tail end of the Bauhaus. The technically correct, 'engineered' image of German design – well-made but boring – is one that many young designers are still trying to escape.

In the UK, the US, the worldwide web and beyond, interest in Dieter Rams and his ten principles for good design seems to have grown enormously. I think this is related to the global economic downturn that began around the same time that I started work on this book, as well as a worldwide, growing eco-anxiety. A burgeoning dissatisfaction with throwaway culture and general tightening of belts has caused consumers to question their indulgent lifestyles. Modesty and thrift are becoming virtues again. The western generation that has never known real hardship or war talks about growing their own vegetables, taking up knitting and repairing rather than throwing away. Dieter Rams's message about making better products of better quality that last longer to help us consume less, resonates with an increasing number of people. Buying a new car and computer every two years, a new printer and camera every year and a new telephone every six months is not and cannot be sustainable. Despite the general acknowledgment of this fact, we have forgotten, or never learned, how to live otherwise. In this context, the attraction of Rams's design principles becomes obvious, especially because they crystallize the thoughts of a designer who clearly practised what he has preached, always working ideologically towards a more socially considered design, putting the user and the environment in all its the meanings before fashion, ego and showy extravagance.

But there is a danger here of oversimplified hero-worship. Dieter Rams is no guru. He is a designer – an excellent designer – who had the good fortune to enter a new profession with a particular company at a particular time: a renaissance moment full of new ideas, new attitudes, new growth, new technologies, new materials and opportunities. His talent comes from a meticulous attention to detail, an unusual sensitivity to form, feel and colour, a consistency in approach once he had found his path and a huge stubborn streak that has kept him on that path for over half a century. But his work is as much part of a system as the objects he designed, co-designed and oversaw. Industrial design is and always has been about team-work. Many people confuse 'Rams design' with 'Braun design' (he has, more than once, been called 'Mr Braun'), but although his was the guiding hand for many years, he was certainly not the only great designer to work for Braun. Hans Gugelot, Gerd Alfred Müller, Reinhold Weiss and many others contributed greatly to the Braun golden era of product design, not to mention all the unnamed technicians and engineers who also played their part, or the vision of the company bosses who initiated and facilitated all the appliances. The Braun hi-fi section for example, which included some of Rams's greatest designs, never made a profit and had to be subsidized by other more successful lines such as the shavers. In another climate, Rams might never have flourished as he did at Braun, nor had the freedom to design for Vitsoe at the same time.

His ten principles of design also emerged from the working environment and system of which he was a part. Rams travelled often in Germany and abroad to talks, conferences and exhibitions, initially on behalf of Braun and then later as president of the German Design Council and as a designer in his own right. Each of the many speeches he gave shows a progression towards a further condensation of thoughts and ideas that were mostly already in place by the early 1960s. As with his products, he just kept refining them until he got down to the ten principles and his favourite axiom: 'Less but Better'. As fashions in design have come and gone, Dieter Rams, his design, and what he has to say about it have remained constant. Thus he has become a symbol of a certain idea of German functional design, an icon, even a brand in our brand-obsessed world. This fact has been facilitated by some fortuitous characteristics – his distinctive, easy-to-pronounce name and memorable appearance, which has changed little over the years except that his impossibly white hair keeps getting even whiter. His inflexibility is his strength but it can also be a weakness: he is not very adaptable and does not suffer fools lightly. Many of his designs are brilliant and deservedly hailed as twentieth-century masterpieces but, one has to admit, he came up with a few turkeys as well. Dieter Rams and his collaboration with Braun and Vitsoe has left us with a valuable and important legacy, a systemic concept for the future of industrial design that is capable of transcending progress. Both the objects he created and his approach to their design are, as Sam Hecht so rightly says, a point of reference for those who follow his path. And that is no mean feat.

Dieter Rams, c.1975

Dieter Rams
in Context

Klaus Klemp

When Queen Victoria opened the Great Exhibition, the first World Fair, in London's Crystal Palace on 1 May 1851, it was immediately clear to the 25,000 guests that the production and consumption of goods had evolved into the dominant paradigm for the economic development of Western societies. Industrialization had already brought wide-ranging social and economic changes and had created a vast and entirely new world of products. But when marvelling at the approximately 100,000 exhibits on show, many of the six million visitors did not realize that all of these things only looked as though they had been made by craftsman using traditional methods. Most of the objects on view cited traditional art forms, glossing over the fact that they used new production systems, which took advantage of the division of labour. At first, both manufacturers and consumers ignored this lack of authenticity in terms of craft and material. In the eighteenth century, the entrepreneur Josiah Wedgwood had already made a success of marketing machine-produced work as 'handmade'. But the next two centuries were to be marked by efforts to find a new machine aesthetic, which led not least to the founding of design as a profession and to the Modern project.

If Dieter Rams's achievements as a designer are to be judged appropriately, it is advisable to look at the philosophy of creative design from the late eighteenth century to the mid-twentieth century. No practitioner operates in a void or is free of received ideas; their drawing board is not a *tabula rasa*; Older traditions continue to exert their influence even after their actual requirements have changed.

The starting point for Dieter Rams's attitude to design is the idealistic philosophy of men such as Immanuel Kant and Friedrich Schiller, who worked mainly on the premise that art and technology – or even art and design – were two separate fields. Immanuel Kant, in his 1790 *Kritik der Urteilskraft* (*Critique of Judgement*) had introduced the concepts of 'free' (independent of purpose) and 'dependent' (purpose-related) beauty, thus establishing an idealistic notion of beauty that placed con-sumer goods and architecture on a lower plane in the arts because they could not be objects of disinterested pleasure. In this interpretation, architectural decoration – because it was not structurally essential – counted as the actual architectural or artistic element. For Friedrich Schiller art, and thus beauty, was the most noble element for man's self-realization. Art was supposed to offer the mental tool that was needed to create a humane society, rather than a 'mechanical life'. To do this, it had to be free from all purposes: 'It is to be directed by the necessities of the spirit, not by the needs of the material', Schiller wrote.' Meanwhile, Goethe warned that art would lose its aura if it were associated with the functional purpose of craft.

By 1935, Walter Benjamin averred that this demythologizing of art was an established fact, and had already led to art's loss of aura and its new ability to function socially. Of course, this switch from artistic work done by hand to reproductive

---

[1]   Friedrich von Schiller, 'Von der Notwendigkeit der Geister, nicht von der Notdurft der Materie will sie ihre Vorschrift empfangen', *Die* ästhetische Erziehung des Menschen (1795), reprinted as the 2nd letter in Sämtliche Werke in 5 Bänden, vol. 5 (Gütersloh, 1955), 323

mechanical work not only led to a re-evaluation of the historical basis of any design activity, but also made possible the new media of photography, film, art prints and gramophone or radio recordings. Despite this, the idealistic tradition in Germany supported a greater division between the fields of art and design in Germany than in the Anglo-American countries. But from the nineteenth century onwards, a new design theory in Germany began to wear down this idea and establish the proposition that aesthetic beauty could arise from an object being bound to a purpose. The art historian Karl Bötticher (1806–89) worked with the concepts of a 'core form' based on function and a decorative 'art form' that was determined historically and therefore superimposed. The history of Modernist design in Germany was to see this core form progressively emancipating itself from the art form so that, by 1949, Max Bill demanded 'a beauty that develops from function and fulfils a function of its own by its beauty'.[2]

However, before this change could take place, a number of conditions were necessary. Two were particularly virulent in Germany, one before and one after the advent of idealistic philosophy. The first was the basic thrust of the early sixteenth-century Reformation, which made a particular impact in Germany, where it led not only to a new Christian denomination, but above all to a fresh system of ethics that rejected formal excess and pictorial qualities in favour of frugality and worldly sobriety. In 1517, Martin Luther's *Ninety Five Theses* had demanded a return to the ethics of biblical Christianity. This process of Christian renewal created a direct relationship between the faithful and God, and also changed the relationship between the faithful and their material world. This process, which went on for about 150 years, had rendered the Church's mediating authorities such as relics, saints, church buildings, pictures and sculptures more or less obsolete. The Protestant church building was no longer sacred, but essentially a neutral space for the faithful to assemble in. This had a lasting effect on ornament and decoration: it was no longer necessary, at least theologically. The new religious aesthetic grounding was the basis of a purpose-related connection with things, which also had a strong political dimension. In the mid-sixteenth century, the legal provision *cuius regio, eius religio* (he who governs the territory decides its religion) demanded an ethic that was uniform throughout a country or region – whether Catholic or Protestant – that was to precipitate the development of regional monocultures in centuries to come. This Protestant grounding of the northern and eastern German states, which had an impact until well into the twentieth century, also applied to southwest regions including Württemberg, Calvinist Switzerland, the Netherlands and the modern Czech Republic, and it is interesting to note that the main impetus for Modernist German design in the twentieth century affected precisely these countries.

[2]   Max Bill, 'Schönheit aus Funktion und als Funktion', *Werk* no. 8 (1949), reprinted in Volker Fischer and Anne Hamilton, eds., Theorien der Gestaltung: Grundlagentexte zum Design, vol. 1 (Frankfurt, 1999), 193

But perhaps the most important basis for overcoming the idealistic approach was established in the mid-nineteenth century by the architects Karl Friedrich Schinkel (1781–1841) and Gottfried Semper (1803–79). They developed the first tenets for appropriate industrial design. Schinkel used principles from antiquity and also from the Gothic period, and provided a prototype for serial and functional building in the form of his 1836 Berlin Bauakademie (School of Architecture). Meanwhile, Semper wrote as early as 1860: 'The solution to modern problems must be developed freely from the requirements of the present day … Each technical product is the result of purpose and material.'[3]

It was above all Semper who laid the theoretical foundations for a fresh approach to design, intending to bring together 'what a false theory had put asunder'. During his four years in London (during and after the Great Exhibition in 1851), Semper addressed John Ruskin and his associates of the Arts and Crafts movement and articulated a coherent and forward-looking theory of the functional.[4] The British Arts and Crafts movement had idealized a craft-orientated Middle Ages and adopted an emphatically anti-industrial stance. This had led to a formal basis for design principles that treated materials 'correctly' and related forms to their function, but it ran counter to the new industrial production conditions. Semper, however, responded to this by arguing for a new connection between art and industry in the shape of an 'art industry' combining technology and aesthetics. According to Semper, the excess of resources created by the sciences and the new industrial technologies were not being treated properly in practice, due to a lack of experience and appropriate heuristics. But he began to theorize about how it could be done: the outward appearance of nature was no longer to provide the model for human artefacts; instead, structures and elemental parts ('primal forms') were to become the basis of design. In his proposed method, design stimulus should come not from the outward form of a leaf or a flower, but from its cell structure or make-up. This legitimized orthogonal, that is, apparently inorganic design. The use of cubes, spheres and other Platonic solids to create an orthogonal architecture had become popular some decades earlier, but for quite different reasons, in the unrealized designs of the 'Utopian revolution architecture' of Claude Nicolas Ledoux and Étienne Louis Boullée. Semper's second important principle, that objects should be appropriate to their material, was also one of the fundamental tenets of the Arts and Crafts movement. But Semper expressly emphasized the effects of the materials and tools used, the place of manufacturers, climate and regional customs, and the social status of the designer and producer on the objects.

[3]   Gottfried Semper, *Der Stil in den technischen und tektonischen Künsten oder praktische Ästhe-tik, Ein Handbuch für Techniker, Künstler und Kunstfreunde* (vol. 1: Frankfurt, 1860; vol. 2: München, 1863), quoted in Fischer and Hamilton, eds., *Theorien der Gestaltung*, 194

[4]   See Gottfried Semper, 'Wissenschaft, Industrie und Kunst. Vorschläge zur Anregung nationalen Kunstgefühles' (London, 1852), reprinted in Fischer and Hamilton, eds., *Theorien der Gestaltung*, 86–89

These design ideas were taken up about 1900 by various reform movements, including the *Wiener Werkstätte* (Vienna Workshops), the *Deutsche Werkstätten* (German Workshops) in Hellerau, Dresden, the *Mathildenhöhe* (Artists' Colony) in Darmstadt and later by the *Deutscher Werkbund* (German Work Federation),[5] and applied to industrial processes with varying degrees of success. The influence of traditional Japanese culture was another factor, first through the woodcut, which provided inspiration for French Modernism from the mid-nineteenth century onwards, and later through knowledge of the Japanese house, with its modular structure and lightness.

The *Deutscher Werkbund*, an association of entrepreneurs, artists and designers devoted to improving the quality of design of German products, became a reservoir of theory and practice from 1907 to the outbreak of World War I in 1914. Its most important early theoretician was the architect Hermann Muthesius (1861–1927), who triggered a long debate in 1907 with his demand for *Sachlichkeit* (objectivity or functionality).[6] This also led to the foundation of the industrially-orientated *Werkbund*, to which the best-known German designers and architects were to belong in the 1910s and 1920s. Muthesius was strongly influenced by British design culture, in part because he was attached to the German embassy in London during 1896–1903. He studied architecture and industry, gaining many ideas from the English country house. The designers of these houses were themselves greatly influenced by the Arts and Crafts movement, and drew their inspiration more from functionality than prestige.

A fundamental debate took place on the occasion of the first major exhibition of the *Werkbund* in Cologne in 1914 between two members, Muthesius and Henry van de Velde. It had been in the air for some time, and was to make a lasting contribution to the perception of design. It subsequently went down in history as the '*Werkbund* dispute' and represented the opposing poles of standardization for product design (Muthesius) and the greatest possible individual freedom for the designer (van de Velde). Muthesius' view was to win out after World War I, but for him standardization did not mean schematization, and was inconceivable without an artistic approach. 'The idea that it is completely sufficient for the engineer for a building, an instrument, a machine that he creates to fulfil a purpose is erroneous, and even more erroneous is the oft-heard statement that if it fulfils a purpose then it is also beautiful at the same time. As such, usefulness has nothing to do with beauty. In the case of beauty it is about a problem of form and of nothing else, and in the case of usefulness [it is] about the simple fulfilment of a service.'[7]

[5] See Joan Campbell, *The German Werkbund: The Politics of Reform in the Applied Arts* (Princeton, 1978)

[6] Hermann Muthesius, 'Die moderne Umbildung unserer ästhetischen Anschauungen', *Kultur und Kunst* (Leipzig, 1904), 74

[7] Hermann Muthesius, 'Die ästhetische Ausbildung der Ingenieurbauten', *Zeitschrift des Vereins Deutscher Ingenieure*, no. 53 (1909), 1212

To this debate, the Viennese architect and theoretician Adolf Loos provided another, radically different voice. He considered the entire arts and crafts reform movement, including the *Wiener Werkstätten*, to be superfluous. Loos made the case for a cathartic movement – albeit with a time limit – during which designers should renounce all stylistic demands and ornamental forms. In the case of the 1910 Steiner House, the architect delivered a purely cubic design without ornament – at least on the garden side of the exterior of the building. As early as 1908 he had defined the lack of ornament as a cultural step in his highly polemical essay 'Ornament und Verbrechen' ('Ornament and Crime'),[8] which became a beacon for his ideas: '… the fact that our times are not able to produce a new ornament is what makes them great. We have conquered the ornament, we have fought our way through to being without ornament … Being without ornament is a sign of mental and spiritual power.'[9]

Loos' radical critique of ornament led to serious efforts aimed at design based on elemental, primary forms. This exemplary statement comes from the 1924 'Werkbund' exhibition: 'Stereometric form: intellectual, cool, bright, alert, crystalline, tames everything instinctive through reason, subjects everything to rigid, rational legitimacy.'[10] However, the anti-ornament debate also led to an extreme functionalism, which itself would later become vulgar as well, hardly concerning itself with form at all. 'It is not about forms, but about the realities of maximum functionality,' wrote Karel Teige in 1925 about the new approach laid down by Constructivism, which was to take over from art and make human needs its measure.'[11] Unfortunately, for a long time this legitimized the worldwide proliferation of slab-construction buildings, which benefited the building industry rather than humanity.

Finally, Peter Behrens (1868–1940) was an important contributor to these ideas, as an influential theoretician and, above all, a practitioner of German Modernism before 1914. Beginning as a painter and graphic artist, Behrens had become an active architect and product designer during his time in the *Mathildenhöhe*, and his first well-known work was the house he built there in 1901. His all-embracing work for the Allgemeine Elektrizitäts-Gesellschaft (AEG) in Berlin from 1907 to 1904 is rightly seen as the first 'corporate design' for a major company.'[12] In his own studio with his own staff, he designed how everything for AEG should look, from the letterhead to the factory building, and almost all of the products of the then-important company.

[8]   Adolf Loos, 'Ornament und Verbrechen' (1908), reprinted in Fischer and Hamilton, eds., *Theorien der Gestaltung* 112–20

[9]   Ibid., 115 and 120

[10]   Walter Riezler, *Form ohne Ornament*, catalogue for the Werkbund exhibition of the same name held in Stuttgart (Berlin, 1924), 9

[11]   Karel Teige, 'Der Konstruktivismus und die Liquidierung der Kunst', *Disk*, no. 2 (1925), reprinted in Fischer and Hamilton, 152–58

[12]   See Tillmann Buddensieg, *Industriekultur. Peter Behrens und die AEG* (Berlin, 1979)

In 1910, Behrens published an essay called 'Kunst und Technik' ('Art and Technology'), in which he stated at first that architects were exclusively historically inclined, and engineers only technically inclined. But as an artist who had become an architect and designer, he wished to achieve a symbiosis of their fields. As Loos has done before him, he drew on the concept of culture as opposed to beauty in his accompanying lecture. 'Technological progress has created a civilization that history had not achieved hitherto, though only a civilization and not, or at least not yet, a culture … because the two fields of technology and art do not touch each other, and indeed touch each other least where they should do most, in building and in the products of large-scale industry.'[13] For Behrens, technology definitely could not produce culture ('no style from construction'): it could come only from 'the language of art'.

However, Behrens also cited the Viennese art historian Alois Riegl and his concept of a 'will to art', which he sets against Semper's 'mechanistic view', with its target- and purpose-driven approach. Where Semper wanted to follow a coolly functional method using 'primal forms', Behrens felt it necessary to argue that design arose from 'the dynamism of great and strong personalities'. In this idea, it is impossible to overlook the influence of Friedrich Nietzsche, probably the most widely read German philosopher around 1900, in both the aim for a new culture and the idea of the 'will'. 'Where from, where to and why all science, if it is not intended to lead to culture?' he asked in his 1873 *Unzeitgemässen Betrachtungen* (*Unmodern Observations14*). For Nietzsche, in this collection of essays, culture meant 'ceasing to be units like human beings' and instead following the Delphic oracle's pronouncement, 'Know thyself'. Everyone must 'organize the chaos in himself, his sound and true character must then at some time strive against always merely repeating, relearning, imitating; he then begins to grasp that culture can be something other than decoration for life, i.e. essentially still nothing but pretence and obfuscation; for all ornament hides what is ornamented.'[15]

Nietzsche's elitism ('mankind's aim cannot lie at the end, but only in its highest exemplars'[16]) can also be read as a criticism of the blind faith in technology of his day, and for many artists and designers it was a challenge to be more self-confident. Behrens certainly took up this challenge, but in his 1910 essay 'Kunst und Technik',

[13]   Peter Behrens, 'Kunst und Technik', lecture delivered at the XVIII annual assembly of the Verband Deutscher Elektrotechniker in Braunschweig (1910), printed in *Elektrotechnische Zeitschrift*, no. 22 (2 June 1910), 21

[14]   The nuances of this title have proved difficult to translate into English. Other attempts have included *Untimely Mediations, Thoughts Out of Season, Untimely Reflections, Untimely Considerations* and *Inopportune Speculations* or, more clearly, *Essays in Sham Smashing*.

[15]   Friedrich Nietzsche, *Unzeitgemäße Betrachtungen* (*Vom Nutzen und Nachteil der Historie*) (Munich, 1984), 145

[16]   Ibid., 134

Behrens also took on other parts of Nietzche's ideas, stating that there were 'valid art laws', for example relating to proportions and three-dimensional quality ('the line is without being, architecture lies in corporeality'). Here, the term 'art laws' does not apply strictly to art, but its auxiliary sciences relating to endowment with form.

In his lecture, he adopted three further positions of importance. He spoke out against an 'individualistic style' and in favour of standardization, which was to become a key theme of the ensuing debate. He called for close cooperation between engineers and designers, but not for an engineer–architect as a single person. In his view, each fields was too complex to be best served by a single individual. Unlike László Moholy-Nagy at the Bauhaus and Hans Gugelot in Ulm, both of whom toyed with the idea of the autonomous designer–engineer, Dieter Rams, like Behrens, was convinced that the two professional spheres should remain separate, but at the same time that those involved should co-operate closely.

Industrial design, or work that is primarily technical, such as car manufacture, and computer, mobile phone or home entertainment production, is now complex enough that it can no longer be done, even theoretically, by a single person. So the challenge to a design of the future, which must be generated not as authored work but as process design, lies in organizing and optimizing communication processes between those involved in each case. This requires designers to have new capabilities, particularly in terms of communication. The line of thinking from Peter Behrens and Walter Gropius to Dieter Rams has been essential to this development.

Ultimately, the Modernist design discussion until the first half of the twentieth century culminates in the concepts of beauty, functionality and sociability. However, of these three ideas, beauty was much discredited in Germany. Kaiser Wilhelm II, who was reactionary in terms of culture, tried at every possible opportunity to assert 'laws of beauty and harmony'[17] that he accepted as correct and valid in their historical derivation. But in denigrating 'gutter art', a phrase he used to allude to modern artists, who wanted to present social hardship as more shocking than it already was, he did not manage to discredit Modernism as a wider art movement – which was anchored in a broad swath of society – but instead to discredit himself and any real discussion about the concept of beauty. Instead, before and after 1914, the avant-garde looked towards things that were fragmentary, incomplete, lacking in harmony or destructive.

Behrens' 1910 essay also contains the significant remark that efforts should be made to provide aesthetically ambitious industrial design for all, for ethical reasons but also for economic ones. However, despite the best efforts of Ikea and H&M, truly democratic design remains to be effectively realized in modern times. So many ideas, such as the reform-led wings of Jugendstil and the Bauhaus, tubular steel

[17]   Kaiser Wilhelm II., speech at the opening of the Siegesallee in Berlin (18 December 1901). See

    Doede, Werner, *Berlin Kunst und Künstler seit 1870*: *Anfänge und Entwicklungen* (Recklinghausen,

    1961), 82

furniture and, of course, Braun radios, started with clear social ambitions and ended up confined to the luxury sector.

Two large projects that had an impact on Rams came out of these discussions and deserve a closer look in this context: the Bauhaus, founded in 1919 by Gropius, and the New Frankfurt, which began in 1925. For a long time, the Bauhaus was considered to be absolutely synonymous with Modernist design. More recent research has offered a relative perspective on this view and pointed out that the institution's early theoretical basis was permeated by esoteric traits deriving from Johannes Itten and Paul Klee in particular, and was definitely not compatible with rationally and scientifically orientated Modernism. Furthermore, the essentials of the tutorial programme had been set out by Otto Bartning in the *Arbeitsrat für Kunst* (Workers' Council for Art), a group of artists formed in the revolutionary atmosphere of post-war Germany. In fact Gropius's initial 'art and craft' approach took its impetus from discussions that occurred prior to 1914, and it was not until 1922 that he changed the Bauhaus motto from 'art and craft' to 'art and technology, a new unity'. This new direction was based not least on the influence of the instigators of two non-German movements that championed abstraction: Dutch De Stijl exponent Theo van Doesburg, who offered private courses in Weimar during 1921–22, and the Russian Constructivists, above all Kasimir Malevich and El Lissitzky. The Bauhaus was a kind of international laboratory, and though many experiments came into it from the outside, it posed its own particular questions about them. However, it was smaller projects, such as children's see-saws, lamps, furniture, applied art, hand-woven textiles, or even a chess set and a little teapot – that came to the fore at the Bauhaus, particularly at the beginning. The Bauhaus never designed a car or a radio, and there was no regular architecture class until Hannes Meyer, its second director, introduced one in 1927–28. Even today, the Bauhaus myth is based above all on the communication skills and assertiveness of its founding director, who can be seen more as a head of marketing and a masterly presenter than the originator of Modernist design. The lasting power of this narrative is due in part to the interpretative sovereignty over the Bauhaus that Gropius continued to exert during his American exile, along with Ludwig Mies van der Rohe, the Bauhaus's last director before the school closed in the wake of the Nazi regime.

The influence of the Bauhaus, however, was very strong and when the Hochschule für Gestaltung was established in Ulm after the War, with Max Bill as its founding director, the Swiss artist had the idea of continuing the Dessau Bauhaus as an institution, a proposition that soon found Gropius's blessing. Other places had similar ambitions, including Rams's alma mater, the Werkkunstschule in Wiesbaden under its own founding director, Hans Soeder. Both Bill and Soeder were indebted to the Bauhaus. In Wiesbaden, the attempt foundered on the hesitancy of the city, which was financially responsible for the school. At the Hochschule für Gestaltung (HfG) Ulm, Tomás Maldonado, a professor at the college, turned away from Bill's artistic approach, forcing the former Bauhaus student out, and pointed the HfG Ulm towards a more academic approach, including methodological design research. However, by this time Rams had completed his education and begun his professional career in Frankfurt.

The city of Frankfurt, home to Braun's headquarters, had developed a major Modernist project, beginning in 1925. It involved nothing less than redefining this historical European city along Modernist lines. The architect and city building director Ernst May, under a liberal-social democrat city government, directed not only the construction of municipal building works and several large housing estates providing 15,000 dwellings, but demanded total control over the design, extending from household effects such as kitchen furnishings to town planning. May was not just a consistent Modernist, committed to a geometrical, rational and ornament-free approach to design; he also succeeded in bringing outstanding designers to Frankfurt for his great experiment. Architects Martin Elsaesser, Walter Gropius, Mart Stam, Adolf Meyer, Ferdinand Kramer and the interior designer Franz Schuster all built and designed here, as did Margarete Schütte-Lihotzky and graphic artists Willi Baumeister, Walter Dexel, Hans Leistikow and Robert Michel. All of this, of course, had a large impact on the city in which Max Braun was to found his company, but the 'New Frankfurt' also exerted an influence well beyond the city – above all from 1926 through a publication of the same name, subtitled 'Monthly magazine for modern design problems', which aimed to provide the overall cultural context and what it called 'honesty in creation'. Mart Stam wrote here in 1928, 'The right scale is at the same time the minimum, as it would not be right to make our cutlery larger and heavier than necessary; it would not be right to make our chairs larger, heavier and imposing. They should simply meet our needs, i.e. they should be light and easy to move ... So the scale of our objects should be a human scale.'[18]

This magazine, aimed at an international audience, addressed all kinds of design questions, from urban development through architecture, furniture and house-hold objects to fine art, film and photography. It mediated between the artistic and the design avant-garde and mass production. Thus, something that had begun in a kind of design laboratory at the Bauhaus came into being through large-scale, serial production in Frankfurt. This, together with publications such as *Die Form* (published by the *Werkbund* from 1925) and the *Bauhaus* (published by the Dessau Bauhaus from 1926), led to a wide-ranging public discussion from the mid-1920s in Germany about the industrial production of objects and the demands of an ever more clearly articulated functionalism, which would impact Dieter Rams.

[18]   Mart Stam, 'Das Maß, das Richtige Maß, das Minimum-Maß', *Das Neue Frankfurt* 2, no. 1 (1928), in Heinz Hirdina, *Neues Bauen Neues Gestalten: Das Neue Frankfurt / Die Neue Stadt; eine Zeitschrift Zwischen 1926 und 1933* (Dresden, 1991), 215

Index

Timeline

1932

– Born in Wiesbaden, Germany

1947

– Began studies in architecture and interior design at the School of Arts & Crafts in Wiesbaden aged 15

1948

– Carpentry apprenticeship completed as best in the State of Hessen

1953

– Graduated with honours from Wiesbaden
– Employed by architects office Otto Apel, collaborating with the American architects Skidmore, Owings and Merrill

1955

– Joined Braun as an architect and interior designer

1956

– First assignments as a product designer at Braun

– 569 table programme
– PA 1 slide projector [1]

– PC 3 record player, W. Wagenfeld, G.A. Muller with D. Rams
– SK 4 radio-audio combination, Hans Gugelot with D. Rams [1]

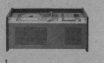

1957

– First furniture designs for Zapf

– transistor 1 portable radio
– 573 bed programme
– 571/72 montage system [1]
– RZ 57 / 570 table programme
– atelier 1 radio-audio combination [2]
– L 1 speaker
– PA 2 automatic projector [3]

– SK 4/1 radio-audio combination, H. Gugelot with D. Rams
– SK 4/1 A radio-audio combination, H. Gugelot with D. Rams
– DL 5, with G. A. Muller [1]

1958

– L 2 speaker [1]
– EF 1 standard electronic flash [2]
– transistor 2 portable radio [3]
– atelier 1 stereo system [4]
– EF 2/NC special electronic flash [5]

– SK 4/2 radio-audio combination, H. Gugelot with D. Rams
– SK 5 radio-audio combination, H. Gugelot with D. Rams [1]
– T 3 transistor radio, with HfG Um [2]

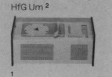

1959

– Formation of the company Vitsœ + Zapf with Otto Zapf, Niels Wiese Vitsœ and Dieter Rams

– Braun products designed by Dieter Rams and the design department acquired for the permanent design Collection of the Museum of Modern Art (MoMA), New York

– CE 12 receiver
– ZL 5 flash wand
– Studio 2 compact sytem
– L 01 speaker [1]
– T 4 transistor radio [2]
– TP 1 radio-audio combination (T 4 and P 1 [3])
– transistor K portable radio [4]
– KTH 1/2 earphones
– atelier 1 compact stereo system [5]
– atelier 1-81 compact stereo system [6]
– P 1 battery record player [7]
– L 02 additional speaker [8]
– L 40 bookshelf speaker [9]
– H 1/11 heater [10]
– F 60/30 flash [11]

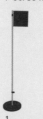

– PC 3 SV record player, W. Wagenfeld, G.A. Muller with D. Rams

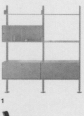

1960

– T 22-C portable radio
– L 02 X additional speaker
– H 2/21 heater
– RZ 60 / 606 universal shelving system [1]
– 601 chair programme [2]
– T 22 portable radio [3]
– T 23 portable radio [4]
– T 24 portable radio [5]
– PCK 4 portable compact stereo [6]
– L 11 speaker for atelier [7]
– F 22 flash [8]

– T 31 transistor radio, with HfG Um
– SK 5 C record player, H. Gugelot with D. Rams
– TP 2 transistor radio combination (T 31 and P 1), with HfG Um [1]
– SK 6 record player, H. Gugelot with D. Rams [2]

1961

– Appointed Head of the Braun design department

– T 220 portable radio
– T 52 portable transistor radio
– T 54 portable radio
– L 60 bookshelf speaker
– L 61 bookshelf speaker
– RT 20 tabletop radio [1]
– RZ 61 / 610 hall stand system [2]
– T 52 portable radio [3]
– PCV 4 portable stereo amplifier combination [4]
– L 12 speaker for atelier [5]
– LE 1 speaker [6]
– L 50 bass reflex speaker [7]
– CSV 13 amplifier [8]
– RCS 9 control unit [9]
– atelier 11 compact system [10]
– atelier 2 compact system [11]
– F 20 flash [12]
– D 40 automatic projector [13]

1

2

3

4

5

6

7

8

9

10

11

12

13

1

1962

1

2

3

4

5

6

7

8

9

10

11

12

13

14

15

16

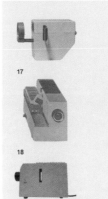

17

18

19

1963

1

2

3

4

5

6

7

8

9

1

2

1964

1

2

3

4

5

6

7

8

- D 21 automatic slide projector, with R. Oberheim
- EA 1 camera, with R. Fischer, R. Oberheim [1]
- FP 1 nizo film projector, wth R. Oberheim [2]
- HUV sun lamp, with R. Wiess, D. Lubs [3]
- FS 60 television set stand, H. Hirche with D. Rams [4]

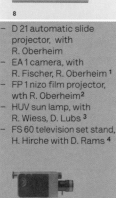

1

2

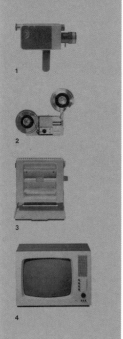

3

4

1965

- Art Award (Industrial Design) 'Junge Generation, Berlin' together with Richard Fischer, Robert Oberheim and Reinhold Weiss from the Braun design dept

- TS 45 / TG 60 / L 450 modular stereo system that could be wall-mounted
- audio 2/3 compact system
- L 700 speaker [1]
- L 700-4 speaker [2]
- L 1000 speaker [3]
- L 300 miniature speaker [4]
- L 450 flat speaker [5]
- CE 1000 receiver [6]
- CSV 1000 amplifier [7]
- PCS 52-E record player [8]
- PS 400 record player [9]
- PS 1000/1000 AS record player [10]
- TG 60 reel-to-reel tape recorder [11]
- LS 75 PA column speaker [12]
- F 200 flash [13]
- F 260 flash [14]
- HZ 1 room thermostat [15]

1

2

3

4

5

6

7

8

9

10

11

12

13

14

15

- KMZ 2 citrus press for KM 2, wth R. Fischer
- KMK 2 coffee grinder for KM 2, with R. Fischer
- FP 1 S nizo film projector, with R. Oberheim [1]
- D 45 slide projector, with R. Oberheim [2]
- KM 2 kitchen machine, with R. Fischer [3]
- H 6 convection heater, R. Fischer with D. Rams [4]

1

2

3

4

1966

- CE 500 receiver
- CE 500 K receiver
- PK 1000 antenna [1]
- L 800 speaker [2]
- L 900 speaker [3]
- CSV 12 amplifier [4]
- CSV 250 amplifier [5]
- FS 600 television set [6]
- F 100 flash [7]
- F 270 flash [8]
- F 650 flash [9]
- F 1000 flash system [10]

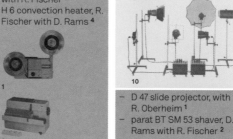

1

2

3

4

5

6

7

8

9

10

- D 47 slide projector, with R. Oberheim [1]
- parat BT SM 53 shaver, D. Rams with R. Fischer [2]

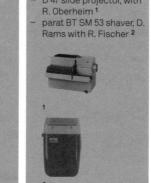

1

2

1967

- L 300/1 miniature speaker
- L 450/1 flat speaker
- CE 250 receiver
- CSV 60-1 amplifier
- TG 504 reel-to-reel tape recorder
- stand for FS 600
- system stand metal base separate for FS
- system stand connecting plates
- system stand record compartment
- DSM 1 disco mixing console
- EVV 600 PA amplifier
- MP 1 stereo mixing console
- EDL 2 PA disco speaker
- L 250 bookshelf speaker [1]
- L 600 bookshelf speaker [2]
- CSV 500 amplifier [3]
- audio 250 compact system [4]
- PS 402 record player [5]
- TG 502/502-4 reel-to-reel tape recorder
- TGF 1 remote control [6]
- FS 1000 television set [7]
- EVS 400 PA control amplifier [8]
- DSV 2 PA high-power amplifier [9]
- EKF 1 PA mains and control unit [10]
- ETG 502/4 PA reel-to-reel tape recorder [11]
- EPL 1 PA recorder player drawer [12]
- EVL 500-1 PA high-power amplifier [13]
- EMM 68-2 PA microphone mixer [14]
- ELF 1 PA ventilator unit [15]
- EVV 600 PA high-power amplifier [16]
- EGZ equipment rack [17]
- ETG 402/4 PA reel-to-reel tape recorder
- SP 1 control console [18]
- ETE 500 PA tuner [19]
- EDL 2 PA disco speaker [20]
- D 46/46 K slide projector [21]

1

2

3

4

5

6

7

8

9

10

11

12

13

14

15

16

17

18

19

20

21

- H 7 heater, R. Weiss with D. Rams [1]
- lectron educational toy, with J. Greubel [2]
- lectron educational toy, with J. Greubel [3]

1

2

3

1968

- Appointed Director of the Braun design department
- Hon. RDI (Honorary Royal Designer for Industry) at the Royal Society of Arts, London, for distinguished design in furniture and light engineering products

- PV 1000 adapter
- L 400 bookshelf speaker
- L 250/1 speaker
- L 450-2 flat speaker
- stand for FS 1000/1010
- ELR 1 PA line array speaker
- 682 chair programme
- T 1000 CD receiver [1]
- L 910 speaker [2]
- CE 1000/2 receiver [3]
- CSV 1000/1 amplifier [4]
- regie 500 control unit [5]
- PS 410 record player [6]
- PS 500/E record player [7]
- TG 550 reel-to-reel tape recorder [8]
- TGF 2 remote control [9]
- F 110 flash [10]
- F 210 flash [11]
- F 700 professional flash [12]
- T 2/TFG 2 cylindric lighter [13]
- HW 1 personal scale [14]
- 680 bed programme [15]
- 681 chair programme [16]

1

2

3

4

5

6

7

8

9

10   11

12

13

14

15

16

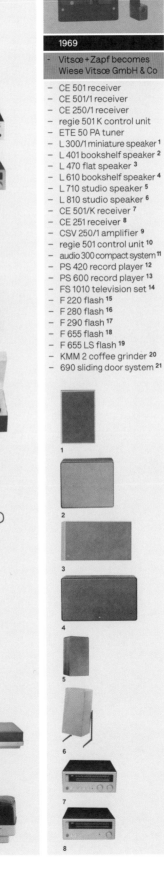

- parat BT SM 53 shaver, D. Rams with R. Fischer

1969

- Vitsœ + Zapf becomes Wiese Vitsœ GmbH & Co

- CE 501 receiver
- CE 501/1 receiver
- CE 250/1 receiver
- regie 501 K control unit
- ETE 50 PA tuner
- L 300/1 miniature speaker [1]
- L 401 bookshelf speaker [2]
- L 470 flat speaker [3]
- L 610 bookshelf speaker [4]
- L 710 studio speaker [5]
- L 810 studio speaker [6]
- CE 501/K receiver [7]
- CE 251 receiver [8]
- CSV 250/1 amplifier [9]
- regie 501 control unit [10]
- audio 300 compact system [11]
- PS 420 record player [12]
- PS 600 record player [13]
- FS 1010 television set [14]
- F 220 flash [15]
- F 280 flash [16]
- F 290 flash [17]
- F 655 flash [18]
- F 655 LS flash [19]
- KMM 2 coffee grinder [20]
- 690 sliding door system [21]

1

2

3

4

5

6

7

8

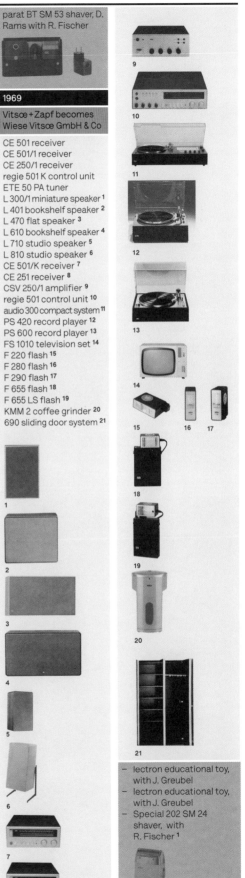

9

10

11

12

13

14

15   16   17

18

19

20

21

- lectron educational toy, with J. Greubel
- lectron educational toy, with J. Greubel
- Special 202 SM 24 shaver, with R. Fischer [1]

1

1970

- 250 SK, compact system
- EDI 3 PA disco speaker
- EL 450 PA speaker
- EL 250 PA speaker
- HLD 4 hairdryer [1]
- L 310 flat speaker [2]
- L 500 bookshelf speaker [3]
- L 550 speaker [4]
- CSV 300 amplifier [5]
- CSV 510 amplifier [6]
- 250 S compact system [7]
- TG1 000/1000/2 tape recorder [8]
- TGF 2 remote control TG 1000 [9]
- TD 1000 cover, TG 1000 [10]
- F 240 LS flash [11]
- F 111 flash [12]
- F410 LS flash [13]
- T3 Domino battery ignition [14]

1

2

3

4

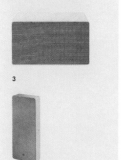

5

6

7

8

9

10

11

12

13

14

- Manulux NC flashlight, R. Weiss with D. Rams

1971

- L 550/1 flat speaker
- L 480 bookshelf speaker
- L500/1 bookshelf speaker [1]
- L 650 bookshelf speaker [2]
- L 620/1 bookshelf speaker [3]
- LV 1020 powered speaker [4]
- audio 310 compact system [5]
- PS 430 record player [6]
- F 16 B flash [7]
- F 17 flash [8]
- F 245 LSR flash [9]
- F 18 LS flash [10]
- F 1 mactron lighter [11]
- 710 container programme [12]

1

2

3

4

5

6

7

8

9

10

11

12

- Phase 1 battery and mains clock, with D. Lubs [1]
- mach 2 lighter, with F. Seiffert [2]

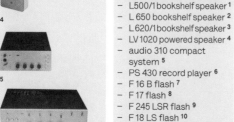

1

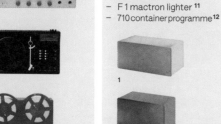

2

1972

- L 810-1 floor-standing speaker [1]
- L 260 speaker for cockpit 250/260 [2]
- L 485 flat speaker [3]
- L 555 flat speaker [4]
- L420 bookshelf speaker [5]
- L 420/1 bookshelf speaker [6]
- L 480/1 bookshelf speaker [7]
- CES 1020 receiver/ pre-amplifier [8]
- regie 510 control unit [9]
- 260 S compact system [10]
- 260 SK compact system [11]
- TG 1000/4 tape recorder [12]
- 720/21 oval table [13]

1

2

3

4

5

6

7

8

9

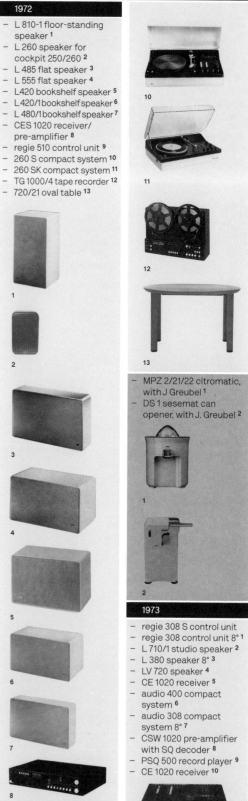

10

11

12

13

- MPZ 2/21/22 citromatic, with J Greubel [1]
- DS 1 sesemat can opener, with J. Greubel [2]

1

2

1973

- regie 308 S control unit
- regie 308 control unit 8° [1]
- L 710/1 studio speaker [2]
- L 380 speaker 8° [3]
- LV 720 speaker [4]
- CE 1020 receiver [5]
- audio 400 compact system [6]
- audio 308 compact system 8° [7]
- CSW 1020 pre-amplifier with SQ decoder [8]
- PSQ 500 record player [9]
- CE 1020 receiver [10]

1

2

3

4

5

6

7

8

9

10

– PS 450 record player, –
  PS 350 record player,
  with R. Oberheim [1]
– PS 358/458 record player,
  with R. Oberheim [2]
– sixtant 8008 shaver,
  with F. Seiffert and
  R. Oberheim[3]
– synchron plus shaver,
  with F. Seiffert,
  R. Oberheim and
  P. Hartwein [4]
– sixtant 6007 shaver, with
  R.Fischer[5]

1

2

3

4

5

1974

– regie 308 F control unit 8°
– TG 1020/4 tape recorder
– L 505 bookshelf speaker [1]
– L 425 bookshelf speaker [2]
– L 625 bookshelf speaker [3]
– regie 520 control unit [4]
– TG 1020 tape recorder [5]
– CD-4 demodulator [6]
– QF 1020 remote
  control unit [7]
– energetic solar lighter [8]
– 740 stacking programme [9]

1

2

3

4

5

6

7

8

9

1975

– L 715 studio speaker
– TGC 450 cassette recorder
– L 530 bookshelf speaker [1]
– L 530 F flat speaker [2]
– L 630 bookshelf speaker [3]
– L 730 bookshelf speaker [4]
– L 830 bookshelf/
  standing speaker [5]
– L 321 bookshelf speaker [6]
– L 100 miniature speaker [7]
– L 322 bookshelf/
  wall speaker [8]
– L 320 bookshelf speaker [9]
– audio 400 S compact
  system [10]
– audio 308 S compact
  system 8° [11]
– KH 500 stereo heaphones [12]
– regie 450 control unit [13]

1

2

3

4

5

6

7

8

9

10

11

12

13

– AB 20 clock, with D. Lubs
– ET 11 calculator, with
  D.Lubs [1]

1

1976

– L 2000 compact
  studio speaker
– regie 450 control unit
– regie 450 E control unit
– L 200 bookshelf/
  wall speaker [1]
– regie 450 S control unit [2]
– regie 550 control unit [3]
– domino lighter with
  piezo ignition [4]
– domino lighter set with
  3 ashtrays [5]

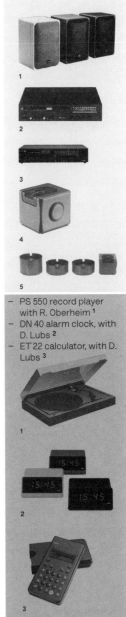

1

2

3

4

5

– PS 550 record player
  with R. Oberheim [1]
– DN 40 alarm clock, with
  D. Lubs [2]
– ET 22 calculator, with D.
  Lubs [3]

1

2

3

1977

– L1030/4 US speaker
– L 530 F flat speaker
– L 350 bookshelf speaker
– CT 1020 receiver
– L 1030 speaker [1]
– L 300 miniature speaker [2]
– regie 525 control unit [3]
– regie 526 control unit [4]
– regie 528 control unit [5]
– regie 530 control unit [6]
– P 4000 audio system [7]
– PC 4000 audio system [8]
– C 4000 audio system [9]

1

- PS 550 S record player, with R. Oberheim [1]
- PDS 550 record player, with R. Oberheim [2]
- DW 20 clock, with D. Lubs [3]
- ET 23 calculator, with D. Lubs [4]
- ET 33 calculator, with D. Lubs [5]

1978

- L1030 speaker
- L1030/8 speaker
- TS 501 and A 501 modular hi-fi audio system
- regie 540 E control unit
- GSL 1030 speaker [1]
- L100 auto car speaker [2]
- SM 1002 speaker [3]
- SM 1003 speaker [4]
- SM 1004 speaker [5]
- SM 1005 speaker [6]
- A301 Amplifier [7]
- regie 550 D control unit [8]
- regie 540 E control unit [9]
- RS 1 control unit [10]

- LC 3 bookshelf speaker, with P. Hartwein [1]
- LW 1 bass speaker, with P. Hartwein [2]
- T 301 receiver, with P. Hartwein [3]
- PC 1 integral studio system, with P. Hartwein [4]
- C 301 cassette recorder, with P. Hartwein [5]
- AB21/S clock, with D. Lubz [6]
- ABR 21 clock radio, with D. Lubs [7]
- ABR 21 FM clock radio, with D. Lubs [8]
- DW 30 LCD digital watch, with D. Lubs [9]
- ET 44 LCD calculator, with D. Lubs [10]

1979

- L 300 miniature speaker
- SM 1006 TC speaker
- SM 1002 S square speaker [1]
- C 301 M cassette recorder, with P. Hartwein
- SM 2150 speaker, with P. Hartwein [1]
- IC 50 speaker, with P. Hartwein [2]
- IC 70 speaker, with P. Hartwein [3]
- IC90 speaker, with P. Hartwein [4]
- PC 1 A record player and cassette recorder, with P. Hartwein [5]
- sixtant 4004/ compact s shaver, with R. Oberheim and R. Ullmann [6]

1980

- Opening of 'Design: Dieter Rams &' exhibition at the Internationales Design Zentrum, Berlin

- IC 80 speaker
- SM 1006 speaker [1]
- AP 701 power amplifier [2]
- dymatic lighter [3]

- T 1 receiver, as head of Braun product design team
- A 1 amplifier, as head of Braun product design team
- P1 record player, as head of Braun product design team
- C 1 cassette recorder, as head of Braun product design team
- L8060 HE speaker, with P. Hartwein
- L8070 HE speaker, with P. Hartwein
- L8080 HE speaker, with P. Hartwein
- BTB 50 teleropa box speaker, with P. Hartwein
- BTB 70 teleropa box speaker, with P. Hartwein
- BTB 90 teleropa box speaker, with P. Hartwein
- ic 1002 speaker, with P. Hartwein
- ic 1003 speaker, with P. Hartwein
- ic 1004 speaker, with P. Hartwein
- ic 1005 speaker, with P. Hartwein
- AC701 receiver, with P. Hartwein
- L 8100 HE speaker, with P. Hartwein [1]
- LA sound bass reflex speaker with, P. Hartwein [2]
- P4/ T2/ C2/ A1/ AF1 hi-fi system, with P. Hartwein [3]

1

2

3

1

2

- ic 60 speaker, with P. Hartwein
- ic 1003 speaker, with P. Hartwein
- ic 1004 speaker, with P. Hartwein
- ic 1005 speaker, with P. Hartwein
- R 1 control unit, as head of Braun product design team, with P. Hartwein
- P 701 record player, with R. Oberheim [1]
- P 501 record player, with P. Hartwein [2]
- ABR 11 megamatic radio, with D. Lubs [3]

1

2

1982

- P 2 record player, as head of Braun design team, with P. Hartwein
- P 3 record player, as head of Braun design team, with P. Hartwein
- AB 22 clock, with D. Lubs [1]

1

1983

- C 3 cassette recorder, as head of Braun product design team, with P. Hartwein

1984

- AB 2 clock, J. Greubel with D. Rams

1985

- 850 conference table

- CD 3, as head of Braun product design team, with P. Hartwein

1986

Vitsœ UK founded

- 860 round-oval table
- rgs-2 FSB 1136 door handle programme
- rgs-3 FSB 1137 door handle programme
- FSB 1495 door handle programme
- FSB 1462 door handle programme
- FSB 0836 door handle programme
- FSB 0838 door handle programme
- FSB 1714 54 door handle programme
- FSB 3631 door handle programme
- FSB 2891 door handle programme
- FSB 0640 door handle programme
- FSB 0641 door handle programme
- rgs-1 FSB 1138 door handle programme [1]

1

- R 2 control unit, as head of Braun product design team, with P. Hartwein
- CD 4 for atelier, as head of Braun product design team, with P. Hartwein
- TV 3 tabletop set, as head of Braun product design team, with P. Hartwein
- RC 1 remote control, as head of Braun product design team, with P. Hartwein
- 862 chair, with J. Greubel

1987

- Aluminium version of the 606 universal shelving system manufactured by De Padova, Milan

- CD 2, as head of Braun product design team, with P. Hartwein
- CD 5 control unit, as head of Braun product design team, with P. Hartwein
- VC 4 videorecorder, P. Hartwein with D. Rams
- CC 4 pre-amplifier/ receiver, as head of Braun product design team, with P. Hartwein
- PA 4 amplifier, as head of Braun product design team, with P. Hartwein
- R 4 control unit, as head of Braun product design team with P. Hartwein
- C4 cassette recorder, as head of Braun product design team, with P. Hartwein
- PHa1 desk lamp, with A. Hackbarth
- ET 66 calculator, with D. Lubs [1]
- ET 77 solar calculator, with D. Lubs [2]

1

2

1988

- Appointed Executive Director of Braun AG

1988-1998
- Chairman of the German Design Council

1991

1991-1995
- Board Member of ICSID, International Council of Societies of Industrial Design

1992

- Awarded the IKEA prize

1995

- Leaves Braun Design Department to become Executive Director of Corporate Identity Affairs at Braun
- Wiese Vitsœ closes
- Vitsœ UK becomes Vitsœ
- sdr+ manufactures Rams's furniture in Germany with designer Thomas Merkel

1997

- Retires from Braun
- Professor Emeritus of the Academy of Fine Arts Hamburg

1999

- becomes Member of the Academy of Arts, Berlin

2001

- 'Dieter Rams Haus' exhibition, Centro Cultural de Belém, Lisbon, Portugal
- 'Tingens Stilla Ordning (The Quiet Order of Things)' exhibition, Skissernas Museum, Lund, Sweden

2002

- Awarded the Verdienst-kreuz des Verdienstor-dens der Bundesrepublik Deutschland (Commander's Cross of the Order of Merit of the Federal Republic of Germany)

- 'Dieter Rams – Weniger aber besser (Less but better)' exhibition, Museum of Applied Arts, Frankfurt, Germany

2003

- Design Award ONDI (Havana, Cuba) for special contribution to industrial design and world culture

- 'Dieter Rams Design – Die Faszination des Einfachen (The Fascination of the Simple)' exhibition, Bremen Design Centre, Germany

---

2005

- 'Dieter Rams/ Less but Better' exhibition in the Kenninji Temple, Kyoto, Japan

2007

- Awarded Design Prize of the Federal Republic of Germany
- Lucky Strike design Award

2008

- Less & More – 'The Design Ethos of Dieter Rams' exhibition opens at the Suntori Museum, Osaka, Japan

2012

- sdr+, Germany, ceases production of Rams-designed furniture

2013

- Vitsœ becomes the exclusive worldwide licensee of Dieter Rams's furniture designs
- 620 Chair Programme and 621 Table are re-engineered and relaunched by Vitsœ and Dieter Rams

2016

- 'Dieter Rams: Modular World' exhibition, Vitra Design Museum, Weil am Rhein, Germany

- 'Rams', a documentary feature-film by American filmmaker Gary Hustwit is released worldwide

2018

- 'Dieter Rams: Principled Design' exhibition, Philadelphia Museum of Art, USA

2021

- 'Dieter Rams – Ein Blick Zurück und Voraus (A Look Back and Ahead)' exhibition opening, Museum of Applied Arts, Frankfurt, Germany

2022

- Ingeborg Kracht-Rams – Rams's wife of over 50 years – dies, aged 91
- Dieter Rams celebrates his 90th birthday

KEY

- Events

- Exhibitions

- Designed by Dieter Rams

- Designed in collaboration with Dieter Rams

About the author:

Sophie Lovell is an editor, consultant and author of several books and magazines on design, architecture and food. With her intergenerational studio_lovell, she emphasises contextual, system-based thinking in all her projects including thecommontable.eu, a platform for food futures that she publishes together with her daughter, the designer Orlando Lovell.

Acknowledgements:

The author would particularly like to thank the following for their time, support, inspiration or just plain patience in the realization of this project: Mark Adams, Helge Asmoneit, Lars Atorf, Michael DiTullo, Naoto Fukasawa, Konstantin Grcic, Jasper Hagenberg, Sam Hecht, Jonathan Ive, Horst Kaupp, Toshiyuki Kita, Klaus Klemp, Asia Kornacki, Ingeborg Kracht-Rams, Joan and Derek Lovell, Orlando Lovell, Antje Lubs, Dietrich Lubs, Susan Lundgren, Jasper Morrison, Daniel Nelson, Beate Preis, Dieter Rams, Penny Sparke, Britte Siepenkothen and Keiko Ueiki, and at Phaidon, Sara Goldsmith for her amazing and intelligent editing, Fiona Shipwright for her assistance in compiling the timeline, and Emilia Terragni.

Photo credits:

Courtesy of Braun: 18, 31, 34-37, 40-43, 56, 59, 61-64, 73, 80, 242-248, 255-256, 262, 285, 290-291, 297-301, 308, 373 Courtesy of Dieter Rams: 2, 20, 30, 32-34, 37-39, 41-42, 53-55, 57-58, 60-61, 65-68, 72, 77-78, 80, 84-87, 143-145, 206-216, 226-229, 243, 257-261, 263-267, 270-280, 282-288, 302-313, 374 Courtesy of Vitsoe: 194-195, 201-205, 211, 219-225, 230

Florian Böhm: 7 & 8, 11 & 12, 15, & 16, 21 & 22, 69-71, 73-80, 89-138, 144, 146-151, 153-186, 231 & 232, 268, 281, 308-309, 315-338, 357 & 358, 375 & 376

Biographies correct as first edition, first published 2011

Phaidon Press Limited
2 Cooperage Yard
London E15 2QR

Phaidon Press Inc.
111 Broadway
New York, NY 10006

www.phaidon.com

First published 2011
Reprinted 2011, 2012, 2014, 2016, 2017 (twice), 2018, 2019
Published in this format in 2024
© 2011 Phaidon Press Limited

ISBN 978 1 83866 909 6

A CIP catalogue record for this book is available from the British Library and the Library of Congress.

Designed by Kobi Benezri
Printed in China